D1576047

DATE DUE

ONE MORE RIVER TO CROSS

KEITH BOYKIN

Anchor Books

DOUBLEDAY

New York   London   Toronto

Sydney   Auckland

ONE MORE

RIVER

TO CROSS

Black and Gay

in America

AN ANCHOR BOOK

PUBLISHED BY DOUBLEDAY

a division of Bantam Doubleday Dell Publishing Group, Inc.
1540 Broadway, New York, New York 10036

ANCHOR BOOKS, DOUBLEDAY, and the portrayal of an anchor
are trademarks of Doubleday, a division of Bantam Doubleday
Dell Publishing Group, Inc.

BOOK DESIGN BY DANA LEIGH TREGLIA

Library of Congress Cataloging-in-Publication Data

Boykin, Keith.
    One more river to cross : Black and gay in America / Keith Boykin.
        p.   cm.
    1. Afro-American gays—Social conditions. 2. Racism—United
States. 3. Homophobia—United States. I. Title.
    HQ76.3.U5B685   1996
    305.9′0664—dc20   96-15995
                                                              CIP

ISBN 0-385-47982-4
Copyright © 1996 by Keith Boykin

10   9   8   7   6   5   4   3   2   1

First Anchor Books Edition: September 1996

To my family, Shirley, Bill, and Krystal,

for teaching me to dream,

and to my godsons,

Jardin and Cameron,

that they may grow up in a world where they are free to soar.

ACKNOWLEDGMENTS

I am forever indebted to the hundreds of people who opened up their lives so this story could be told. To improve society, we need more people to come out and follow your courageous examples.

Special thanks and my eternal love go to John King, for everything you did to help me finish this book and especially for those things that I neglected to acknowledge. I also want to single out Phill Wilson and E. Lynn Harris, for believing in me and supporting me through difficult times.

Thanks to my best friend Norris Case, for always knowing the right thing to say, and to my friends Sabrina Sojourner, Greg Hutchings, Neil Stanley, and Russell Binion. who comforted me and endured my endless complaints as I was writing.

Thanks to the people who read and commented on my manuscript: Maurice Franklin, Julia Gordon, Franz Freeman, Robert Raben, and Bobby Dexter. I accept all the blame for the faults of this book, but they get at least part of the credit for its virtues.

Thanks to those who gave valuable advice or provided critical information. Chief among these people is Dr. Ron Simmons, the real expert on being black and gay in America. Thanks also to the Servicemembers Legal Defense Network, for supplying great information about gays in the military. A big hug and thanks to my agent, Faith Childs, for teaching me the ropes of publishing and the art of patience.

Thanks to all those who believed, including Doris Jackson, Delores and Michael Teague, Levia Hoppszallern, Patricia Scott, Linda Singer, Fay Williams, Dave Sanchez, Ray Gordon, James Esseks, Craig Washington, Wilma Splawn, Marjorie Shoaff, and Linda Denny.

Thanks to Derrick Bell, just for being available and down-to-earth. Thanks to Mario Cooper, for your support. Thanks to the members, staff, and Board of Directors of the National Black Gay & Lesbian Leadership Forum, for allowing me the space to complete this book, and particularly to Emery Smith, Lenore Rivers, Rene Miranda, Blaine Teamer, Lawrence Denson, and Anthony Salas.

Thanks to the current and past leaders of the major lesbian and gay organizations, Melinda Paras, Elizabeth Birch, and Tim McFeeley, for your time.

Thanks to the officials in the federal government who took time out to talk to me, including Representative Barney Frank, Representative Eleanor Holmes Norton, National AIDS Policy Director Patricia Fleming, Assistant to the President Alexis Herman, Deputy Assistant to the President Marsha Scott, Special Assistant to the President Flo McAfee, and Assistant Attorney General for Civil Rights Deval Patrick, my idol.

Thanks to Chris Georges of *The Wall Street Journal,* for acting as my unofficial publicist for my first novel.

Finally, thanks to Charles Flowers, my very patient editor, for guiding me ever so gently from start to finish.

CONTENTS

Acknowledgments   *vi*

Preface   *xi*

ONE: In Search of Home   *3*

TWO: Are Blacks and Gays the Same?   *30*

THREE: Black and Gay in America   *85*

FOUR: Bearing Witness: Faith in the Lives of
Black Lesbians and Gays   *123*

FIVE: Black Homophobia   *155*

SIX: Gay Racism   *212*

SEVEN: Déjà Vu: The Common Language of
Racism and Homophobia   *236*

EIGHT: One More River to Cross   *261*

PREFACE

As I watched the look of surprise flush over my colleague's face, I realized I had said something provocative. Her raised eyebrows and dropped mouth told me I had struck a deep and sensitive nerve. Her reaction would soon become typical as I told others. Their mouths would drop too. Their eyes would widen with shock and then gracefully recover to hide their surprise. Some would struggle silently to determine the meaning of what I had said. A few would ask me to repeat myself, as if their minds could not verify what their ears had heard.

And what was the remark that elicited these sharp responses? I simply said I was writing this book.

One More River to Cross chronicles the experiences of hundreds of black lesbians and gay men and explores their interactions with the white gay community and the straight black community. It begins with a chapter on my own "coming out" story, followed by subsequent chapters that discuss the lives of the hundreds of people I interviewed.

In April 1991, as a twenty-five-year-old student at Harvard Law School, I came out of the closet. I knew very little about lesbians and gays, and even less about black lesbians and gays. As a black gay man, I started to question the similarities and differences between race and sexual orientation. When I graduated from law school the next year, after working several months for the Clinton-Gore campaign, I landed in the White House as a special assistant to the President. I was hired in January 1993 by presidential adviser George Stephanopoulos—who knew about my sexual orientation—to work on media issues, not lesbian and gay issues. However, in the midst of the controversy about President Clinton's plan to lift the ban on gays in the military, I volunteered to help with the communications strategy. Eventually, I was drawn into other lesbian and gay issues, and participated in Clinton's historic April 1993 meeting with leaders of lesbian and gay organizations. I soon began taking notes and discussing issues of race and sexual orientation with friends and colleagues I had met in law school and the Administration. I became very frustrated by the misleading and simplistic arguments I heard in the media and among the public, and by autumn 1994 I was ready to leave the White House to write this book and tell the stories of the people the media neglected.

As I told more people about this project, I underwent a "coming out" process. I found that people I had worked or associated with for a long time still did not know my sexual orientation. Not because they had not listened but because I had not told them. For example, I had been a loyal client of my barber's for a year and had engaged him in deeply personal conversations about *his* girlfriend and *his* aspirations for *his* future. But I never gave him an inkling about my own lover or my sexual orientation until I told him I was quitting my job to write this book.

At a White House holiday party the same week, I told a black reporter and his date. She reacted warmly and promised to buy the book once it was published. But he, the reporter, looked troubled, cryptically telling me he had "known" all along and had been meaning to talk to me about it. He put his arm around my shoulder and, with an avuncular tone, advised me that provocation for the sake of provocation was not always wise. "I'm still your friend," he said with a grin, "but I think you should think about this some more."

Shortly after I began writing this book, the Republican Party took control of the U.S. Congress and Newt Gingrich became Speaker of the House of Representatives. Beholden to the radical right wing that elected them, many in the Republican majority began a mean-spirited campaign to change public policy on affirmative action, immigration, reproductive choice, and "family values." Their targets are blacks, Hispanics, women, and gays, and they hope to divide these oppressed communities by convincing us that we have more to fear from each other than from a racist, xenophobic, misogynist, and heterosexist society. In this politically charged climate, I accepted my current position in September 1995 as executive director of the National Black Gay & Lesbian Leadership Forum, an organization that represents people who are both black and lesbian or gay.

I continued researching and writing this book after I began my new job. As I traveled across the country, I interviewed blacks and whites, heterosexuals and homosexuals, about their experiences with race and sexual orientation. I quickly learned to question my own assumptions and stereotypes. I found that most generalizations about blacks and gays fail to provide complete answers. For example, the attitudes and experiences of openly lesbians and gay men often differ markedly from those of closeted homosexuals. The attitudes and experiences of black and white homosexuals and of male and female homosexuals differ as well. The shared experience of homosexuality is not so great that it eliminates all other differences between people of various races, genders, ethnicities, and backgrounds.

I also discovered an enormous amount of denial, both by heterosexual blacks who denied the existence of large numbers of black lesbians and gays and by white lesbians and gays who denied the existence of racism in their community. Most disturbing were the denials about the face of AIDS, both from heterosexual blacks and from white lesbians and gays, who see it primarily as a white gay disease. The reality is that AIDS is the leading cause of death for black males between the ages of twenty-five and forty-four, and this is not likely to change until the black community, the lesbian and gay community, and the black lesbian and gay community learn to deal honestly with their fears and biases about race and sexuality. If this book begins a dialogue that helps save one life, it will have been more than worth the effort.

March 1996
Washington, D.C.

ONE MORE RIVER TO CROSS

CHAPTER ONE

In Search of Home

"It's a boy," said the man in a white lab coat. Standing in the delivery room of the Homer G. Phillips Hospital in St. Louis, the doctor lifted the newborn and legally declared me alive and "Negro" four hours and thirteen minutes into Saturday, the twenty-eighth day of August, 1965.

I have always felt something special about August 28. My last boyfriend was also born on that date, as was the first known openly gay rights advocate, Karl Heinrich Ulrichs, in 1825. Most important, exactly two years before the day I was born, Dr. Martin Luther King, Jr., stood at the steps of the Lincoln Memorial and shared his dream with the world.

He dreamed that one day his four children would live in a nation where they would be judged by the content of their character rather than by the color of their skin. And he dreamed that this nation would one day "rise up and live out the true meaning of its creed . . . that all men are created equal." Right from my childhood, I took Dr. King's words to heart and always imagined a life involved in civil rights, one dedicated to the pursuit of his dreams.

I was born to upwardly mobile black parents in a lower-income black community in St. Louis. My father, Bill, began his career as a bus driver before becoming an insurance salesman and then a computer salesman, but he was too restless to work for any company for very long and soon started his own businesses. My mother, Shirley, on the other hand, has spent nearly her entire adult life working in military procurement for the federal government. My sister and only sibling, Krystal, was born thirteen months after I was.

Soon after Krystal was born, our family left the inner city for an apartment in the mostly white suburbs of St. Louis County and then moved to a nearby middle-class home with a dog and two cars. I was lucky to have a family that believed in my dreams, and I suffered no lack of creativity in my fantasies. Often I would close my bedroom door and dream about anything and everything, from what it would be like to go to college, to imagining the life of the President, to picturing my future wife and kids, to worrying whether I would ever be able to live as well as my parents did.

One childhood fantasy involved a Mickey Mouse watch my parents bought me at Walt Disney World. It came in a long, slender black case. In my bedroom, I would place the case on the red shag carpet and roll it around as if it were a chauffeur-driven limousine and I were the President of the United States or some other high official. I would imagine being shuttled from place to place to make speeches and attend important meetings of some sort. At the time, I knew little about the President except that he made speeches and rode around in a limousine. I knew he was important because he was always on TV and everybody knew who he was.

My family never knew about the toy limousine, but they always knew I was interested in politics. I started running for office in fifth grade, when I was elected student-body president of my mostly white grade school. I later became student-government president of my mostly white high school—something of a novelty for a black student in the 1970s and '80s. My family felt as proud as I did about my accomplishments, as well as my goals, and at times they would joke with me about my ambition. "That boy is gonna become the first black President," they would say. My aunt, who often accused me of being "cheap," would tease me: "Keith, when you become President, don't forget your auntie. All I want is some tickets to the Inaugural Ball." All of us dreamed of a future where a young black boy from Missouri could grow up to become the leader of a white-majority nation.

Another fantasy from my childhood remains just as vivid. When I was seven years old, soon after my family moved into our first house, I became friends with Eric, an older, white boy who lived directly across the street in the only other house in our dead end. Eric and I would hang out at his house, playing poker inside the family room or wrestling outside on the lawn. Away from the house, we would shoot targets with our BB guns, climb buildings, hike through the nearby cornfield, and do other things that boys do. By the time I was thirteen or fourteen, Eric and I had grown apart and did not spend as much time together. As I was reaching puberty, he was maturing into a young man. He was entering high school and getting interested in cars and girls, while I was entering junior high and becoming increasingly introverted. Although I was never jealous of Eric's new female friends, I did envy him, and I assumed I would begin to date girls when I became his age. In fact, in elementary school I had had a "crush" on a pretty, long-haired black girl named Robin. Robin was a friend of my sister's and she had spent the night at our house a couple of times during slumber parties my sister would throw. Unlike Eric's interactions with his female friends, I never approached Robin and we never went out on a date.

When I was thirteen, my view of Eric changed dramatically one day when I looked out my window and saw him across the street. He was pushing a lawn mower while wearing jeans but no shirt, exposing a sleek, muscular torso. I stopped and stared through the window for several minutes. Before then, I had never noticed his body. I reflected on our wrestling matches of a few years earlier, and I began to imagine what it would be like to wrestle him again now that he was obviously bigger and stronger. Within a few weeks, these thoughts consumed me, and I imagined various moves he had used and how he might use them now. Eric had always had a shirt on when we actually wrestled, but in my fantasy contests, he wrestled shirtless, although I would keep my shirt on, since I was too skinny and embarrassed to remove it in public. In my favorite scenario, he would toss me on my back, prop his knees on my arms, and pin me.

These fantasy contests continued in my head until I moved away from St. Louis, when I turned fifteen. Yet despite the sexual nature of these fantasies, I never once thought about having sex with Eric, or even kissing him or any other man. My interest in wrestling was based on sport, not on sex. While I hardly knew what sex meant when I was in junior high school, I didn't tell anyone about these fantasies. Did other boys fantasize about wrestling muscular friends? I wondered. I did not understand why I was having the fantasies, but I knew better than to ask.

During this same time period, my family and I saw *The Wiz,* the African-American film adaptation of the classic *Wizard of Oz.* The cast included Diana Ross as Dorothy, Lena Horne as the Good Witch, Richard Pryor as the Wiz, Nipsey Russell as the Tin Man, and Michael Jackson as the Scarecrow. My parents videotaped the film, and I watched it over and over again for months, memorizing many of the scenes and songs. I understood Dorothy's ambivalent feelings toward her family because I, too, felt I was experiencing changes in my life that my family could not really understand.

As a black person in a white community, I always knew I was different, but it was a difference I shared with the rest of my family. We were all different from the majority of our neighbors. But something else was different about me, and I felt it distinguished me not only from my friends but from my family as well. I did not understand what made me different or why I had to be that way, but as I reached adolescence I knew that something inside me was happening, and I was frightened that I would not be able to deal with it.

My parents had separated from each other when I was still in elementary school. I lived with my father, while my mother lived in a nearby suburb; I would see her on weekends and during the summer. Then in February 1980, when I was fifteen, my life changed completely. My maternal grandmother and my paternal great-grandmother both died a week apart. The two women who had helped raise me and my sister as children—often taking care of us during the summer and disciplining us when we were out of line—were gone. My maternal grandmother had raised my mother and her eight foster siblings in the same house where she helped raise me and my sister. Her only biological son, Michael, inherited the house. Four months later, he was dead too.

A popular church organist and gospel musician, Uncle Michael was a flamboyant gay man. Although he had lived in my grandmother's house all his life and often brought men home with him, I never heard anyone say a disparaging word about him. My parents never told me to avoid him when they would drop me and my sister off at our grandmother's house for long weekends or other occasions. In fact, I did not even know at the time that he was gay or, for that matter, what it meant to be gay. I only knew that his hair was processed and that he wore tight-fitting colorful pants, and shirts unbuttoned to his waist. He was shot and killed in his own bedroom by someone he had let inside the house, and the murderer was never apprehended.

A few months after Uncle Michael's death, my parents moved away from St. Louis, each embarked on a separate journey of renewal, discovery, and self-awareness. My mother transferred from her government position in downtown St. Louis to an Army depot in Stockton, California, while my father, my sister, and I moved to Clearwater, Florida, where my father started a black beauty-supply business. Since I was separated from my mother by an entire continent, our visits together became less frequent, although she continued to play a central role in my life.

I dated two girls while I was in high school in Clearwater. The first, Angela, a black classmate, was a cheerleader at my school, while the other, Trina, also black but older than I, was a cheerleader for a rival high school. In a parking lot outside a local teen dance, Trina taught me to French-kiss. The new and pleasant sensation of her tongue twirling inside my mouth was the most sexual experience of my young life. But unlike many boys my age, I never wanted to have sex with either of my girlfriends. We went out on dates, took romantic midnight strolls along the beach, hugged, and caressed and kissed, but we never went much further than that. Privately, I feared what would happen next and worried whether I could get or maintain an erection. Although the dating continued for months at a time, I graduated high school exactly as I began—a virgin.

During high school, I had also developed an active interest in men's bodies and in wrestling. I had been a member of the wrestling team in ninth grade in St. Louis but chose not to join the team when I moved to Clearwater for the tenth grade. I was afraid that my new classmates would think I was gay if I joined the wrestling team, and I was very concerned about making a positive impression on them. Moving allowed me to change my reputation for being introverted and to become more popular than I had been in St. Louis. As a runner on the track team and a member of the student government, I often stayed late after school, and during wrestling season I would occasionally sneak over to the practice room and peek through the small rectangular window in the door. My two favorite wrestlers were, like most of the people in the school, white. Both had Italian names, dark curly hair, dark features, and slim but muscular bodies. Both played starring roles in my continuing wrestling fantasies, replacing my friend Eric from St. Louis. Despite my obsession, I never befriended either of them or told them about my fantasies.

A few days after I graduated from high school, in June 1983, I began to keep a journal in a notebook given to me as a graduation present by a teacher. Familiar with my early penchant for colorful language, the teacher inscribed a note saying that I could "write any amount of 'flowery' words . . . and never have to worry about a grade on them." In one of my first journal entries, I wrote a poem about the confusion and uncertainty in life, partly related to my high school graduation. In the most "depressing" verse of the forty-eight-line poem, I wrote, "My life right now is unusual / Bewilderment is now my guide / My regret about my life / Is that happiness has abandoned my side." In a later journal entry, I wondered about college and wrote, "Can I possibly make it with so much strife? / Must I begin a whole new life?" Bewilderment and strife served as euphemisms for my more concrete concerns (sex and money and insecurity), which I did not know how to describe when I was eighteen. In each entry where I complained, I would at some point write that I would try to find solace in God, but I spent a great deal of energy beating around the bush and concealing my innermost fears, not only from myself but from anyone else who might ever read my journal.

I moved to Hanover, New Hampshire, to attend college at the same time my father left Clearwater and moved to Atlanta to try to start a different business. After my first semester at Dartmouth College, in the fall of 1983, I stopped keeping my journal for several years, until my junior year. Although I was in my prime as a male, my sexual activity had not advanced beyond masturbation, and I made myself too busy with extra-curricular activities to pursue anything more serious. My sexual frustration began to boil to the surface in February 1986, when I was twenty years old. My roommate, a freshman, was making out with his girlfriend in the next room. Writing in my journal, I mused obliquely upon my nonexistent sex life: "Life has treated me pretty unevenly in that I feel great about some aspects and hopeless about others." I felt hopeless about whether I could ever be involved in a long-term intimate rela-tionship with a woman. Family and societal pressures had pushed me into dating, but I never felt as comfortable as some of my friends appeared to be. Even in college, I tried to avoid sex because I was terrified that I would not be able to perform in bed. I was terrified that some woman would discover what I considered my secret inadequacy.

Not until 1989, three years after my first journal entry about sex, did I again write about anything remotely sexual. During the three-year interlude, I had busily occupied my time: graduating from college in June 1987; working in Boston on the Dukakis presidential campaign through November 1988; and then, later that fall, moving home with my father in Atlanta and applying to law school. Defeated in the election, broke, and unemployed, I found time to reflect on, and write about, personal matters once again.

In late January 1989, I wrote a long, sweeping journal entry in which I described one of my college track teammates as "strikingly beautiful." This was the first time I had ever used those words to describe another man. A few weeks later, I wrote about my experiences as a high school wrestler. To con-vince myself that I was writing from a "sportsman's" view-point, I took pains to distinguish my interest in wrestling from a sexual desire for other men. "I never publicly acknowledged my interest in wrestling," I wrote. "Perhaps I feared that peo-ple would think of me as a sexual pervert, or worse, gay . . . I have long associated wrestling with homosexuality, and I thought others did too." Then I began the rationalization. I wrote, "It was not until well after college that I realized that half the adult male population [pure speculation] enjoys wrestling, and most sexually secure and mature individuals are not afraid of the sport."

For several weeks afterward, my journal entries focused exclusively on pseudosexual topics such as wrestling, weight-lifting, and men's bodies. Then the essays stopped. In the winter of 1989, I took a job as a high school teacher, and being gainfully occupied, I did not have the time for my journal anymore. Instead, I focused on the tedious tasks of creating daily lesson plans and grading papers. During this time, I continued to wonder why I felt so excluded from some of my male friends' conversations. True, I had always abstained from discussions about attractive women, dating, and sexual practices. But this, I thought, was understandable given my lack of experience (I was, after all, still a virgin after college). I attributed this lack of experience to my "complex" racial identity.

As a shy, smart black kid raised in the white suburbs, I never felt fully comfortable in either the black or the white community when I was growing up. The majority of the black students at my schools were bused in from poorer, mostly black areas, so I felt I had little in common with them other than skin color. On the other hand, my white classmates had little or no understanding of what it was like to grow up black. We listened to different music, worshipped at different churches, and grew up in very different families. I was not so suburbanized that I considered myself white or even wanted to be white. I clearly thought of myself as black, and I was un-abashedly "pro-black" politically. But because I did not fit completely into the social strata of either racial group at school, I seldom dated. I felt that white girls would never accept me, since I was black; and that black girls would never accept me, since I was "not black enough."

I found other reasons to avoid talking about sex. I convinced myself that I was more mature than the other guys because I did not objectify women or kiss and tell. I thought people who boasted about their sexual conquests had not really had much experience and were compensating with their hyperbole. But people who were sexually secure in their identities and their abilities, I reasoned, had no need to boast.

Although I still believe some of these statements, I eventually realized there was a more basic, if less conscious, reason for my never taking part in conversations about women. I did not participate because I was not interested. I liked men instead.

Society's negative stereotype of homosexuals had been so ingrained in me that I failed to see myself as one. Communicated mostly in subtle ways, the message reinforced traditional gender roles. "Don't hold your books up to your chest like a girl," I was told. "Don't cross your legs like a sissy," I heard. "You're switching [moving your hips] like a woman," an uncle warned. Thinking that gay men did all these things I was told not to do, I believed that if I avoided the taboos, I would not be gay. I learned to adapt my behavior to conform to the male expectation. In college, after being called Michael Jackson by my white classmates, I cut off my Jheri curl to appear more conservative and preempt any speculation about whether I was gay. Perhaps to overcompensate for the possibility of being seen in that way, I participated in traditional male activities. I ran track, joined a fraternity, and became a reporter for the college daily. Since I was not particularly effeminate and had never desired to dress in women's clothes, I thought I could not possibly be gay. I identified homosexuality not by sexual behavior but primarily by failure to conform to gender roles. Even when I did consider the sexual aspect of homosexuality, I was able to deny my own orientation because I felt no desire to sleep with men and was repulsed by the appearance of male genitalia. While I had spent years masturbating to the image of wrestling with muscular men, I so thoroughly deceived myself that I never considered these thoughts to be sexual.

As with most lesbians and gays, the first and most difficult step in coming to terms with my sexual orientation was acknowledging myself to be gay. This fact became obvious when I "fell in love" for the first time, in early 1991, while I was still at Harvard. I met Andy when we began working together on a joint forum on Black-Korean relations sponsored by the Black Law Students Association (BLSA) and the Asian American Law Students Association. From the moment I first laid eyes on him—that first day when he walked into the BLSA office for an organizational meeting—I thought he was beautiful. Korean-American and a few years younger than I, he had milky-smooth skin, and he wore jeans and a tight-fitting sweater. It took so much energy not to stare at him during the meeting that I could not focus on what we were supposed to be doing. Soon I started noticing him at other places: in the library, in the hallways, at the gym. The gym was the most pleasurable place to run into Andy because he usually wore a form-fitting white tank top that accented his perfectly carved chest. It also pained me to see him there because I was afraid to express the strong physical desire I felt. Nevertheless, I would quickly adjust my schedule so I could watch him work out. One time on my way to campus, I saw him going into the gym building. I turned and ran three blocks to my apartment to get my gym bag, then raced back to the gym so I could watch him while I "worked out."

With each conversation we had—about politics, weight-lifting techniques, whatever—I melted. I became his secret admirer. I never told him about my feelings, and I never asked if he was gay. But after several weeks of obsession, I finally admitted to myself what was going on. I described my feelings and activities in my journal, and I wrote, "I think this means I'm gay." A few weeks later, having never had sexual intercourse with a man or a woman, I decided to come out and acknowledge my homosexuality.

To be honest, I had had sex with women, but it never involved intercourse. Even when I became sexually aroused, I never desired to penetrate them and always feared that I could not. With men, I had had only one sexual experience, which I so fully denied after it happened that I virtually forgot it within a few months. While I spent the summer of 1989 in St. Louis, I worked out at a local gym and developed an acquaintance with a tall, muscular black man named Mike. He stared into my eyes every time we spoke and often suggested that we "get together" some time, a suggestion I ignored until the last time I worked out that summer. When I told him I was off to law school in a week, he knew an opportunity would be lost and moved quickly. "We've been talking about getting together for the longest time," he said. "What are you doing tonight?"

"Nothing," I said.

"Why don't we hang out?"

"Sure, what do you want to do?"

"We can just hang out. Come on over to my place for a while," he said.

I agreed, and when we left the gym, I followed him in my car to his house. We walked through the family room, where he yelled to someone in the kitchen that he was home. He led me to his bedroom, and I asked if the person who answered was his roommate. "No, that's my wife," he told me. I felt strangely comforted by this knowledge, feeling safe that his wife was in the house. But then he locked the door, turned on the television, and sat on the edge of the bed next to a chair where I was seated. He stared at me with seductive eyes as I became nervous and confused. A few minutes into an awkward, unmemorable conversation, he reached out and touched my hand, caressing my palm with his middle finger. His simple gesture caused a rush of conflicting emotions: guilt that I was feeling the touch of another man's hand, pleasure that this was the first time any man had touched me in this way, and confusion about what I was doing in this man's house in the first place.

The touching continued silently until he asked me to sit next to him on the bed. I got up and moved, smiling awkwardly, and then he moved his hands from mine and began touching my shoulders and back. He put one hand under my shirt and moved it up to and around my chest. Soon he removed my shirt and took off his and lay on top of me. As he vibrated over me, my erection grew larger and larger until I quickly ejaculated. I pushed him off me. I did not want him to know that my pants were wet, so I moved away from him and searched frantically for my shirt.

"What's a matter?" he asked.

"I have to go."

"Why, you just got here."

"No, you don't understand. This is, this is not for me," I stuttered. "I have never done this before, and I'm not about to start right now. I can't do this. I have to, uh, go home, right now."

We talked back and forth for several minutes until he realized I was actually leaving. "Okay," he said, relenting. But he sensed that this would not be my last experience with a man, and his final, prophetic words were, "You'll be back."

"I don't think so," I protested, and walked out the door.

I struggled with that incident for several weeks, and even called my mother once to talk about it, but I did not have the courage to go through with it and tell her what had happened. When I started law school, I managed to replace the memory with more pressing concerns about my studies. Eventually I denied to myself that the incident had ever taken place—until I came out in April 1991.

That spring, I turned to religion to help me come out. Although my parents had not required my sister and me to go to church every Sunday, religion had always played an important role in my life. When we did go to church, we worshiped with various black Protestant faiths and denominations. As a preteen, I was initially drawn to the musical experience of the black churches, which typically place a heavier emphasis on choir performance than white churches do. As I grew older, I started to understand and appreciate the words of the spirituals and hymns. With lyrics like "The Lord's gonna work it out" and "What a mighty God we serve" accompanying an upbeat gospel tempo, the music preached a message of hope to me and to others struggling with life's concerns.

Since the beginning of my political consciousness as a teen-ager, my religious beliefs had complemented my political phi-losophy. In junior high, after watching a television movie about Jesus, I started studying the Bible, and particularly the New Testament, on my own. I was impressed by Jesus' Sermon on the Mount when I read "Blessed are the meek: for they shall inherit the earth." The theme of redistributing power seemed consistent with my liberal, almost socialist, political view of the world. As a pacifist opposed to the nuclear arms buildup of the early 1980s and as an opponent of capital punishment, I found strong meaning in Jesus' message to turn the other cheek and avoid vengeance. The Bible's message of love and community seemed to contradict the ethnocentric, jingoistic rantings of Jerry Falwell's Moral Majority and Phyllis Schlafly's Eagle Fo-rum. Some American religious conservatives were suggesting that the nuclear bomb was God's gift to America, but I found comfort in Jesus' words "Blessed are the peacemakers." Al-though the right-wing religious rhetoric contradicted my un-derstanding of the Bible, it taught me early on how dema-gogues could use the Bible to pervert a message of love into one of hate.

The Bible's message of love resonated most with me. When I started praying in church for guidance, I did not ask God to decide whether I was gay, for on some level I already knew I was. I did not ask him to change what he had already created and to make me "straight." I went to church to pray for strength in facing the unknown and the then unforeseeable challenges I would encounter as an openly gay black man. At the time, I knew that homosexuality was widely despised, but I had rarely been to a black church where anyone had said as much. Most of the religious-based hatred I had heard came from the mouths of white ministers and televangelists, not from black ones.

After two consecutive weeks of intense prayer at church and at home, I was ready to share my identity with the world (or at least a small, politically correct part of it) so I could get on with the rest of my life. I felt the logical first step was to come out to my close relatives and friends. But I hesitated, deeply concerned with the social and political consequences of this decision. I feared that, at worst, I would be ostracized by my friends and disqualified from opportunities in politics and public life. My two fantasies from childhood—running for President and wrestling with a shirtless Eric—suddenly felt at odds with each other. I could not acknowledge my homosexuality and continue my political ambitions, I thought. I felt I had to decide which desire was more important to me, and I decided that living my life honestly was more important than holding public office. I imagined the misery I would feel at sixty if I realized that I had never been in love. Even as a successful progressive politician, what would I have accomplished if I had helped change society but had failed to change myself? If my political goals meant anything, I reasoned, then they meant that my personal life would make a political statement as well. Just being myself, and learning to be unafraid in doing so, would be the ultimate political accomplishment.

My first acts of coming out were tentative. During Bisexual, Gay, Lesbian Awareness Week at Harvard, I attended a forum on "Divided Loyalties" about gay people of color. This was the first gay-related event I had attended. Two nights later, I walked into a Harvard Square bookstore, positioned myself in front of the "Gay and Lesbian" section, and searched for a how-to book on being gay. I settled on the psychoanalytic *Being Homosexual: Gay Men and Their Development*. I read through it that night. Although I was twenty-five years old and a second-year student in law school, it was the first book about homosexuality I had read.

The next night, I decided to come out to my mother. I sat by the phone, repeatedly picking up the receiver and dialing a few digits. I anxiously rehearsed what I would say, how I would say it, and at what point in the conversation I would bring it up. I paced around my apartment wondering how she would react, but I was unable to think clearly enough to imagine an entire conversation. Finally, I threw caution to the wind and called her. My heart beat rapidly when she answered. "Hi, Mom, how you doing?" The conversation began as usual, but eventually took an unusual turn. I nervously took a deep breath and mustered up the courage to say, "Mom, I want to tell you something." Then I knew I had crossed the point of no return. I had to tell her something important, not something trivial about the weather or my classes. I rambled on for a few moments before finally managing to sandwich the words "I'm gay" into a convoluted sentence.

"Are you sure?" she asked.

"Yes, it took me a long time to realize it, but I'm sure."

My mother asked me all the typical questions. "Have you tried dating women?" "How long have you known this?" "Is it something I did?" I explained that I was sure about my feelings, that I had unconsciously tried to suppress them for twelve years, that I had dated women, and that it had nothing to do with my upbringing or my family environment. Although she said she had long suspected I might be gay, she seemed unwilling to accept the finality of my declaration. I think she held out hope that I was only going through a phase or that I would change. But she tried to be supportive and assured me that she still loved me. She ended the conversation with an admonition to "be careful," which she often says to me even now.

My mom and I are great friends, so it seemed natural that she would be the first person I would come out to. But for two months, she was the only family member I told. In fact, during the first six months after my decision, I came out to my roommate, my law school friends, my old college buddies, my summer employer in San Francisco, and my workmates in San

Francisco and Washington, D.C.—but not to most family members. My method of coming out was deliberately untheatrical and low-key. I wanted people to know about this part of my life, but I did not want to put on a big production. Except with relatives and close friends, I have always preferred not to sit people down to tell them I'm gay. I have adopted a more casual approach that integrates my sexual identity into the rest of my being, just as straight people will matter-of-factly discuss their lovers or spouses.

Fortunately, as I was going through the first phase of being openly gay, I had the luxury of dating James, who was white. We met when he was my editor at the *Harvard Civil Rights–Civil Liberties Law Review*. He was the first openly gay man I knew who appeared "normal" and was comfortable with his identity. With my consent, James told his friends we were dating, and his gossip spared me the task of actually coming out to many of our mutual friends.

Coming out to my family members, I found, was much more difficult than coming out to my friends. Because my family had known me longer than my friends had, I thought they at least deserved to hear the words "I'm gay" from my own lips rather than from a third party. For years they had known (or rather assumed) me to be heterosexual, so to change my public identity without telling them would have been callous. On the other hand, precisely because my family had known and loved me as one person, I worried that they might not accept me as another. Would they think I had deceived them for years? Would such deception offend them? I asked myself.

When months later I reflected on my early fears about coming out to my family, I came to appreciate their importance in my life. I realized that the concerns my mother had expressed about my safety and health and those my grandmother had subsequently expressed about my spiritual salvation were born out of the same sort of "tough love" that Dorothy learned about in *The Wiz*. Dorothy's mother warned her that she sometimes lost her patience because she had so many dreams she wanted Dorothy to fulfill. I think this explains why my grand-mother feared my going public with my homosexuality—she did not want me to be hurt or my dreams to be broken.

My experience growing up in a mostly white suburb had taught me that black parents were often more protective of their children, and therefore stricter disciplinarians, than white parents were. Black parents often taught their children what I call black survival. Having felt the sting of racism and discrimination in society, they did not permit their kids to wear rose-colored glasses to face the cruel world. They wanted them to know that white society would not tolerate from black children the same "indiscretions" it accepted from white kids. We were always taught we had to be twice as good as our white counter-parts.

Today, I think it is this same concern that leads our parents to discourage what the majority of white society considers socially inappropriate behavior, sexual or otherwise. They know from experience that white society will use any excuse it can to deny a black person an education, a job, a promotion, or a fair break. Therefore, rather than merely accepting homosexual children with comforting words of advice, our parents often warn us that society will mistreat us if we acknowledge that we are both black and gay. Although I have been lucky to have supportive parents, I know they remain concerned about my openness as a gay man. As my mother used to tell me every time we discussed gay issues, "Just be careful!" She meant, I can accept the fact that you're gay, but be discreet. She was concerned not only about AIDS but also about gay-bashing and jeopardizing my career and other problems often associated with being "openly" gay—the dangers of visibility.

After coming out to my mother, I tried not to deny my sexual identity to the rest of my family, but only if someone else raised the issue. I quickly realized that my duplicity made me into two different people living two very different lives. My persona at home in St. Louis differed starkly from my persona everywhere else. I hinted that I was gay rather than announcing it. Accepting a summer job in San Francisco (despite having no relatives in the city) and visiting St. Louis with a long, dangling earring were signals, but no one dared acknowledge to me that they saw any significance in these things. I think their reactions (or nonreactions) reflected the same assumption that prejudiced my perception of homosexuality. They could not imagine (or did not want to believe) that a successful, respectable member of their family could be gay. Although my deceased Uncle Michael had been gay, he had fit the homosexual stereotype. The image of a straitlaced, Harvard-educated lawyer, on the other hand, challenged my family's—not to mention my own—preconceptions about sexual orientation.

The first few times I visited St. Louis after partially coming out, I felt traumatized. The initial visit was on the Friday before Memorial Day Weekend, 1991, on my way from Boston to San Francisco and my summer job. I had scheduled my flight with a four-hour layover in St. Louis so I could see my family. My relatives seemed to come out of the woodwork. My father was in town, and my cousins and aunts and uncles who lived in the area showed up too. During the conversation at my grandmother's house, my family tried to convince me to change my flight and stay for the entire holiday weekend. After a year in the dehumanizing pressure cooker of law school, I sincerely wanted to, but I changed my mind soon after the conversation turned to the topic of marriage.

"Are you seeing anyone?" one relative asked.

"No," I said, and smiled, hoping my curt response would foreclose this line of questioning. But the questions and comments continued.

"I know Keith," said one female relative. "He's probably got him some white woman."

"He better *not* bring home some white woman," said another, only half-jokingly.

The conversation progressed slowly, and minutes began to feel like hours. I felt a lump in my throat, and my palms started to sweat. It was my first time in St. Louis since I'd come out at school, and now even typical, previously innocuous conversations seemed oppressive. Being "closeted," although only for a few hours, felt as if a lifetime of oppression were being thrown back at me. Without revealing my sexual orientation to my family as I had to my classmates and friends, I felt I was living a lie. Before returning to St. Louis, I had actually considered coming out to my father and grandmother during my brief layover in the city, but the conversation that day quickly dissuaded me from doing so. There were too many people around, I thought, who were probably not ready for such a disclosure.

It would take time for my family to grow and accept my openness as a homosexual. I did not condemn them for having failed to create a more supportive environment for me as a child because they had never known I needed such an atmosphere. That was their world. And since it had taken me twelve years to find myself, I did not expect my family to adapt more quickly than I had. So when I did come out to them, I decided to reveal my sexual orientation on a "need to know" basis. For example, when my sister announced that she wanted to visit me during my summer in San Francisco, I decided she had to be told, since I refused to hide my identity in my own home. I had a gay poster and gay newspapers in my living room, and I had a boyfriend living a few blocks from me whom I still planned to see while my sister was in town.

Over the phone, I told my sister I was gay and she accepted it very supportively. Her most intrusive question about my boyfriend was predictable. "Is he black or white?" she asked. "White," I sheepishly responded. That simple question led me to examine whether my family would react more favorably to my being involved with a black man than with a white woman. Homosexual and interracial relationships raise many of the same concerns to black families, including continuation of the family, humiliation of the family, and commitment to the race. A black man who dates only men raises the specter of the extinction of the family name, potentially causes embarrassment to the family, and often suggests an irresponsible disregard for the need to create strong black families. Dating a white woman raises similar concerns, compromising the racial purity of the family and the couple's offspring. Black homosexuals dating each other raises concerns too, but at least suggests some appreciation of the beauty within the race; it does not seem as much an abandonment of blackness as does interracial dating. The shared racial identity develops a much stronger family bond than any presumed identity based on sexual orientation. I never polled my family members, but ultimately I decided that some would be more disturbed by my dating a white woman, while others would be more upset by my dating a black man. This confusion helped me realize that I had to live my life for myself, not for my family.

After I had come out to my mother and my sister but before I came out to any of my relatives who still lived in Missouri, I made a five-day trip to St. Louis. My sister drove in from Atlanta to see me and the rest of the family. On my own, I explored the city with newly opened eyes to get a feel for its gay culture. But when I picked up the local gay newspaper at a newsstand and when I saw a movie during a gay film festival, I felt strangely guilty, as if I were violating some unspoken family law. I felt as if my great-grandmother, who had passed away a decade earlier, were looking down on me, shaking her head in obvious disappointment. So I surreptitiously planned my daily activities, and I did not tell my family how I spent that time. All this felt odd but not entirely oppressive, since I did not think of myself as lying to anyone. It was not until the night before I was to leave St. Louis that I fully realized the size of the gulf separating what I had become from what I had been. Raised in a simple, traditional family with suburban Midwestern values, I'd become a complex, untraditional urban dweller whose very existence challenged the conservative teachings of the Midwest.

Sitting at a relative's home late that last night, someone mentioned Richard Roundtree, the actor who starred in *Shaft*.

He was appalled that Roundtree had played a gay character in a recent edition of the television show *Roc.* "You couldn't *pay* me enough money to play that role," he said. Soon the topic shifted from actors playing homosexual roles to the subject of homosexuals themselves. Another relative mentioned a party she had attended recently where several of the guests wore drag. She and her husband seemed both amused and disgusted in describing the party. The words "faggot" and "fag" slipped off their tongues effortlessly, and at one point she said, "They didn't like you to call them fags either." She sounded surprised that gay people would object to an offensive term the way blacks object to racial epithets. "They wanted to be called, what's that word?" She paused. "Gay," she said. I stared at her, my mouth agape. Surely, she had heard the word "gay" before, I thought. Yet as she spoke with a sense of innocent detachment from the entire gay world, I felt the same sort of shock I had experienced when white people revealed their infuriating ignorance about black people.

As I caught a glimpse of my sister, Krystal, she joined in the conversation and tried to educate my family. She interjected, "You should see this movie, *Paris Is Burning.*" She described it as a documentary about part of the African-American and Puerto Rican gay community in New York. "Haven't you seen it, Keith?" She turned to me.

"Yes," I responded, surprised, but in a voice calm enough to disguise my nervousness. "It's very good," I added, for effect. I was pleased to hear Krystal's voice of reason, but I remained virtually silent as I rotated on my swivel chair to face each person as he or she spoke. Thoughts about coming out raced through my head, but I beat them back, deciding that I was not prepared yet for this step. I had not rehearsed what I would say, and I felt that a declaration of my homosexuality at this point would cause an uproar of some sort, and I was in no mood for a scene. All I wanted was to make it through the last night of my trip and return to Harvard, where discussions were less emotional and more intellectual. I had never felt so uncomfortable with my own family as I did that night. Although I had left Cambridge eager to get away from law school, I gladly returned there the next day.

When I finally did come out to other members of my family, not everyone reacted positively. My grandmother, for example, told me she had become weak and sick thinking about my "lifestyle." The conflict between us rose to a climax when she came to Cambridge for my law school graduation. I had broken up with my first boyfriend after he graduated and moved to San Francisco, and by the time of my own graduation the following year, I had become involved with someone else, an attractive black gay man named Lee. Lee accompanied me to the commencement exercises, but he had to sit with my family when the graduates were seated in their special section near the front of the stage. During the ceremony, as I learned later, my grandmother and another relative accosted Lee, telling him they did not approve of my lifestyle. They also asked Lee what his parents thought about *his* lifestyle and asked for their phone number in Chicago, which he supplied. When I learned about the incident later that day, I confronted my grandmother and told her that I did not appreciate her behavior. I asked her not to call Lee's parents, and I challenged her to tell me what there was about my "lifestyle" that she disapproved of. I tried to explain to her that she knew nothing about it; she knew only about my sexual orientation. But in spite of this confrontation, it would take years before she would begin to change her attitude about my homosexuality.

Unable to determine my appropriate role in my biological family, I began to look for comfort in some alternative families. I looked to the gay community, the black community, and then to the black gay community for support. Independently, the first two groups could not fully accept me. I found racism and racial ignorance in the white gay community, and homophobia and heterosexism in the black community. Only in the black gay community did I find a group with which I felt completely at home.

I have often been asked by blacks and gays alike which group I most closely identify with. I have been black for far longer than I have known I am gay, so I think I *understand* African-American culture better than gay culture. In addition, the gay community, politically and socially, has long been dominated by white men, so as a black person I have felt ostracized by that world. But at the same time, I do not believe many in the black community fully understand or accept me either. As a result, I've spent a great deal of my time and energy as an openly gay black man shuttling back and forth between my two identities.

It took time to learn about the dark realities of both communities. I had felt so liberated when I first came out that I began to immerse myself in the so-called gay lifestyle, slowly, unknowingly, destructively and absorbing characteristics of a culture that devalued me because of my color. I later learned how white gays had excluded African Americans, denying them entry into nightclubs, ignoring their contributions to the gay political movement, and reinforcing straight society's stereotypes and prejudices.

At the same time, the black community made my life difficult as well. When I lived in the closet, I suffered the oppression of living a lie, and once I came out, I faced a different prejudice, one based on fear and dislike. The more out I was, the more at risk I became. At first, some "straight" black men I knew observed me from afar with both curiosity and trepidation, as though they were examining a dangerous animal in the jungle. Others seemed afraid even to talk to me, apparently fearing that they, too, would be labeled gay by their association with me. When I hung out with certain black male classmates in law school, some would almost immediately begin talking about their girlfriends, as if to let me know they were straight. Being out, I learned, sometimes meant being marginalized by one's own communities.

Nevertheless, unlike many African-American lesbians and gays, I enjoyed the luxury of being able to come out with few real negative consequences. Out lesbians and gay men abounded at Harvard Law School and at my San Francisco law firm and in Democratic Party politics, so the threat of being penalized felt less significant in these places than it might have elsewhere.

Prodded by questions and anecdotes from newfound black gay friends, I began to challenge the white gay mainstream just as I had already questioned the black community. Ultimately, it was the black lesbian and gay community that reaffirmed my existence, helped me to love other black men and women, and taught me to love myself as a mirror image of these others. Within this group, I felt I could be a whole person rather than just a gay man or just a black man. I felt the comfort of unqualified love and acceptance that I had never really felt in other communities. Many of the black lesbians and gay men I met came from backgrounds different from my own. We had different jobs, interests, and desires. Yet I did not feel ostracized for not being "black enough" or for not being "gay enough."

I remember the exhilaration I felt when I visited my first gay nightclub, a dance palace called Colossus in San Francisco's SOMA district. There I discovered hundreds of men—strong and sexy, masculine and effeminate, stereotypical and unstereotypical—many of whom my hormone-sensitive eyes thought were gorgeous. They were dancing together, comfortably, openly, and naturally, and I did not feel guilty to be among them, cruising and being cruised. The pleasure I felt at that first gay nightclub was far surpassed, however, by what I experienced at my first black gay nightclub. On a Sunday night in July 1991 at a sprawling complex called Tracks in the District of Columbia, I found thousands of young black lesbians and gay men. At times, as I walked around the three dance floors, it seemed as though everyone in Washington were gay. The men I had spotted at the gym, the parishioners at the church, the salespeople at the department stores, even the guards at the White House, were there. But here, unlike at many white gay clubs, the patrons appreciated, and in fact reveled in, black beauty. For the first time, I felt not only desirous of others but desirable to them as well.

Years of hiding my sexual identity from myself and others had diminished my sense of self-worth. But in the black gay community I found a support group, if not a family, willing to love me and accept my love for them regardless of our differences. At the end of her long journey to Oz, Dorothy came to understand what had eluded her before: what and where is home? She learned to think of home as a place of abundant, unqualified love. In a strange way, she spoke for me as a black gay man deciding whether to come out of the closet. On the one hand, I wanted to return home to my family and to the black community; but on the other hand, I was unsure whether I would be welcomed by either once they learned who I really was. I followed the road in my heart, and I started on my way home.

I soon learned that the assumptions I had made were not always accurate. By assuming my family would react negatively to my homosexuality, I made this reality somewhat self-fulfilling. By dodging and tiptoeing around the issue, I thought I could protect both myself and them from the painful and bitter discussions that gay friends had told me about. Instead, by not challenging anyone to confront the reality of my identity and my place in the family, I only made it harder for us all. But as I began to come out to family members, I learned to do something I had never been able to do before—to love. I learned to love myself enough so that I could open up and love other people, and I learned to love my family enough to be honest with them in spite of the consequences.

In February 1995, my grandmother called me from St. Louis. She knew I would be traveling to Los Angeles and she wanted to wish me well. "What's going on in Los Angeles?" she asked.

"The Black Gay and Lesbian Leadership Forum," I answered.

"So you're going to be interviewing people out there?"

"I sure hope so," I said.

"You think you can find anybody in St. Louis to interview, so you can come and see me?"

"I'm sure I can," I told her. "I'm sure I can."

CHAPTER TWO

Are Blacks and Gays the Same?

Advancing down Pennsylvania Avenue like an army of the unwanted, legions of lesbian and gay marchers repeated a mantra-like chant: "Gay, straight, black, white: same struggle, same fight." The organizers of the event—the 1993 National March on Washington for Lesbian, Gay, and Bi Equal Rights and Liberation—liberally invoked the name of Dr. Martin Luther King, Jr., and freely conjured up memories of the historic March on Washington for Jobs and Freedom thirty years earlier. By labeling their march "A Simple Matter of Justice" and positioning themselves as the natural successors to the civil rights movement's legacy of protest, the

1993 marchers were challenging the black community and the public-at-large to welcome them into the mainstream of the American civil rights tradition for social justice. Although the lesbian and gay movement had won the support of high-profile black leaders such as Coretta Scott King, the Reverend Jesse Jackson, and NAACP executive director Benjamin Chavis, conservatives in the black religious community balked, and since the black church had led the three-hundred-year struggle against the nation's most pernicious inequity, black religious leaders spoke with unparalleled credibility when they rejected any comparisons between blacks and gays.

By marching on Washington, lesbians and gays launched a major volley in the battle to reclaim the civil rights mantle, but they did so with the same strategy employed by their opponents. All the various factions—including the conservative religious community, the conservative military, and a relatively progressive black community that jealously guards the memory of the black struggle—have fought to extort, exploit, and appropriate the good name of the civil rights movement and its most visible icons. Each side, quoting selectively from history and speeches, portrays itself as the direct descendant of Dr. Martin Luther King's dream. White religious conservatives, who have discovered a fund-raising jackpot by exploiting homosexuals, seek to divide blacks against gays by playing on the black community's worst fears, telling blacks that their "legitimate" civil rights are threatened by the "special rights" requests of lesbians and gays. The religious conservatives, many of whom had not favored civil rights for blacks in the 1960s, suddenly call out the name of Dr. King to *oppose* gay rights as freely as King's widow uses his name to *support* gay rights.

While many mainline black civil rights leaders have endorsed in words, if not in deeds, the principle of equal rights for lesbians and gays, not everyone in the black elite agrees. General Colin Powell, former chairman of the Joint Chiefs of Staff, has become the most visible African-American opponent of the comparison between blacks and gays. In rejecting what he called the "attempts to draw parallels" between the ban on gays in the military and the segregation of black soldiers, Powell positioned himself in the tradition of Dr. King's vision when he wrote in May 1992 to white liberal representative Patricia Schroeder: "I can assure you that I need no reminders concerning the history of African Americans in the defense of their nation and the tribulations they faced. I am part of that history."

Powell dismissively rejected the comparison between blacks and gays with three simple sentences: "Skin color is a benign, non-behavioral characteristic. Sexual orientation is perhaps the most profound of human behavioral characteristics. Comparison of the two is a convenient but invalid argument." Although the general spoke with the clarity and brevity that usually convey authority, each of his three statements can be proved wrong. Race is not merely a matter of skin color, nor has it ever been considered benign or nonbehavioral. The whole history of America's troubled race relations contradicts such rose-colored historical revisionism. In addition, sexual orientation is not just about behavior. To assume that sexual orientation is merely behavioral suggests that individuals have no sexual orientation when they are not behaving sexually. While the act of having sex, whether heterosexual or homosexual, is certainly behavioral, the mere orientation toward one gender or another is not. Finally, the comparison of race with sexual orientation is not only a convenient argument but a valid one, not because the two characteristics are exactly the same but because most people have misunderstood them. In his letter, Powell himself misunderstood the two and failed to consider that race is not only about blacks and that sexual orientation is not only about gays. Nevertheless, even Powell recognized some similarities between the plight of the two groups when he told President Clinton privately that he would oppose the segregation of homosexual soldiers if the gay ban were lifted.

In many ways, Colin Powell's public opposition to gays in

the military shut off the debate prematurely. Coming from the nation's highest-ranking black soldier, his analysis allowed white conservatives to hide behind his unquestionable credibility and discouraged white liberals from challenging him directly. The general's comments deprived the country of a much-needed discussion about race and sexual orientation and allowed us to retreat to the safety of our cocoons, where we did not need to think for ourselves because someone had already done our thinking for us.

Rather than educating or leading the public about gays and blacks in the military, Powell's analysis simply echoed the popularly perceived distinctions between race and sexual orientation. In fact, much of the division between blacks and homosexuals can be traced to fundamental misconceptions that each group holds about the other. Arguing from positions of raw emotion, blacks and homosexuals and others often ignore the complexity involved in comparing race with sexual orientation. We find ourselves hopelessly mired in simplistic sloganeering rather than seriously considering similarities and differences of identity, behavior, mutability, and oppression. Only when we examine carefully how race and sexual orientation are defined and (mis)understood in this country can we better determine what common ground, if any, exists between blacks and gays.

Comparing Identity

Race and sexual orientation are not easily identified or defined. We discover the first problem when we attempt to define blackness itself. Despite the widespread use of skin color as a racial indicator, natural varieties and gradations of color arising from centuries of interracial mingling have diminished its usefulness in defining race for blacks and whites. If we judged blackness solely by skin color, we might find ourselves including darker-skinned Hispanics, Asians, Indians, and even European Mediterraneans—who claim no identity as black people—and excluding some lighter-skinned blacks who appear to be white. A study by the National Center for Health Statistics found that 5.8 percent of the people who called themselves black were seen as white by census interviewers. If skin color alone were used to measure blackness, it would alter our understanding of existing racial categories.

In 1986, the U.S. Supreme Court let stand a lower court's ruling that a visibly white Louisiana woman was actually black because her great-great-great-great-grandmother had been a black slave in the eighteenth century. The woman thought of herself as white, was raised as white, lived in the white community, looked white, and had been married twice to men who thought she was white. But she said she discovered in 1977 that the Louisiana Bureau of Vital Statistics had listed her as "colored." She took her case to court to prove that she was white, but lost. The Supreme Court, without hearing the case, effectively affirmed the principle known as the "one-drop rule"—that anyone with any trace of black blood in them is to be considered black. As UCLA professor G. Reginald Daniel told Lawrence Wright in a 1994 article for *The New Yorker,* "We are the only country in the world that applies the one-drop rule, and the only group that the one-drop rule applies to is people of African descent."

Despite our country's long-standing obsession with race, it was not until 1977 that the federal government issued uniform standards to define what we mean by race. In a government report on higher education for Chicanos, Puerto Ricans, and American Indians, the Federal Interagency Committee on Education (FICE) recommended developing common definitions for racial and ethnic groups to replace duplicative and incompatible information in use at the time. The standard was later articulated in a memorandum from the President's Office of Management and Budget called OMB's Statistical Policy Directive No. 15.

Directive No. 15 established four races (American Indian

or Alaskan Native, Asian or Pacific Islander, Black, and White) and two ethnicities (Hispanic Origin and Not of Hispanic Origin) for all government classification purposes. It defined as black any person who has "origins in any of the black racial groups of Africa," but curiously defined as white those with origins in North Africa, Europe, or the Middle East. But as University of Michigan professor C. Loring Brace told *Newsweek* magazine in February 1995, "There is no organizing principle by which you could put 5 billion people into so few categories in a way that would tell you anything important about humankind's diversity."

The problems compound when we consider the classification of multiracial people. For example, a white man with curly hair, somewhat full lips, and Mediterranean skin described himself to me as "European African." One of his parents, he said, is from Cameroon in western Africa and the other is from a European country. Although he does not look stereotypically African, he complained, "I have a closer connection to Africa than a lot of these other people around here who call themselves African American."

When we ask multiracial people to self-identify in our bipolar racial dyad, we are asking them to choose which part of themselves is most important. In a sense, we are asking them to box themselves into neatly wrapped categories that make our worlds easier to understand. Multiracial people, therefore, often end up ostracized by one or both races. This was the case in February 1994 when the principal of a high school in Wedowee, Alabama, reportedly told a multiracial student that she was a "mistake" and threatened to cancel the school's prom if interracial couples planned to attend. Because the world is not as simple as we would like it to be, coercive categorization into racial groupings leads us to overlook actual differences that exist within the races.

The debate about definitions exposes a disturbing reality about the meaning of race in America. Although we often talk about race as though everyone agreed on the basic terms, more than two hundred years after the founding of the nation, no one—not even the federal government—has yet to develop a widely acceptable definition of what it means to be black. For anyone, therefore, to speak of race as benign skin color is to misunderstand how race is misunderstood.

America also fails to recognize how homosexuality is defined and misunderstood. Because we usually only know someone is lesbian or gay if she or he tells us so, self-identification raises unique challenges. The authors of a 1994 study conducted at the University of Chicago found differences in homosexual self-identification based on race, geography, and education, determining that whites, urban residents, and well-educated people were more likely to *consider* themselves homosexuals than others who are not part of these categories but who still engage in homosexual activity. "To quantify or count something requires unambiguous definition," the authors wrote. "And we lack this in speaking of homosexuality."

Polls and public opinion surveys that purport to measure the prevalence of homosexuality actually measure only the prevalence of people who, for whatever reason, are willing to *acknowledge* their homosexuality. Despite pollsters' assurance of anonymity, many closeted lesbians and gays will not admit their homosexuality to a stranger on the telephone. As San Francisco supervisor Susan Leal explained to a reporter, "Not everyone will come out of the closet in a survey taken in a shopping mall or wherever." In addition, polls do not reflect people who deny their homosexuality to themselves or those who have not yet come to terms with it. Instead of measuring the percentage of homosexuals, what these polls often measure is the percentage of people who have recognized their homosexuality, acknowledged it to themselves, and become comfortable enough with it to admit it to at least one other person when asked. This may be a small subset of the overall population of homosexuals.

The self-closeting that homosexuals engage in can be divided into two categories: (1) failure to disclose and (2) affirmative misrepresentation. The failure to disclose sexual orientation is typically what outsiders see when they describe the invisibility of lesbians and gays as a benefit. This usually occurs in millions of everyday situations when someone wrongly assumes that the person they are dealing with is heterosexual. "Your girlfriend will love to see you wear this," the salesman might say to the gay man, but few gay men would correct the salesman by interjecting "boyfriend." On the other hand, affirmative misrepresentation occurs when the lesbian or gay man plays along and contributes to the lie. "Yes, I think she would like this," the gay man might respond to the salesman.

In an effort to avoid either controversy or detection, lesbians and gays play title roles in this affirmative conspiracy of silence. When our families ask if we are dating, we don't just confirm that we are; instead, we make up gender-appropriate names for our loved ones and substitute pronouns to hide the same-sex identity of our lovers. Homosexuals do not self-identify for many reasons. Some do not want to be homosexual in the first place, while others fear the consequences of being open about their sexual orientation. Either way, their denial of identity represents a form of internalized homophobia. While only a small percentage of blacks actually pass as white, the overwhelming majority of homosexuals pass as heterosexual. Even "out" lesbians and gays—unless they wear a button or a T-shirt that clearly labels them—do not self-identify in some contexts.

Outsiders, including many blacks who reject comparisons between blacks and gays, may view this ability to pass as lessening the oppression felt by homosexuals, but many lesbians and gays experience it as profoundly disempowering and dishonest, forcing them to "live a lie." Barbara Smith, an author and openly lesbian black woman, compares the oppression of the closet with that of the black woman who straightens or dyes her hair to make it look more like white hair. "People are *deciding* that they want to go that way," she says, "but if there was suddenly a community expectation that every person of color had to try to look as Caucasian as possible, I think there would be a lot of problems with that."

When we do not know or cannot tell someone's race, we often wait to see how she identifies herself. Generally, we consider someone black if she tells us she is black, even though she appears to be white. But what do we do with someone who says she is white but looks black? Often we ridicule that person for not accepting her identity. These contrary responses reflect our understanding of race, power, and prejudice. While we perceive dozens of benefits that would accrue to someone who chooses to pass as white, we fail to see the benefit of passing as black. Why else, we ask, would anyone surrender the privileges of presumed whiteness unless she really was not white?

Similarly, widespread homophobia among lesbians and gays complicates the problem of identifying them. The various ways in which people self-identify their sexual orientation reveal the layers of secrecy and privacy we have to unfold in order to see the reality. For example, a few years ago, when I asked a friend about his sexual orientation, he refused to assign a label to himself, but he denied that he was gay. Eventually, I learned that he had been involved in a long-term intimate relationship with another man at the time I had asked the question. "How could you say you're not gay," I asked him later. "Well, I'm still attracted to women," he said. "I just happen to be dating a man." A young man I met at a gay nightclub in Washington responded similarly: "I just fool around." A third man told me that he did not consider himself gay because he still felt "emotionally" attracted to women, although his physical and sexual attraction was to men. "Sexual orientation is about your *sexual* orientation, not your emotional orientation, so doesn't that make you gay?" I asked him. He did not budge from his opinion.

As we can see from these examples, self-identification will not always provide clear answers to the question of sexual orientation. I do not suggest that self-identification is useless in determining someone's sexual orientation; in fact, it can be the

most important determinant. But given the multiplicity of definitions of homosexuality, especially among homosexuals themselves, we may have trouble determining if we are all talking
about the same thing. For one person, being homosexual
means participating in a stereotypically flamboyant "gay lifestyle," while for another it means taking part in *any* type of
intimate behavior with someone of the same gender. Many of
the people who engage in same-sex sexual behavior do not
consider themselves homosexual, for one of three reasons: because they do not identify with other homosexuals, because
they only take part in homosexual behavior in certain limited
circumstances, or because they also have sex with people of the
opposite sex.

Because of our biases and fears about being gay, self-identification may be most useful as an inclusive device rather than
an exclusive one when it comes to identifying homosexuals.
We cannot always assume that everyone who denies he is gay is
actually not gay. Societal pressures to conform to expected
behavior often prejudice our images of self, sweeping closeted
homosexuals and bisexuals into the broad swath of presumed
heterosexuality. However, using the same logic we employ with
racial identity, we can usually safely assume that most people
who acknowledge they are homosexual honestly believe they
are homosexual. As with race, we reflect our visions of power,
prejudice, and identity when we ask, "Why else would anyone
volunteer to bear the wrath of homophobia if they were
not gay? Why else would anyone choose to surrender the privileges of presumed heterosexuality unless they really were not
heterosexual?"

Comparing Behavior

"Most people think of racial identity as a matter of (racial)
status, but they respond to it as behavior," writes Henry Louis
Gates, Jr., in *The New Yorker*. In contrast, he adds, "most

people think of sexual identity as a matter of (sexual) behavior, but they respond to it as a status." As a result, we think of blacks based on their racial status, but we assign stereotypical behavior to them. On the other hand, Gates writes, disapproval of gay sexual practice "is transmuted into the demonization of a sexual species." For both groups, there is a status and a behavior component to their identity. For Colin Powell, therefore, to suggest that sexual orientation is about behavior and race is not is to misunderstand both characteristics and to ignore the similarities in the behavioral stereotypes.

While race may appear to be benign and nonbehavioral when we think of it in comparison to sexual orientation, such comparisons often overlook the history of stereotypical behaviors that have been, and in many cases still are, assigned to race. As black historian Roger Wilkins has noted, "In an earlier era—and perhaps still today—skin color evoked a host of behavioral stereotypes that were barriers to black advancement."

Blackness is still associated with a host of negative behaviors, from criminality to sexual promiscuity, a reputation that has lingered since slavery, when black men were considered sexual predators toward white women and black women were thought of as nymphomaniacs to justify their rape by white men. In fact, when we think of blacks, we are more likely to conjure up images of lazy workers, criminals, and sexually active welfare mothers than of industrious, law-abiding, entrepreneurs. The Reverend Jesse Jackson acknowledged that blacks themselves internalize the stereotypes when he said, "There is nothing more painful to me . . . than to walk down the street and hear footsteps and start thinking about robbery, then look around and see somebody white and feel relieved."

So profound are the behavioral stereotypes assigned to blacks that in some instances society does not even wait for the expected behavior to take place before harassing us. In Union Point, Georgia, a town of 1,750 people, the authorities responded to a shoplifting problem by publishing a list of twenty-one *suspected* shoplifters and banned them all from entering local businesses. In a town that is only 43 percent black, every one of the twenty-one suspects was black. Similarly, in Springfield, Illinois, a sign at the Lincoln Yellow Cab Company in November 1995 warned the drivers: EFFECTIVE IMMEDIATELY DO NOT PICK UP ANY BLACK MALES UNLESS YOU FEEL IT IS SAFE. When the company's lawyer told the manager to change the sign after a reporter had spotted it and asked questions, the manager replaced the sign with one that said DO NOT PICK UP ANY SUSPICIOUS-LOOKING PERSONS. Since the seed had already been planted in the minds of the drivers, "suspicious-looking" would be interpreted as "black male" and the effect of the new sign would be the same as the first, demonstrating the subtle mechanisms by which racism perpetuates itself even when it is challenged. In effect, the local businesses and the cab company were punishing blacks, and particularly black men, for their status and for what they assumed that status implied about their behavior.

Quite similarly, when we think of lesbians and gays, we tend to confuse status with behavior or conduct. In a colloquy between BET talk show host Bev Smith, the Reverend Lester James, and other guests on an October 1995 broadcast, Smith asked the minister, "If you had a son or a daughter and they came to you and said, 'Daddy, I'm gay, I'm a lesbian,' what would you do? How would you handle it?"

"I would love that child but I would always stand against their lifestyle," James responded.

"What is their lifestyle," I and several other panelists asked.

"What is the homosexual lifestyle? It is the direct opposite of *heterosexual,*" James said, lowering his voice to a whisper on the last word.

"What does that mean," I asked.

"You want me to spell it out?"

"Yes, please spell it out."

"First of all, anal intercourse," he said, and left it at that. That exchange illustrates a common and fundamental problem in our understanding of sexual orientation: our minds cannot separate homosexuality from behavior. When most of us think of homosexuality, we conjure up a whole set of images and behaviors that may offend our moral sensibility. Perhaps the most powerfully offputting image depicts two men engaged in anal intercourse. The sight of a woman performing cunnilingus on another woman may stimulate similarly negative feelings. Some of us imagine men dressed as women and women dressed as men. Some remember pictures of ACT UP protesters hurling condoms after Mass at St. Patrick's Cathedral in New York, while others may think of bare-breasted women parading through the streets in San Francisco's gay pride parade.

Whatever image we visualize, when we think of homosexuality we think of behavior, and the behavior we think of is usually sexual. On the other hand, heterosexual sexual orientation has become so ingrained in our social custom, so destigmatized of our fears about sex, that we often fail to make any connection between heterosexuality and sex. Wedding rings, pregnancies, spousal office photos, and other badges of heterosexuality often conjure up no images of the sex act between the two heterosexual partners, but just the mention of someone's homosexual sexual orientation starts us thinking about "the unthinkable."

Our media, in the form of literature, television, radio, film, and theater, reinforce this image by constantly connecting homosexuals with sex. For example, the annual *Compendium of American Public Opinion* compiles results of numerous public opinion surveys into chapters ranging from health to media to religion. The chapter on "Minorities" deals with blacks, Jews, and immigrants, but not with homosexuals. Instead, they can be found in the chapter on "Sex," along with premarital and extramarital sex, pornography, and prostitution. On picture-obsessed television, news stories are often told with "B-roll" footage that runs on the screen as the on-air reporter or anchorperson speaks. For local stories about lesbians and gays, the most often used footage (gathered by sending a camera crew to the gay part of town) shows men or women holding hands with people of the same sex. Likewise, with gay pride parades, the cameras always focus on people who appear to be gay or who are doing something that seemingly identifies them as gay. Camera footage of thousands of "average-looking" people walking down a street would not convince anyone that the marchers were gay. The only way television knows how to show lesbians or gay men is to portray them engaging in some form of "homosexual" behavior.

Although the stereotypes persist about blacks as well, society has grown less tolerant of many racial behavioral assumptions. In fact, we would criticize a television news program that showed blacks dancing or eating watermelon every time it ran a story about African Americans. However, the invisibility of sexual orientation almost guarantees that lesbians and gays will be identified by their behavior rather than by their appearance, thus reducing homosexuals to their behavior alone.

In a twenty-minute antigay video called *The Gay Agenda,* Dr. Stanley Monteith, a member of the ultraconservative John Birch Society, says, "Most Americans would be highly offended if they really knew what was involved" in the gay lifestyle. Monteith claims that gay men commonly ingest feces and urine as part of their sexual behavior, that the average homosexual has between 20 and 106 sexual partners a year, and that 28 percent engage in sodomy with more than 1,000 partners over the course of their lives. But as the Anti-Defamation League (ADL) reveals in its publication *The Religious Right,* Monteith's claims are based entirely on a study comprised of interviews with a mere forty-one individuals. The study itself was conducted by Paul Cameron, whom the ADL identifies as an "anti-gay extremist" expelled from the American Psychological Association and denounced by the American Sociological Association for having "consistently misinterpreted and misrepresented sociological research." Still, Cameron's assertions resonate with an uninformed public that often fails to see beyond the rhetoric.

Stereotypes about gay sexual behavior ignore the variety of sexual practices engaged in by people of all sexual orientations. For example, during the May 1993 Senate hearings on gays in the military, octogenarian South Carolina senator Strom Thurmond asked Senator John Kerry if homosexuals engaged in anal intercourse. "Some do," Kerry responded. Thurmond then zeroed in to make his point, saying, "Heterosexuals don't practice sodomy." A red-faced Kerry broke the news to an even redder-faced Thurmond that some heterosexuals do engage in oral and anal sex.

While we might excuse an eighty-year-old Southerner for his lack of familiarity with various sexual practices, what explains the ignorance of so many younger and supposedly better informed people? Many of us, heterosexual and homosexual alike, still labor under a delusion that limits sex to notions of specific behavior. For heterosexuals, that stereotypical behavior means the "missionary position"; for homosexuals, it means anal sex. But these generalizations not only misrepresent the practices of some heterosexuals, they misrepresent the practices of many homosexuals as well. While many gay men do engage in anal intercourse, others do not. In an age of increasing concern about sexually transmitted diseases such as AIDS, a growing number of male homosexuals choose to avoid anal intercourse altogether and instead find fulfillment in other sexual activities. The generalizations also contribute to phallocentric visions of sexuality that exclude many women's sexual practices and needs from consideration. Both heterosexual and homosexual men foster this devaluation of women's sexuality by assuming that the only "real" sexual activity involves a man's penis.

Other behavioral assumptions about homosexuality prove equally problematic. For example, the image of the limp-wristed, flamboyant queen is not only distortive but in some ways also outdated. This is not to say that flamboyant male homosexuals do not exist, but with the evolution of gay male culture, they have become marginalized. Replacing the effeminate man as the new archetypal preference is the image of the rough or supermacho man. The attire of choice for many of these men revolves around jeans, workboots, baseball caps, and form-fitting shirts that expose beefed-up bodies (often accessorized with a thin veil of attitude). Similarly, many lesbians do not subscribe to the stereotypical "butch" image that heterosexuals imagine; instead, they embrace a more traditional "femme" identity. The point of debunking the stereotypes is not to suggest that they have no value in determining who might be homosexual (in fact, many homosexuals themselves use the same stereotypes to label or identify one another). The point is that stereotypes have limited utility. They may appear innocent and harmless when we joke among ourselves, but stereotypes take on a more insidious connotation when policymakers, lawmakers, and people who call themselves thinkers use them to make decisions. What both gay and straight people need to recognize is that just as there is no uniform gay lifestyle or culture, there is no universal gay behavior either.

Despite the absence of a universal gay reality, we find no shortage of antigay critics stirring up controversy and feigning expertise about a so-called gay lifestyle. Conflating sexual orientation with sexual practice and behavior, the Reverend Kenneth Henry told the *Atlanta Journal-Constitution* in August 1993, "I do not accept homosexuality as an acceptable lifestyle." This lifestyle argument follows the pattern of what philosophers call the "converse fallacy of accident" because it attempts to establish a rule by picking out a few unrepresentative examples. For instance, a July 29, 1994, press release from the right-wing Traditional Values Coalition contends that "the homosexual community is on an admitted national public relations campaign to force acceptance of their lifestyle upon American society and culture . . ." And what is that lifestyle? As the Reverend Jerry Falwell explains, it involves "those bare-breasted women flaunting themselves in the streets in front of the White House . . . and the homosexual perverts simulating sex on each other in public—in front of national television cameras—for innocent children to witness . . . and the transvestites—and the child molesters . . ." As others describe the gay lifestyle, it means picking up hundreds of sexual partners a year at seedy gay bars and in public parks.

Just as homosexuals cannot be stereotyped into simplistic negative stereotypes, neither can they be stereotyped into simplistic positive ones. We need only scan the television channels to find examples of exhibitionists, nymphomaniacs, transvestites, and child molesters of either sexual orientation. In other words, some homosexuals do fit into categories of stereotypical lifestyles, but some do not. What does that prove except that the gay community, like the straight community, is made up of diverse people? But the tone of Falwell's rhetoric suggests that Americans should be so repulsed at the mere suggestion of homosexuality that they should close down all mental functioning and allow religious bigots like himself to dictate their thoughts. Falwell would have his followers believe that a few isolated examples selected by the antigay right wing reflect the norm of homosexual behavior, and because of this, all decent God-fearing Americans should cringe at the mere thought of homosexuality. For instance, in a fund-raising letter to "Christian friends," Falwell attacks openly gay federal employee Bob Hattoy because he *proudly declared that he is a homosexual—* AND THAT HE HAS AIDS!" (The emphasis in the letter is Falwell's, not mine.) Apparently, Falwell would prefer that homosexuals and people with AIDS lead lives of shame rather than accept their status. Later in the letter, he asks for donations of $25 or more so he can personally "keep President Clinton from hiring more homosexuals like Roberta Achtenberg, Leonard Hirsch, and Keith Boykin—into the federal government." I have never met Jerry Falwell, so his attack on me cannot be based on personal knowledge but instead on some assumption that my homosexuality equates to my participation in a particular lifestyle he does not support. But since I have never "flaunted" myself in front of the White House or simulated sex in front of television cameras or been a transvestite or child molester, I am not certain I know what he means when he objects to my lifestyle.

The perverse effect of men of the cloth (who act in the name of Christ) attacking others merely for being who they are is that they may actually help to create the lifestyle they claim to deplore. By contributing to an atmosphere of intolerance, these religious leaders may encourage homosexuals to express their sexual desires as part of a secretive, underground culture. Eager to avoid persecution, homosexuals may select this surreptitious lifestyle over healthier, open expressions of their sexuality. Instead of developing self-love for who they are, they may then struggle with low self-esteem and engage in increasingly risky and self-destructive behavior.

Perhaps because of the widespread condemnation they experience, problems of low self-esteem and self-abusive behavior seem more pervasive among homosexuals than many gay people would like to acknowledge. The inclination to deny or paper over this issue is a tactical mistake made by some gay activists, who would prefer to create a false image of the homosexual population as well-adjusted, unthreatening next-door-neighbor types. There are two major problems with this approach. First, it inaccurately portrays our (presumably heterosexual) neighbors as free of affliction and places them on a pedestal, in a position above all homosexuals. Rather than aspiring to be just like stereotypes of other people, lesbians and gays should aspire to be comfortable with themselves. Second, by avoiding the real problems within the community, gays themselves may lead some troubled homosexuals to delay the recognition of their need for treatment. Instead of denying the self-abusive behavior, the gay community might better acknowledge the problem and then point the finger of blame where it properly belongs—not at homosexuality but at homophobia. As some antigay zealots claim, homosexuals lead lonely, miserable lives, but these zealots are the very ones who want nothing more than to make homosexual life miserable so they can continue their chastisement.

Disturbingly, many in the black community have been unknowingly co-opted into this scheme. In an effort to confuse and anger African Americans, the religious right has embarked on a campaign to convince blacks that homosexuals are claiming to be exactly like they are. Many blacks, understandably hesitant after years of struggle against racist oppression, are reluctant to be compared and "reduced" to the level of an even more disfavored group in society. "I don't want to be put in that bag," a forty-seven-year-old black carpenter told *The Wall Street Journal* in October 1994. Homosexuality is different from blackness, he said, because homosexuality is wrong. He did not question why homosexuality is considered wrong, nor did he remember how blacks were once thought to be immoral. Like so many others, the carpenter seemed merely to repeat what he had been told without examining its truthfulness or meaning. Nevertheless, the comparison between blacks and gays is a red herring.

Although lesbian and gay activists often compare the struggles against racism and homophobia, they usually do not equate blacks with gays. No one I interviewed—gay or straight, "militant" activist or closeted homosexual, white or black— said blacks and gays were exactly the same. "How can we even compare that when we have a whole section of gay America that is black?" That response, posed by Elizabeth Birch, the executive director of the nation's largest national lesbian and gay organization, the Human Rights Campaign, typifies other comments by homosexuals themselves, all of whom denied that blacks and gays are the same. What, then, is the source of the comparison? A misreading of the lesbian and gay community's rhetoric. When the lesbian and gay marches chant "Gay, straight, black, white: same struggle, same fight," they are not saying that blacks and gays are the same. Instead, they are saying the two communities' struggles for liberation are the same. This is still a questionable claim, given the differences between the black civil rights movement and the lesbian and gay movement, but it does make sense if we interpret it to mean that the fight against all oppression shares a common nexus.

The radical religious right takes the gay community's own language one step further and, purposefully or not, twists it to incense blacks. A typical press release issued by the conservative Traditional Values Coalition begins with the headline THERE IS NO COMPARISON: HOMOSEXUALS ARE NOT THE SAME AS RACIAL MINORITIES (July 29, 1994). The Coalition makes its point by setting up a straw opponent and then attacking that nonexistent enemy for its outrageous views. But in the case of blacks and gays, something more sinister appears at work than the use of cheap argumentative tricks. Instead, the aim is to divide two oppressed minority groups from each another, outwardly to weaken the homosexual movement but actually to splinter all those with whom the right disagrees. Bumper stickers reportedly sold at a recent convention of Republican women demonstrate the common enemies of the radical right. WORK—IT'S THE WHITE THING TO DO, says one antiblack bumper sticker, according to Kentucky's gay paper, *The Letter.* Not far away, an antigay bumper sticker compared Presidents Clinton and Roosevelt: ROOSEVELT—A CHICKEN IN EVERY POT; CLINTON—A FAG IN EVERY PUP TENT. What the radical right won't tell you is that the same conservative religious movement that now opposes gay rights opposed the extension of civil rights to African Americans a generation ago.

Perhaps the clearest example of the similarity between gay and black behavioral stereotypes can be found in the military. This fact should not surprise General Powell, especially since he reminds us that he is a part of the history of struggle against racial discrimination in the armed forces. With the U.S. military's "don't ask, don't tell" policy, the behavior that people oppose is simply the declaration of one's sexual orientation. Senator Sam Nunn, for example, asked, "When someone announces [they are gay], isn't that also stating a basic tendency for sodomy?" In Nunn's mind, the statement of one's status has been transformed into behavior itself. The mere status of being gay communicates a whole host of assumptions about one's conduct in the military.

The same behavioral assumptions Nunn and Powell today assign to lesbians and gays were previously assigned to African Americans. Making assumptions based on intelligence, performance, criminal propensity, and even promiscuity, defenders of the status quo fifty years ago opposed integration of blacks into the military. In 1942, the chairman of the General Board of the Navy wrote that his branch of the service was all-white because "those in control have believed and experience has demonstrated that the white man is more adaptable and more efficient in the various conditions which are involved in the making of an effective man-of-war." These behavioral assumptions make even less sense when applied to homosexuals, who, unlike blacks in the 1940s, are already integrated into the military, though they serve in the closet.

Much of the debate over gays in the military has focused on the distinction between status and conduct, with gay rights advocates now arguing in court that one's status as a homosexual does not necessarily suggest that that person will engage in homosexual activity. Yet at other points in the debate the same advocates maintain that it is unfair to expect gay people to serve without allowing them to act on their sexual orientation, since this would mean asking them not to be gay. Similarly, gay rights advocates maintain that criminalizing homosexual sodomy constitutes punishing homosexuals merely because of their status. This is not the case. What sodomy laws criminalize is acting on one's sexuality, which is behavior, not the status of being sexually oriented toward a particular gender. Of course, singling out a group and punishing them for acting on their sexual desires with other consenting adults is unfair, but unless one assumes that sexual orientation and sexual behavior are essentially linked, status itself remains unpunished. In fact, gay rights advocates often seem to make conflicting arguments about the connection between homosexuality and homosexual sex. They seem to be arguing that engaging in gay sexual conduct is the essence of being gay at the same time they argue that it has nothing to do with being gay.

Opponents of gay rights often commit the same type of mistake. On the one hand, conservative religious leaders claim gay people are unavoidably afflicted with a perversion that compels them to do wicked things and molest children; on the other hand, they claim to hate only the sin and not the sinner. But because they imagine an unbreakable link between homosexuality and perversion, they cannot very well claim that homosexual conduct is their target as opposed to homosexuals themselves. Similarly, secular gay rights opponents simply assume that gay sex is the natural end product of the gathering of any more than one homosexual. For example, in one typical legal case, a judge voted against allowing the University of Missouri to permit the creation of a gay campus organization, using the logic that "the First Amendment does not require a University to extend formal recognition to a campus organization that will engage in criminal activity." Presumably, the criminal activity of which he spoke was the act of sodomy, which he apparently believed flowed inevitably from any educational or political gathering of homosexuals, be they male or female, sexually active or not.

To compare gay behavior with black behavior is merely to compare one stereotype with another, and on that score we find common ground. Members of both groups are identified by assumptions that connect their status with some sort of unflattering behavior. The specific behaviors themselves may differ, but the nature of the stereotyping is exactly the same.

Comparing Mutability

In Living Color, a popular television comedy show, featured two stereotypical gay men in a series called "Men on Film." The two men, Blaine and Antoine, dressed in fabulous flowing chiffon, bell-bottoms, and women's haltertops, sat on stools with their legs crossed and their wrists limp as they reviewed motion pictures in their chatty, homoerotic style. The theme continued for several episodes until Blaine was struck by a falling sandbag in the studio. When his partner leaned over to see if he was all right, Blaine arose a new man: heterosexual and virile. He no longer desired men and instead scouted out sexy women. In the next episode, Antoine became so frustrated by Blaine's heterosexuality that he eventually hit Blaine over the head with a frying pan, a cinder block, and a right hook to change him back. It worked, at least on television.

Many Americans still view homosexuality as being caused by some accident or tragedy: a domineering mother, a sexually abusive father, spending too much time with the opposite sex as a child, being brainwashed by a stronger corrupting influence. The debate over the immutability of homosexuality focuses on these and other theories to determine its origin. Of course, not nearly so much attention has been focused on the origin of heterosexuality. Nor do we question the fact that race, whether black or white, is immutable. The whole issue of mutability, like much of the debate on sexual orientation, boils down to one simple question: Is homosexuality a choice?

For many opponents of gay rights, homosexuality is clearly a choice. Drawing a comparison with African Americans, they say blacks are born black, but homosexuals choose to be that way. Joe Rogers, staff counsel to Republican senator Hank Brown of Colorado, put it this way in a *Washington Times* column: "Unlike the behavior of homosexuality, which a person may practice or not practice, African-Americans' status as black remains with us always." In his haste to paper over any possible similarities between the two groups, Rogers inadvertently reveals why this distinction matters. For those who believe homosexuality is a choice, discrimination against lesbians and gays can amount to little more than providing incentives for all people to resist temptation and avoid socially inappropriate conduct. Prejudice, then, is nothing more harmful than the expression of a societal preference for heterosexuality. Similarly, criminalizing gay sex is not the same as penalizing status or punishing fundamental expressive conduct, because gay people could always choose not to engage in the proscribed conduct. If these same gay rights opponents could be convinced that homosexuality is not a choice, then if they wished to be logically consistent in their arguments, they would have to acknowledge that their biases are not harmless, since the very people they hope to influence would be, by definition, uninfluenceable. Of course, they could argue honestly that the purpose of denying gay rights would be to punish people for their status, but that belief contradicts the core principles, at least in theory, of our laws and our concepts of fairness. In America, we consider it unfair to punish someone merely because of his or her status without any accompanying conduct. This is why we don't punish drug addicts or alcoholics unless they have engaged in some criminal behavior, such as driving under the influence of one of these substances.

Because Americans still like to believe in the fairness of their country, open advocacy of unfair practices would likely face a cold reception by the public. Therefore, the antigay forces, even as they advocate bigotry toward homosexuals, constantly attempt to prove their belief in fairness toward all. Public opinion surveys indicate that Americans are more likely to support gay rights if they think that homosexuality is not a choice. This explains why so many gay rights advocates hang their faith on the hopes of convincing straight America that homosexuality is immutable. As some lesbians and gays argue, the only choice they make is not to lie to themselves and feel miserable about their sexual orientation.

Much of our misunderstanding derives from the myth that

families shape sexual orientation. While families may help to define a child's environment, they alone do not appear to determine sexual orientation. Heterosexual parents often give birth to homosexual children, and homosexual parents give birth to heterosexual children. Similarly, conservative, religious families are no more likely to produce heterosexual children than are liberal, irreligious families. The children of intolerant and repressive environments may be more likely to become intolerant and repressed, but not necessarily heterosexual. Repression merely breeds repression, not sexual orientation.

A major barrier to our understanding of sexual orientation is that we have been conditioned to look at only half the equation. When we discuss sexual orientation, we often think about homosexual orientation and neglect the fact that heterosexuality is an orientation as well. Although scientific evidence seems to support the conclusion that sexual orientation is not entirely genetically determined, this does not mean that homosexuality or heterosexuality is a choice. Most evidence still supports the conclusion that sexual orientation, however it is determined, usually cannot be changed once it is established.

To say that homosexuality is a choice, therefore, is to say that heterosexuality is a choice as well. But if you acknowledge that all sexual orientation is a choice, then the whole foundation of antigay bias comes crashing down because heterosexuality can no longer be seen as morally superior: it becomes merely the majority's preference.

The debate over the immutability of homosexuality reveals several layers of thought. Some gay rights opponents concede that homosexuality itself is not a choice, but that acting on that homosexuality is. Apparently, this decision to act on one's unchosen homosexual orientation is somehow different from a heterosexual's choice to act on his or her unchosen sexual orientation. Another group of gay rights opponents apparently recognizes the possibility that even acting on one's homosexual orientation does not in and of itself merit condemnation, but they then chastise those homosexuals who fall prey to the so-called antifamily gay culture. For example, the editors of *Peninsula,* a right-wing publication at Harvard, argue that "submitting" to the homosexual "lifestyle" can destroy individuals "emotionally, physically, and spiritually." Given the complexity of interpreting what homosexual choice means, it is important to determine whether the debate focuses on homosexuality itself as a choice, on acting on it as a choice, or on participating in a stereotypical lifestyle as a choice. These many definitions of choice are often mistakenly confused by both sides in the debate over homosexuality.

Whether or not scientists can prove homosexuality to be immutable or genetic, such a determination may not even matter in comparing the discrimination felt by blacks with that felt by gays. Although many valid arguments may be raised to show that both race and sexual orientation are immutable, race has a certainty of intergenerational transmission that gives it a transcendent permanence. And so far, even the most gay-positive studies do not suggest that sexual orientation is exclusively and directly transferred in the same way as race. Being gay may or may not be immutable, but a 1989 *San Francisco Examiner* poll found that for *most* lesbians and gays, this belief appears to be a core part of their identity.

The immutability of one's status does not eliminate discrimination against a disfavored minority. After all, the fact that blackness is immutable has not put an end to discrimination against blacks. In another example, an Australian woman, claiming that nature produces the same percentage of left-handed people as gay people, explained that when she was a child, left-handed females could not be schoolteachers because they were thought to be unnatural and might negatively influence schoolkids. Even the knowledge that hand orientation is genetically determined was not enough to end prejudice against these women. So why should we expect prejudice directed at lesbians and gays to disappear if some well-meaning scientist proves conclusively that homosexuality is genetic or biologically determined before birth? Instead, the more likely result is that homophobia and heterosexism will persist. The mutability debate not only diverts attention from recognizing gay dignity regardless of homosexuality's cause, it fools the gay community into thinking that a conclusive study might be a panacea to our woes.

Nevertheless, to prove that homosexuality is genetically or biologically determined is not without some real value. Since the legal system penalizes only conduct and not status, a genetic explanation for homosexuality might mean that homosexual sex would be seen as a natural outgrowth of an unpunishable status rather than as chosen criminal conduct. Of course, this argument carries no guarantee that it will persuade decision makers as long as fear, religious teachings, and prejudice lead them to support discriminatory treatment and laws. But armed with the knowledge that homosexuality is not merely a lifestyle or a choice, lesbians and gays could more easily invoke the protection of a legal system that bifurcates status from conduct. Establishing the immutability of sexual orientation is not an end in itself but a means to achieve the greater end of outlawing discrimination against lesbians and gays.

Comparing Oppression

The basic elements of oppression are the same for nearly every group, including blacks and gays. Virtually all oppressed groups suffer from three types of oppression: internal oppression as the individual struggles with his or her identity; group-based oppression from others in the same category; and external oppression from those who dislike the group. Of course, the specific manifestations of oppression differ from group to group, so racism differs from anti-Semitism, which differs from sexism, which differs from homophobia. One group is enslaved and segregated, another is "exterminated," a third is dominated, and the last is "bashed."

Despite the differences, the experience of dealing with prejudice is, perhaps, the defining attribute of both blackness and homosexuality. Racial prejudice, whether they choose to realize it or not, affects all African Americans, including black lesbians and gays. Of course, not all blacks feel they have suffered discrimination, and some say they have not been *overtly* victimized by racism. Similarly, although some homosexuals say they have not experienced discrimination or prejudice, the overwhelming majority of lesbians and gays are affected by antigay bias. Consciously or not, they often make changes in their appearance or behavior to conceal their identity and prevent discrimination, and this self-policing becomes a form of discrimination when it prevents them from being themselves.

Black heterosexuals might better understand the oppression experienced by homosexuals if they tried to put themselves in the position of lesbians and gays. In fact, the whole comparison between blacks and gays is better understood by substituting the word "black" for "gay" whether we talk about oppression, behavior, mutability, visibility, or discrimination. When we hear someone complaining "Why do gays have to be so vocal and militant?" we might as well ask "Why do *blacks* have to be so vocal and militant?" When black straight people laugh at "fag" or "dyke" jokes, they should remember how they feel when white people laugh at "nigger" jokes. When blacks find themselves complaining that gays have taken over or ruined their neighborhoods, think how similar that rhetoric sounds to the oft-heard complaint that *blacks* are taking over or ruining white neighborhoods. One of the most enduring qualities of oppression is not only that it teaches the oppressed to hate themselves but also that it teaches them to hate one another, pitting minority against minority in a senseless contest to replicate the oppressor. Remarkably, the oppressed absorb and accept the values of the oppressor. The external oppression directed at minority groups from outsiders becomes internalized both in the culture of the minority and in the individual's self-esteem. Thus, blacks and homosexuals learn to hate themselves and each other, and to overcome this hatred requires conscious reprogramming of their self-images.

The internal oppression suffered by individual blacks and gays, even as we recognize obvious differences in specifics, suggests similarities in how they experience oppression. Both are taught to see themselves as second-class citizens, often undeserving of society's acceptance unless they live up to the highest standards and assimilate into the majority culture's stereotypical view of itself.

Internalized racism seeps deep into the psyche of black people and their understanding of themselves. Nowhere is this phenomenon more evident than in our obsession with the various hues in our skin color, which we mistakenly use as a measure of attractiveness, intelligence, sophistication, class, racial purity, and racial identity. As law professor and author Patricia Williams observes in her essay "Alchemical Notes: Reconstructing Ideals from Deconstructed Rights," "The simple matter of the color of one's skin so profoundly affects the way one is treated, so radically shapes what one is allowed to think and feel about this society, that the decision to generalize from that division is valid." What Williams seems to articulate is a black self-identity not independently chosen but rather thrust upon us by the treatment we receive from nonblacks.

As with African Americans, many homosexuals carry a unique set of psychological baggage with them. For example, a gay military man described to me the terror he experienced when he had to be interviewed for a top-secret security clearance. He had joined the military at a young age and did not then recognize his sexual orientation. But by the time of the security clearance interview, he knew that he was gay. He walked into the interview petrified that he would be hooked up to a machine or some mysterious device that would somehow read his mind to discover his homosexual thoughts. Another closeted gay man told me he had declined to sign up for sleep studies conducted by a university because he feared the electrodes would somehow telegraph his homosexual desires to the researchers. In these examples, homosexuals internalize the oppression of the larger society and conform their behavior accordingly, even before they come in contact with outsiders.

For African Americans, internalized racism encourages conformity of appearance, which leads some of us to lighten our skin color or straighten our hair so we can pass as white, just as internalized homophobia encourages many homosexuals to pass as heterosexual. Any group that respects itself and its uniqueness will not need to define its status based on its assumed similarity to another group. However, my own mother, with natural, unrelaxed hair, once confided in me her reluctance to join our family for the winter holidays because she knew the other women in the family would chide her about her hair. "Girl, when you gonna get rid of those naps?" they would ask; or they would tell her, "I know you're not going anywhere with me looking like that." These messages reinforce Eurocentric images of beauty and underscore the internalized racism still suffered even by proud black women and men.

The fact that blacks divide themselves along color lines suggests two things: first, that skin color is not benign; and second, that internalized racism stigmatizes not only individuals but whole groups as well. With group-based internalized prejudice, a whole group or its leaders attempt to define themselves by drawing lines that include what they are and exclude what they are not, often borrowing the definitions of their oppressors. On the slave plantations of the Old South, lighter-skinned blacks were often selected to perform the master's household duties, while darker-skinned blacks were left to work in the fields. Because white was the highest standard, the lighter slaves were considered more refined by blacks as well as whites. Though white slaveowners probably never held either light- or dark-skinned blacks anywhere close to the white level, in the hierarchy among slaves the lighter-skinned blacks could claim some pride and superiority over their darker-skinned brothers and sisters.

The antebellum slave mentality toward color has not disap-peared entirely from American black thought. In a landmark legal case in 1989, a black woman in Georgia filed a lawsuit against her employer, alleging that her black supervisor had her fired because of her skin color. The lighter-skinned black employee, a clerk-typist for the Internal Revenue Service, claimed that her darker-skinned black supervisor constantly harassed her. "She told me I needed some sun . . . that I'd had life too easy and I was going to have to work for my position under her," the employee testified in court.

Black people constantly divide themselves based on skin color, creating exclusive social cliques such as "brown paper bag" clubs, which restrict membership to those blacks with skin color lighter than a standard grocery bag. We even allow our skin color to affect our perception of ourselves. In my family, for example, I was always thought of as light-skinned because I was a shade or two lighter than others in the family. It was not until years later that my own perception of my skin color changed, when a darker-skinned friend described me as having a skin color similar to his own. My first inclination was to protest my friend's label by objecting that I was not as dark as he, but I resisted the temptation when I realized it reflected my own bias about skin color. I eventually no longer thought of myself as light-skinned.

Lesbians and gays, like everyone else in society, are bom-barded with images of gender conformity from their families, their employers, their friends, and, especially, the media. The images tell young people that men may be intimate only with women, not with other men. They teach little girls to play with dolls and little boys to play with toy soldiers. They instruct children that men are tough and don't cry, while women are emotional and do cry. Most disturbingly, the pursuit of these images ultimately punishes even young practitioners of gender nonconformity with epithets and labels such as "sissy," "tom-boy," "punk," "faggot," and "dyke." By using these terms to challenge outward expressions of gender role difference, society regulates the perception of the pervasiveness of homosexuality. Society's compulsory heterosexuality, as well as the related risk for those who challenge the norm, ensures that fewer homosexually oriented persons than actually exist will choose to identify themselves as such.

Group-based oppression leads to the difficult question of who decides exactly who or what is an acceptable part of the group. For instance, at a Harlem press conference after New Alliance Party presidential candidate Lenora Fulani shouted down then Arkansas governor Bill Clinton, a man in the audience interrupted her remarks: "I came here to hear him," the *New York Times* reported. When she told the man that she was speaking up for black people, he shot back, "Don't tell me about black people. I've been black all my life."

To challenge another's blackness requires confidence in knowing just what that blackness consists of, yet can we agree on what it means to be black in America? What is uniquely black in thought, culture, and experience? Is it a blue-collar family in the projects of Chicago, or is it an upper-middle-class family in a brownstone in Brooklyn? Is it a family at all? Who represents black values? Is it the millions of Sunday worshippers praying to Jesus, or is it the millions of Muslims turning East to bow to Allah? Is it the couple working two jobs to support a family of four kids, or is it the stereotypical single mother watching soap operas and talk shows at home with her boyfriend? And who represents black political values? Do blacks agree more with former Supreme Court Justice Thurgood Marshall or with current Justice Clarence Thomas? What is the essence of blackness anyway? Is it the color of the skin, the shape of the nose, the curvature of the lips, the size of the butt, the kinkiness of the hair? Is it the soul food, the R&B music, or the mud cloth scarf that makes someone black?

We experience the same problems when we attempt to define homosexuality. What does it mean to be gay in America? What is uniquely gay in thought, culture, and experience? Is homosexuality ultimately reducible to a simple sexual act? If

so, what is that act and how do we classify self-identified lesbians and gays who do not engage in it? How do we define
people who engage in same-sex sexual behavior but do not
consider themselves gay? Are those who live in stereotypical
urban "gay ghettos" more gay than those who live outside
these enclaves? Is gay marriage a betrayal of gay liberation or
an affirmation of homosexual responsibility? Do lesbians and
gays identify more with radical ACT UP protesters or with
conservative Log Cabin Republican Club members? Who decides what is or is not gay, and to whom are they accountable?

The fact that we ask these questions of ourselves with any
expectation of acceptable answers reflects an internalized prejudice that disrespects the diversity of our many different people. Often in an effort to put forward a "positive" image for
our oppressors, we foolishly attempt to construct a single image of blackness or homosexuality to incorporate millions of
different people. Rather than challenging the oppression that
such values represent, our efforts to present "positive" images
reinforce the dominance of cultural values with which minority
communities may disagree. For blacks, this desire to project
"positive" images sets up a tension between the need to include all black people in the struggle and the need to exclude
certain blacks from the projected image. Therefore, we criticize
those blacks who self-exclude from the community and simul-
taneously exclude and ostracize blacks who we believe do not
fit our own stereotypes and biases about what it means to be
black.

Of course, most blacks are fairly well settled with what it
means to be black: it means our day-to-day experiences. But
this does not stop us from—in fact, it may encourage—challenging the experiences of other blacks as being less authentic
than our own. A poor black person living in the "hood" might
label another black person living in a prosperous *black* suburb
as an "Uncle Tom," but the black suburbanite might label still
another black person as an "incog negro" because that person
lives in an all-*white* suburb. By creating our subjective hierar-

chies of black authenticity, we arbitrarily divide ourselves into acceptable and unacceptable categories of racial identification. Although we may think we understand what it means to be black based on our own experience, this thinking often clouds, rather than clarifies, what it means for our race as a whole.

Lesbians and gays are not immune from the same divisions that plague black people. We, too, create hierarchies of authenticity and criticize those who self-exclude from the community as "closeted" or unable to deal with their homosexuality. For both blacks and gays, we start to see the ridiculous nature of our litmus tests when we realize that we end up excluding not only blacks who are not black enough and gays who are not gay enough but also those thought to be "too black" or "too gay." We blacks, for example, call ourselves "niggers," joke among ourselves about our stereotypical behavior, and even distance ourselves from those who "show their color." We homosexuals call ourselves "fags" and "dykes," sometimes in an effort to reclaim the language of our oppressor, but just as often to criticize one another. "I hate fags," one gay man said to me, as if to distance himself from his own identity.

At times, black people seem to shoulder the burden of the entire race whenever another black person makes a spectacle of himself in front of whites. When a stereotypical black homeless man strolls onto a city bus and begins to talk loudly to himself, some blacks admit that they internalize the expected perception of the white passengers on board. This is why we half-jokingly say that someone has "set back the entire race," as though any one individual could or should be allowed to cause such damage. Many black parents, therefore, have taught their children to act the way white people want them to behave or to dress in a way that makes whites feel comfortable and unthreatened. Not surprisingly, homosexuals shoulder similar burdens, distancing themselves from "flamboyant" gay men, "butch" lesbians, drag queens, or whoever does not fit the image we want to project about our identity.

Group-based censorship of "negative" images takes on

heightened proportions among lesbians and gays because the community actually buys into many of the dominant culture's stereotypes about itself. The frequently raised question of whether to include bisexuals and transgendered people in the lesbian and gay community highlights this tension. Bisexuals are thought to portray the wrong image because their existence suggests that homosexuality might be a choice rather than an orientation. Transgendered people, including transvestites and transsexuals, project the image that lesbians and gays are actually just confused about their gender. The mainstream lesbian and gay community fears both of these groups because they confirm the larger society's stereotypes about homosexuality. As with the black community, the gay community seeks to present not an accurate image of who its members are but, instead, a questionably "positive" one that ignores the group's diversity.

Some African Americans, like some lesbians and gays, would prefer to assimilate and do not feel oppressed by responding to societal pressure. Black writer Shelby Steele, for example, has discouraged the black search for difference from white society and encouraged a more color-blind, racial-less attitude. Similarly, in the gay community, columnist Andrew Sullivan argues for gay marriage not only because it legitimates gay unions but because it facilitates the process of assimilation into the dominant culture.

I do not want to understate the potential value of creating a "positive" image in terms of shaping public opinion. If the goal of the gay rights movement is to pass laws that protect average-looking, mainstream lesbians and gays, then "positive" images will help. However, if the movement's goal is to liberate and challenge the larger culture to welcome and celebrate all types of difference, then the use of only "positive" imagery will backfire. Virtually all minority communities, including blacks and gays, wrestle with the conflict between assimilation and liberation as they struggle for their freedom. Few minority groups are sufficiently homogeneous to advance their entire community's goals with only one strategy. It makes sense to use "positive" images if they facilitate the passage of antidiscrimination legislation that protects the entire community, but it also increases the need for the movement to go beyond political transformation into social transformation so that the people not included in the legislative promotion campaign are not left behind.

How we choose to define ourselves is important because the descriptive informs the prescriptive: what we *prescribe* to heal our many wounds as a people depends on how we *describe* the injury or the wounded.

Comparing the famous 1963 March on Washington with its 1993 lesbian and gay counterpart reveals the strengths and weaknesses of the assimilation strategy. The 1993 march participants consciously borrowed from the rhetoric of the 1960s civil rights demonstrations, but they planned their event without the rigidity that characterized the 1963 march.

Bayard Rustin, the black gay man who coordinated the 1963 march, scripted every detail down to the second. He scheduled the buses, plotted the route, and threatened the speakers with embarrassing removal if they did not stick to their time limits and their approved remarks. Male participants wore shirts and ties, and female participants wore skirts or dresses. Black New York City police officers were designated to serve as marshals, lobby visits were supervised by march organizers, and the banners and placards were produced by the march staff. The theme of the march was carefully focused on "jobs and freedom," and the marchers' demands included passage of President Kennedy's civil rights bill, a $2 minimum wage, desegregation of schools, a federal public works program, and federal action to bar racial discrimination in employment practices. (All these demands were accomplished in a matter of years.) Rustin even accepted a lower title and less visible role because some civil rights leaders feared he projected the wrong image as a gay man. All these things were designed to send a message that black people should be given their civil rights because they are just like everyone else in America.

The 1993 March on Washington was quite different. It was arranged by a four-person, cogender, biracial cochair coordinating structure, under the guidance of a 250-person nationwide steering committee. The speakers' remarks were not scripted or reviewed in advance for approval, and even though the entire event was broadcast live on C-SPAN, a lesbian comedian told jokes that many Americans must have considered offensive, including one about "fucking" the First Lady. Another speaker, AIDS activist Larry Kramer, had been excluded from the speakers list but managed to speak anyway by orchestrating a temporary coup with the marshals, who physically blocked a march cochair from the stage. There was no dress code for the speakers, let alone for the participants, who came in T-shirts, tank tops, bare chests, and even bare breasts. The march organizers presented a list of seven demands and fifty-five related items, ranging from lifting the ban on gays in the military and passing a federal antidiscrimination bill to finding a cure for AIDS, ending sexist oppression, and implementing graduated age-of-consent laws. (None of these demands has been accomplished.)

Although the nonthreatening assimilation strategy employed by the black community paid off in legislative victories, the social revolution necessary to transform America's attitudes toward blacks never took place. The same negative stereotypes have persisted long after passage of civil rights legislation, and the socioeconomic changes that enabled the black middle class to develop did little to eliminate the prejudice against the black underclass. In other words, it became acceptable to be black and prosperous and well educated, but poor, undereducated blacks were still despised. Similarly, we might expect that a homosexual assimilation strategy that puts forward only "positive" images of lesbians and gays will leave behind the parts of the community that suffer double and triple discrimination because of other differences based on race, class, gender, appearance, or education.

The arguments within minority groups about assimilation are as old as their particular struggles. In 1890, before Marcus Garvey's separatist movement encouraged blacks to return to Africa, black national organizations splintered over the question of white membership. Some blacks objected to the all-black composition of the Afro-American League and thus formed the American Citizens' Equal Rights Association the same year. The issue has doggedly persisted throughout the years as the NAACP and other black organizations have been criticized for allowing whites to play influential roles.

The similarity between the two movements' debates about assimilation should not blind us to their differences. One major difference is that the gay political movement often seems hopelessly mired in a perpetual conflict between its racy social identity and its sobering political identity. For example, the 1993 march organizers estimated that more than a million people came to Washington for the weekend, but many of them did not participate in the march itself and came primarily for social events. "The timing of the 1993 march had a lot to do with the party atmosphere that developed," remembers Gregory Adams, who served as communications director for the march. "Bill Clinton had just been elected and we had a mistaken sense of confidence that the world was going to change overnight." Even with the election of John F. Kennedy, who was somewhat sympathetic to the civil rights movement, the social-political conflict was not a problem for the black civil rights leadership, although rank-and-file blacks divided themselves along the same social and political divide.

Today, white religious activists tell blacks they should be offended by the analogy that gay people have drawn between themselves and blacks. Calling homosexuality a behavior, unlike race, they contend that blacks should be wary of lesbians and gays seeking to join the civil rights bandwagon. But perhaps blacks should be more offended at white people telling them how to think. The idea that one group, because they are temporarily favored by society, holds a proprietary interest over the rhetoric of freedom should insult all disempowered citizens. This selfish reasoning allows conservative white religious leaders to divide and conquer minority communities that, if aligned, might better challenge the entire power structure. Bernice Johnson Reagon, writing in an essay included in the anthology *Home Girls* (1983), opines more colorfully:

> The Civil Rights movement was the first powerful movement of our era. Black folks started it, Black folks did it, so everything you've done politically rests on the efforts of my people . . . So once we did what we did, then you've got women, you've got Chicanos, you've got the Native Americans, and you've got homosexuals, and you got all of these people who also got sick of somebody being on their neck. And maybe if they come together, they can do something about it.

Reagon ascribes part of the problem to group myopia and self-importance. "Many of us take ourselves too seriously," she says. "We think that what we think is the cutting line . . . You think that what you've got to say is special and somebody needs to hear it. That is arrogance. That is egotism, and the only checking line is when you have somebody to pull your coattails." But Reagon saves much of her dissatisfaction for people unwilling to compromise in coalitions: "Watch these mono-issue people. They ain't gonna do you no good."

Even if we accept the fact that blacks and gays are different, they both experience prejudice and oppression, and the fact that the oppressions differ in nature or even severity does not mean that members of one group are less deserving of protection than another. Surely, American law has never counted homosexuals as three-fifths of a person, enslaved them, segregated them, and psychologically wounded them in the way that it has blacks. But neither has American law or custom established slavery based on gender, ethnicity, religion, or disability. Yet in all these cases we still protect the individual from discrimination. What matters is that no one should be denied a job or kicked out of their home or arrested or beaten merely for existing, for being who they are.

When we look at external oppression, over and over again we hear the same stories of indignity, injustice, and unfairness directed at blacks and gays. A black professional woman in Maryland, in an interview, described a recent incident that began as her son walked down the street wearing a hat and sunglasses. When he walked by a local bank, he looked in the window and smiled at a teller who was looking out at him. He continued walking to the end of the street, whereupon a phalanx of police officers surrounded him in their squad cars, then jumped out pointing their guns at him. He was ordered to the ground, told to place his hands over his head, handcuffed, and carried off to the police station. At the station, the officers informed him he was being charged with armed robbery of the very bank that he had passed only a few minutes earlier. He learned that the white bank teller had identified him as being the suspect who had robbed the bank only a few days earlier.

Reflecting on the episode months after it happened, the mother said her family had been humiliated by the incident. They tried vainly to convince the police that the bank teller had misidentified the young man. Ultimately, the mother was forced to take out a loan to pay a lawyer and a bondsman to secure her son's release from jail. After a great deal of frustration, and time and money spent by the family, the charges were dropped.

The mother's story is not unusual, only more dramatic than others. In fact, nearly every black person I interviewed defined his or her blackness at least in part based on the experience of prejudice suffered historically or currently by black people. Father John Payne, a black Roman Catholic priest in the nation's capital, told me, "I could be dressed in blue jeans and a shirt, a coat and tie, or a Roman collar, and I still can't get a cab." Mario Cooper, a black public relations executive in New York, remembered growing up in Alabama, where he had to sit in the balcony of movie theaters because blacks were not permitted on the main floor. Sherry Harris, a former Seattle City Council member and a black woman, described childhood experiences in Newark, where she could not enter the homes of white friends. Tom Morgan, a former reporter for the *New York Times, Miami Herald,* and *Washington Post,* remembered how he and another black student integrated the Rittenour, Missouri, public schools in 1956 and 1957. Vallerie Wagner, a political activist, described the steely-eyed scorn heaped upon her as a little girl in Shreveport, Louisiana, when she unthinkingly took a drink from a "whites only" water fountain at the eye doctor's office. R. Paul Richard, an Ivy-educated lawyer at the Equal Employment Opportunity Commission, told how his high school counselor assumed that he would not go to college, or if that he did go, he would choose only a black college. Sabrina Sojourner, a Washington, D.C., writer and activist, described the feeling of having white people yell "nigger" at her. Even the nation's chief civil rights lawyer, U.S. Assistant Attorney General for Civil Rights Deval Patrick, while sitting in the same office once occupied by FBI Director J. Edgar Hoover, told me that he is often followed by department store security officers when he goes shopping.

Many whites still deny the prevalence of racism, arguing that affirmative action has meant that discrimination is more often directed at white men than at nonwhites. Multimillionaire Donald Trump, for example, once told NBC News, "If I were starting off today, I would love to be a well-educated Black because I really believe they do have an actual advantage today." The "actual advantage" that I enjoyed as a "well-educated black" was that I could almost never catch a cab when I went home from my job at the White House each day. I always wore a business suit, but I would have little luck finding a cab

if there was a single white person on the same street also looking for one. No matter where I positioned myself, no matter
how the white person was dressed, and regardless of who got
to the curb first, the white person always got the cab. This
experience reinforced to me America's social ordering and,
purposefully or not, put me in my place as a black man. That a
conservatively dressed Harvard-educated lawyer could walk
out of the most powerful office in the land and then be insulted
by a cab driver directly results from the white privilege that
men like Donald Trump have grown so accustomed to that
they don't even realize its existence.

As the images of overt discrimination—the segregated
lunch counters, the firefighters training their powerful hoses on
young black boys and girls—have faded into the world of television documentaries and out of our daily consciousness, more
and more whites see racism as part of America's past. But
many blacks still feel haunted by its omnipresent specter.
Often below the radar screen of public observation, nonwhites
are being constantly insulted and reminded of their "place" in
society.

A law professor has compared the feeling of being a minority today to going through life with a huge magnet attached to
one's body. Walking down the street, one picks up iron scraps
and soda cans and all sorts of trash. Soon one realizes that the
world is full of metal, lurking everywhere in places never before imagined. But the person without the magnet often does
not see this metal, since he or she is not directly affected by it.
This magnet metaphor captures the increasingly subtle nature
of prejudice in America.

In the guise of academics, books such as *The Bell Curve*
(1995) by Charles Murray and Richard Herrnstein suggest that
because blacks score lower than whites on standardized test
scores, they are inherently intellectually inferior. They do not
present other statistics, however, such as those presented in
Andrew Hacker's *Two Nations* (1992), that show wide varia-

tions even among whites by ethnic group. Instead, the authors resurrect long-dormant arguments used to justify the enslavement and oppression of African Americans.

"It's not 'spic' and 'nigger' anymore," Congressman Charlie Rangel told a preelection rally in 1994. "They say, 'Let's cut taxes' . . . You don't have to be a social scientist to understand that if you're going to reduce taxes it's going to impact on the poor, and the poor happen to be blacks and other minorities." As we see, racism is alive and well, but has recreated itself in the image of neutral academics, simple classism, and race-blindness.

In the same way that challenging open expressions of racism has pushed racists underground and made them more clever in their practices, so too have homophobes become more sophisticated in their techniques. Even the most vicious quickly deny charges of homophobia with transparent excuses about loving the sinner and hating the sin. They do not argue that society should discriminate against lesbians and gays but, rather, that gays don't need any "special rights" to protect them from discrimination. Prejudice and discrimination, even when directed at lesbians and gays, have become dirty words in our culture. As a result, no one wants to be a bigot, even when their actions are clearly bigoted.

Oppression is some times unintentional, but this does not lessen its impact. The mechanisms of antigay oppression are so subtle that we not only label them with the term "homophobia" but also employ the term "heterosexism," in which society imposes a presumption of heterosexuality on all its members. When families refuse to recognize or acknowledge that a family member is lesbian or gay, they may think they are saving the person the difficulty of dealing with her or his sexual orientation. They may be making assumptions based on their years of knowing the individual. They may have already invested in the person certain qualities of personality and character that contradict lesbian and gay stereotypes. Regardless of their benign motives, the simple act of maintaining a myth perpetuates a distorted perception of reality that disempowers the individual from a sense of self-identity.

Much of the prejudice directed at gays is purposeful, direct, and malicious. When people hurl epithets like "fag," "sissy," "punk," and "dyke," they usually do so with full knowledge of what the words mean and how they can be used to hurt someone. When rowdy "straight" men hide out near gay clubs to attack unsuspecting patrons, they know what they're doing, even if they have to get drunk to do it. Because the culture of oppression often teaches the oppressors to see their victims as subhuman, antigay conduct becomes destigmatized of its prejudice or violence or criminality. Rather than attacking a human being, they find themselves only attacking a "fag" or a "nigger" or a "bitch," or some other dehumanized thing not worthy of compassion or concern.

Ernest Dillon, a black postal worker in Detroit, spent four peaceful years in his job until a coworker suspected he was gay. Dillon began to experience constant harassment and found what he calls nasty, vulgar, hurtful, and hostile messages plastered on the walls of the office and in the mail trucks. When he reported the incidents to his supervisors, they told him there was nothing they could do. As Dillon testified in a July 1994 hearing in Congress, "Then one day, while on the job, my coworker cornered me—and I thought he would kill me. He threw me down on the ground, kicked me, and beat me until I was unconscious. He left me in a pool of blood, with two black eyes, a severely bruised sternum, and gashes in my forehead."

Once we have demonized blacks and gays, society finds it relatively easy to ignore their suffering. We saw this occur when four white Los Angeles police officers, unknowingly videotaped while brutally beating Rodney King, an unarmed black motorist, were acquitted of all charges against them by a jury that had no black members. The jury's refusal to convict demonstrated how the legal system devalues the significance of the lives of minority crime victims. The same flawed legal system acquitted former San Francisco supervisor Dan White of murdering the city's first openly gay supervisor, Harvey Milk, and convicted him of the lesser charge of voluntary manslaughter. After the jury failed to convict White of murder, San Francisco erupted into riots, just as Los Angeles erupted into riots after the four policemen who beat Rodney King were acquitted.

Despite similarities in the way they are treated by society, in some ways lesbians and gays suffer more today than blacks do. This is a difficult argument to digest because immediately our minds contrast the stereotypes of the poor black family in the ghetto with the more affluent white gay male professional. If we can get beyond the stereotypes, at the very least we will find that lesbians and gays suffer from *unique* forms of oppression that distinguish them from African Americans, including prejudice from deeply closeted homosexuals. Because the price of detection of one's homosexuality is often quite high, many closeted lesbians and gays themselves gay-bash in an effort to avoid speculation about their own sexual orientation. This gay bashing complicates the problem of identifying how much of the homophobia is internal and how much is external. Conservative lawyer Roy Cohn, for example, was notorious for his dislike of homosexuals, and even though he engaged in homosexual practices himself, he reportedly did not consider himself to be gay. The same could be said for J. Edgar Hoover, whose cross-dressing behavior only surfaced years after the Federal Bureau of Investigation, which he led, had persecuted homosexuals and gender nonconformists. More recently, George Stallings, the black bishop of the Imani Temple Church in Washington, criticized "milquetoast sissy faggot[s]," even though he himself has been the victim of antigay rhetoric. In fact, the loudest critics of homosexuals are sometimes those who fear being labeled homosexual themselves, and the volume of their rhetoric is often designed to drown out charges against them.

The identification of sexual orientation, unlike race, conveys a certain power to the oppressor in deciding whether or not to accept the oppressed person's own definition of self. The power to identify is the power to control. A few "heterosexual" people I interviewed told me they did not *believe* in homosexuality. "Does that mean you don't believe homosexuality exists, or that you don't agree with it?" I asked.

"I don't believe there are any real homosexuals," one of them replied.

"You mean it's a choice?"

"The so-called homosexuals don't know any better. They just think they are homosexual, but they are not. God didn't create any homosexuals."

Does it make any sense that out of 5 billion people on earth, not one of them might honestly be attracted to someone of the same gender? Since biologists have determined that homosexuality exists in the animal kingdom, where there are no cultural influences or peer pressure, the unwillingness to acknowledge human homosexuality seems to deny to thinking human beings the same autonomy we recognize in animals. Moreover, such responses deny homosexuals the self-autonomy that most heterosexuals take for granted. No parent would ever ask a daughter if she was sure she was heterosexual. "Have you tried dating women yet? Maybe you're just going through a phase of heterosexuality." But these are comments that homosexuals hear all the time from their friends and relatives, reflecting the extent to which personal experience influences our sense of sexuality. If we find ourselves attracted exclusively to one sex or another, we often find it difficult to understand how anyone could possibly think differently. After all, sexual attraction indicates our deeply personal and subjective ideas about beauty and desire.

But the fact that we don't understand each other cannot mean that the other does not exist. Rarely do we consider how little we actually know about human sexuality. When we reflect on the arrogance involved in lecturing a woman about what type of *man* she should or should not be attracted to, then we might also see the arrogance behind our attempts to identify everyone else's sexual orientation as being exactly like ours.

Another example of how homophobia may be worse than racism is in its public acceptability. Bishop Carl Bean, the black gay founder of the Unity Fellowship Church, based in Los Angeles, explains: "We [homosexuals] are the most ostracized group in society because even a murderer on death row can call us a 'faggot.' Everyone has license to say 'faggot' as if it's the absolute lowest thing one could be. We might be the most upstanding citizen. We might have the education, and the one that's the prisoner who has done everything that society says one shouldn't still feels he has the right to say 'bulldagger' or 'faggot.' " In fact, in February 1996, in Pensacola, Florida, Judge Joseph Tarbuck awarded primary custody of an eleven-year-old girl to her father, a convicted murderer, rather than to the girl's forty-six-year-old mother, a lesbian. Although the father had spent nine years in prison for killing his first wife as they argued over custody of their children, Judge Tarbuck focused on the mother: "This child should be given the opportunity and the option to live in a nonlesbian world." In comparing the fitness of the two parents, the judge seems to have concluded that the mere status of being a lesbian, no matter how law-abiding, is worse than being a murderer.

According to a 1994 report from the American Association of Physicians for Human Rights, a Vermont medical faculty member told a medical student, "I've gotten used to Blacks and Jews, but I can't get used to homos." In addition, some homosexual patients reported being called "dyke" and "sissy" and other derogatory names, while others report being denied treatment altogether. What most Americans do not realize is that such discrimination, no matter how blatant and unfair, is usually legal. Only nine states and the District of Columbia outlaw discrimination against lesbians and gays. In other words, in forty-one states it is still perfectly legal to fire us, deny us a job, mentally abuse us, or deny us certain services merely because we are gay.

Cheryl Summerville learned this lesson the hard way when in 1991 she was fired from her job as a cook at a Cracker Barrel restaurant in a suburb of Atlanta. Her notice of separation read, "This employee is being terminated due to violation of company policy. The employee is gay." Her employer acknowledged that she was a good worker, and the letter made no attempt to justify the company's decision by any other reason or pretext; it was enough simply to state that she was a lesbian. It also did not matter whether she had any control or choice over her sexual orientation or even whether she had engaged in any homosexual behavior. The only thing that mattered was her status, not her conduct, as a homosexual. Who could imagine a large company like Cracker Barrel writing such a letter to an African American today?—"The employee violated company policy. The employee is black." A smoking gun for a lawsuit. In an era when civil rights laws have forced employers to develop highly sophisticated arguments and procedures for racist employment decisions, homophobes, on the other hand, do not even need to hide their prejudice. That is because they know that antigay discrimination is not just tolerated—it is often condoned by religion and encouraged by society, and is usually legal.

In June 1993 while I was working at the White House, I received a letter addressed to me from a minister in Michigan. Apparently without knowledge of my sexual orientation, the minister asked me to tell President Clinton to start *executing* homosexuals: "According to the Bible, the Word of the living God, homosexuals are criminals like murderers . . . worse than adulterers, worse than rapists . . . who need to be executed to protect the rest." That a Christian minister, invoking the name of God, would advocate execution of anyone merely for loving a person of the same sex suggests how disturbingly pathetic some on the religious right have become. In fact, I might have been inclined to pity the minister rather than condemn him had not his words been the kind likely to encourage violence against homosexuals. Yet the religious bigotry of that minister is exactly the type of rhetoric that continues to occur daily in the most public and sacred spaces of America.

While we as a society quickly condemn open expressions of racism, when homophobia rears its ugly head, condemnation is often nowhere to be found. Unlike racism, homophobia is so widespread that we often do not even flinch when we hear homophobic jokes or comments, as we would with racist ones. Recent political developments such as the backlash against Pat Buchanan's political rise have somewhat reduced public tolerance of homophobia. Rabid antihomosexual sentiment is becoming rarer among well-respected politicians, but many politicians still find themselves tiptoeing along a thin line of distinction between bigotry and promotion of so-called traditional values. These politicians want to appeal to the right wing by showing their support for antigay measures but do not want to lose their moderate supporters by singling out homosexuals for mistreatment. As a result, they learn to speak with elaborate semantic gymnastics that appeal to demagoguery without sounding demagogic. Senate Majority Leader Bob Dole, for example, was so stung by the right-wing critical response to his statement that "everyone should be treated alike, whether they're black or brown or disabled or homosexual," that he rushed off a letter to the conservative *Washington Times* to contradict himself: "To protect the rights we treasure, we must avoid creating special rights for special groups." But the "special rights" he cited included the right of lesbians and gays to serve their country in the military and not to be discriminated against because of their sexual orientation. By falsely framing the issue as one of special rights instead of equal rights, Dole and others are able to pose as defenders of traditional values without acquiring reputations as bigots. But just because the rhetoric has been cleaned up, we should not make the mistake of assuming the bigotry has disappeared.

Conservative religious leaders provide political cover and a moral imprimatur to elected officials' homophobia by using sophisticated verbal gymnastics of their own. Although they speak with passionate animosity toward lesbians and gays, they often couch their language in the voice of concern for the misguided homosexuals. Other ministers are not so sophisticated in the expression of their vitriol. Christian religious leaders advocating death for anyone should cause alarm to all who hear their words. Instead, such religious leaders wrap themselves behind the First Amendment's protection of speech and religion. This is their right, but as with other examples of excessive and intolerant speech, we should expect that cooler heads would stand up against this bigotry. Ironically, the Michigan minister would spare from death those docile homosexuals who accept his judgment, but those lesbians and gays "who would publicly campaign for nondiscriminatory treatment or advocate homosexuality as an appropriate alternative life-style should be executed *without mercy*" (emphasis added). In other words, just for exercising the same free speech the religious right wants to protect for itself, homosexuals should be killed.

If we substituted the word "black" for "gay," we might more easily understand the contrast between the public acceptability of racism and of homophobia. Who could imagine a minister in the 1990s publicly advocating death to blacks solely because of their racial status? For that matter, who could imagine society tolerating a family that disowned a child because he was born with brown eyes or an employer who openly refused to hire black workers? Such overt bias has been disdained or even outlawed, but it is similar to that which lesbians and gays still endure repeatedly. But because most Americans, including homosexuals themselves, have been conditioned to believe that homosexuality is immoral, we tolerate a whole array of bigotry without bothering to challenge it. As a result of this conditioning, many do not even believe or recognize that the hatred directed at homosexuals can be considered prejudice. Instead, they expect it as part of what they believe to be the natural order of things. Society should be no more tolerant of homosexuals than of adulterers or prostitutes or rapists, they say. But rarely do they delve to answer the deeper questions. Why, for example, should consensual intimacy between two adults merit the approbation assigned to cheating or violence? Why should such intimacy concern the government? Why should society discriminate against adults because of the people they choose to love?

The connection between the antigay rhetoric of some religious leaders and the violent actions of their religious followers is direct. Proceeding down Pennsylvania Avenue during the 1993 March on Washington, I spotted a band of young white men bearing antigay placards with phrases such as GOD HATES FAGS and REPENT OR BURN IN HELL. The marchers responded by chanting "Shame! Shame! Shame!" as they pointed at the protesters, but what would a sole gay person have done had he confronted the same group of young men without the protection of hundreds of thousands of other homosexuals? Like many homosexuals, he might have been attacked, or gay-bashed. The widespread tolerance for religious homophobia under the rubric of free speech or religious conviction inevitably leads to violence against lesbians and gays. In preparation for her novel *The Drowning of Stephan Jones,* Bette Greene interviewed four hundred young men arrested for gay bashing. In an interview with the *Boston Globe,* she said she found that gay bashers often felt their religious leaders and traditions sanctioned their behavior. The nexus between antigay rhetoric and antigay violence is not difficult to see.

For homosexuals who have come out, the fear of gay bashing influences everyday decisions and actions that many heterosexuals take for granted. The oppression may involve uncertainty about who actually knows and does not know about their sexual orientation. It often requires them to identify their sexual orientation to someone they meet, if only to avoid the awkward possibility that the new person may do or say something homophobic in their presence. Some open homosexuals return to the closet in certain situations as they try to make others comfortable with who they are. Homosexuals also face life-threatening decisions, such as whether to hold hands with their lovers in public. And some experience oppression as they determine at what point they should speak up against the homophobia they hear daily in their lives and whether speaking up against prejudice will get them labeled as troublemakers.

Many gay people understandably react to these situations by doing or saying nothing, thereby remaining closeted. While a homosexual has the choice to remain closeted in these circumstances, this choice does not lessen the pain of being verbally assaulted or having one's existence challenged. As Professor Sylvia Law explains in a 1988 law review article, "Sexual orientation is not readily observable and hence is not persistently stigmatizing in the way race and sex are, although the costs of avoiding discovery of sexual orientation are great." In fact, one could argue that homosexuals are *more burdened* than blacks *because of* their ability to pass. Because blackness is so clearly identifiable, many white racists do not express their racism in the company of blacks. But with lesbians and gays, society's assumption of heterosexuality, along with its toleration of homophobia, causes both closeted and openly gay people to be exposed to a much higher degree of insensitivity and overt prejudice than that experienced by blacks. If you've ever overheard someone criticize you behind your back, you know that the hurt is just as painful as if the person were pointing a finger at you directly.

Being closeted also means being ignored or neglected. The novelist Ralph Ellison wrote:

> I am an invisible man . . . I am invisible, understand, simply because people refuse to see me . . . When they approach me they see only my surroundings, themselves, or figments of their imagination—indeed, everything and anything except me.

Ellison's description of the American Negro could easily be read as a description of modern homosexuals—invisible simply because people refuse to see them. As Adrienne Rich notes in an essay on "compulsory heterosexuality," straight society operates under an assumption of heterosexuality, "whereby all persons—except the most openly and outlandishly gay—are presumed to be heterosexual." But unlike the invisibility of blackness, this elaborate deception continues with the complicity of the oppressed—the millions of homosexuals who are unwilling to risk the uncertain consequences of "coming out." For reasons both noble and simple, these millions remain silent when their coworkers tell homophobic jokes, they masquerade their lovers as roommates when their family members visit, and in conversation they carefully avoid gender-specific references about their girlfriends or boyfriends.

Racial prejudice often responds to the unique visibility associated with being an identifiable minority. Nearly every black person has encountered an experience in which a white person misidentified him or her for another black person who looked nothing alike. The misidentification reflects the centrality of race as an identifying marker: the two black people often share nothing else in common but their skin color. The tendency to reduce blacks and gays to simple, one-dimensional characteristics also reveals how outsiders view minorities. Many lesbians and gays understand this, particularly if they have been "fixed up" on blind dates by well-meaning heterosexuals eager to match the only two homosexuals they know. African Americans in predominantly white communities also experience this problem when white people with good intentions try to match up the few blacks they know.

The support networks available to blacks often are not available to homosexuals. Any black child who has been called "nigger" knows the comfort his parents or family provided. But to whom does a child turn if he is called "faggot" by his classmates? If he has any idea what the word means, he will not likely seek the comfort of his parents. For while race is transmitted directly from parent to child, creating bonds of understanding based on shared experiences, sexual orientation is different. The boy who has been called a "punk" by his teammates and the girl who has been called a "dyke" by her classmates may feel too much shame and guilt to acknowledge this to their families. "Well, what did you do to make them think that?" the parents might ask.

After comparing and contrasting the oppression experienced by lesbians and gays with that of African Americans, we find plenty of common ground on which to stand. Individually, both blacks and gays torment themselves with the internalized prejudices of the larger society. As groups, both communities attempt to regulate their public image in an effort to portray a "positive" face that ultimately disempowers their cultural diversity. And when they are not busy bashing themselves, both blacks and gays find themselves bashed by outsiders. Certainly, lesbians and gays have not suffered a history of state-sanctioned slavery and segregation, but in some ways lesbians and gays still suffer today where blacks are no longer victimized. Ultimately, we must ask ourselves what this comparison of oppression proves anyway. No two groups suffer in exactly the same way, so it makes little sense to compare the Holocaust with the slave trade. But even if we acknowledge that blacks have suffered more than lesbians and gays, does that mean that blacks should be entitled to equal protection of the law and lesbians and gays should not? Should justice be limited only to those groups who are most despised, and if so, don't we impose a new form of injustice on those who are left out? As Harvard professor Henry Louis Gates, Jr., asks, "Why should oppression, however it's measured, be a prerequisite for legal protection?"

Are Blacks and Gays the Same?

We cannot make a perfect match between blacks and gays to prove the two groups are the same, but some of their differences suggest that lesbians and gays are actually more oppressed than blacks are today. Society still tolerates homophobia in places where racism has long been discouraged. Discrimination against blacks in employment and housing is against the law everywhere in the United States, while discrimination against lesbians and gays is perfectly legal in most of the country. Simple daily decisions like holding hands in a park are taken for granted by most African Americans, but lesbians and gays experience them as potentially life-threatening. Young lesbians and gays usually lack the family-based support structure available to young African Americans in dealing with prejudice. And although sexual orientation is usually not visible, the decision not to reveal one's sexual orientation involves a different, although no less stigmatizing, oppression for lesbians and gays.

In some other ways, because of the nation's history of racism, blacks seem to be far more oppressed than lesbians and gays, but regardless of who feels most oppressed, blacks and gays need to know more about each other, to begin a dialogue of understanding. On one hand, white lesbians and gays need to know that race is not the same as sexual orientation and that the civil rights movement of the 1960s is not the same as the gay rights movement today. On the other hand, African Americans need to know that homosexuality is not about behavior or lifestyle and that the struggle for justice does not end with black people.

Although blacks and gays are not the same, their movements are not the same, and even racism and homophobia are not the same, ultimately there is one shared experience that should unite blacks and gays: the members of both groups know what it means to be oppressed. As Melvin Boozer told the 1980 Democratic National Convention, "I know what it feels like to be called 'nigger' and I know what it feels like to be called 'faggot' and I can sum up the difference in one word: none."

CHAPTER THREE

Black and Gay in America

Twenty people, mostly women, are jammed into the living room in the Washington, D.C., home of Sabrina Sojourner and Letitia Gomez. Sabrina is a black lesbian writer and activist, and Letitia, a Latina lesbian, is her partner. The group has come together for a Kwanzaa celebration on New Year's Day, 1996. Sabrina and Leti's home is modestly furnished, but the decor is festive for the occasion. Black, red, and green Kwanzaa candles are mounted on the wooden *kinara* as the smell of burning frankincense and myrrh fills the air. The furniture is arranged in a circle, and seven or eight couples are spread out across the room. Nearly all the couples are lesbians in interracial relationships. One woman, a black lesbian, has two children with her, including a newborn baby. Another child, a nine-year-old boy, is playing with a remote-operated toy motorcycle, and two or three other children are playing in the kitchen before the ceremony begins.

Sabrina begins the Kwanzaa commemoration with a reading from her book *Psychic Scars* and then calls the children to the center of the room to light the *mishumbaa saba* (seven candles). After explaining each of the seven Kwanzaa principles, Sabrina asks one of the children to light the appropriate candle on the *kinara.* With the candles lit, she passes the *kikombe cha umoja* (communal cup of unity) and instructs everyone in the room to take a sip from the cup and to tell the group about their hopes for 1996 and what they would like to release from 1995. It takes about half an hour for the cup to pass around the room. A trend develops in the statements from the participants, several people speaking about their continued love and commitment for their partners as their hope for 1996.

Across town, another New Year's Day party is taking place at the same time. In the tony Gold Coast section of upper Northwest Washington, a group of twenty black gay men, mostly in their thirties and forties, have assembled at the home of a Washington lawyer. Unlike the group of lesbians, most of the gay men at this affair are single. There are no women, no children, and no Kwanzaa symbols. The huge, tastefully furnished living room is divided into three parts, where several conversations are taking place. The group in the center are talking about home mortgage rates; another group, in the rear, are seated on Queen Anne chairs and discussing music. Following a buffet dinner, everyone files into the living room for a musical performance by two of the guests. One man sings and the other accompanies him on the viola.

These two New Year's Day celebrations reflect two very different cultures, one female and the other male, one communal and the other more individual, one exclusive and the other inclusive. What they share in common is that the participants are mostly black and homosexual, but through their differences they offer windows on some of the many places and spaces in which we find black lesbians and gay men. The differences reflect the diversity of what it means to be black and gay in America.

Much of the public debate about race and sexual orientation assumes that all blacks are straight and all gays are white. When we compare or contrast blacks with gays, we sometimes overlook people who are part of both communities: black lesbians and gay men. Just as there is no universal black lifestyle and no universal lesbian or gay lifestyle, black lesbians and gay men share no universal lifestyle either. Some—like Linda Villarosa, the executive editor of *Essence* magazine; Dr. Marjorie Hill, former liaison to the lesbian and gay community for New York City's first black Mayor, David Dinkins; and Phill Wilson, former Los Angeles City AIDS coordinator for Mayor Tom Bradley—have risen to the pinnacle of the power establishment. However, dozens of black lesbians and gay men living at the seat of power in Washington say they have never even set foot in the Capitol building, the White House, or the Supreme Court. Contrary to the assumption that black lesbians and gay men live in only a few places in the country, I found them in every community I visited, including St. Louis, Chicago, Detroit, Dallas, Houston, Austin, Atlanta, Little Rock, Tampa, Oakland, San Francisco, Los Angeles, Washington, Philadelphia, New York, Boston, and Hartford. Although most of those I met are city dwellers, many others live in small towns and rural communities far from the sprawling urban centers. One black lesbian interviewed lives in Honolulu, Hawaii, and one black gay man interviewed lives in Anchorage, Alaska. A few black gay men I met in Washington are wealthy, well-educated Republicans, while a man I met in Little Rock worked part-time at the YMCA and depended on food stamps to make ends meet. Some black homosexuals are unabashed denizens of the nightclub scene, while others feel uncomfortable in that ambience and avoid it. A large number regularly

attend church, sing in the choirs, and serve as ushers and deacons, but quite a few others are turned off by religion altogether. For every stereotype about black lesbians and gay
men—where they live, how they dress, how they socialize, how
they worship—I found someone who contradicted it.

Diversity is the touchstone of black homosexual identity.
Black lesbians and gay men range from black-identified to gay-
identified to those who identify with both communities to
those who identify with neither. When a gay business tried to
win an account with the National Black Gay & Lesbian Leadership Forum, of which I am currently director, its pitch em-
phasized that it was the best gay-owned firm in the area. The
pitch was helpful, but not entirely what I wanted for the Forum. In my judgment, a white gay firm would rank no higher
than a straight black firm, because our identity is not tied solely
to the white lesbian and gay community. A black gay business
would have been ideal. When given the choice between our
black identity and our gay identity, many blacks who are
openly lesbian or gay still find more comfort among straight
blacks than among white lesbians and gay. Partly because African Americans tend to be more disadvantaged than whites, we
often prefer to deal with straight, nonhomophobic blacks than
with white lesbians and gays, many of whom have trouble understanding this concept. For white lesbians and gays, sexual
orientation identification is usually more important than their
racial identification. They tend to see the world through the
lens of their lesbian and gay eyes, while black lesbians and gays
see it through a prism of colors. Therefore, when black lesbians and gays look into the eyes of a white gay businessman,
many of us see power and privilege that are not typically found
in the black community, straight or gay.

Two incidents related to my former position as White
House director of specialty press illustrate my own experience
with identity assumptions. A few weeks after the inauguration
of President Clinton, I picked up a copy of the *Washington
Blade* with a story lamenting the dearth of openly gay members

in the Administration. I contacted the editor and asked her what the article meant, since the newspaper would have had no way of knowing who was lesbian or gay unless they had surveyed all the officials in the Administration. As no one had asked me about my sexual orientation and I considered myself openly gay, I felt slighted to be omitted from the article. The *Blade* got its information from a list maintained by Coalition '93, a fairly effective coalition of white gay organizations that did not represent many black lesbians and gays. Those who did not get their jobs through the coalition were not identified on the list of gay appointees unless they contacted the organization.

Two years later, after I had already left the White House, a friend handed me a copy of a gay publication run by ACT UP that identified me as a "press apologist" for the Administration. Beneath a huge blowup of my face, the full-page broadsheet centerfold carried my name and home telephone number, and quoted a comment I had made to a reporter months earlier in a different context: "I'm still with the administration and I'm proud to be with the administration." The ad urged readers to call me and other Administration officials to complain that "our lives are more important than their jobs." Because I had quit my job at the White House several months earlier, I called the editors of the publication to object to the implication that I was still working there. The editors justified their attack by telling me that I was guilty of genocide for my complicity in the Administration and that I had a responsibility to speak out publicly against the President, since I had only gotten my job because of my homosexuality and as a cover for the Administration. I had never before been accused of benefiting from my sexual orientation, and the comment struck me as particularly ironic, since the gay community did not even know I was gay until I told them. But the suggestion that I had benefited from gay affirmative action indicated just how myopically some white gays see their sexual orientation, projecting onto nonwhite homosexuals the false notion that sexual orientation is the centerpiece of their identities. This is not to suggest that sexual orientation is less important than race to black lesbians and gays, but even when it is equally important, it is still not the only part of their identity that makes them a minority.

Perhaps because of their multiplicity of identities, black homosexuals seem less likely than white homosexuals to be openly gay or to consider themselves out of the closet. For many white homosexuals, particularly men, their sexual orientation is all that distinguishes them from the dominant white population. Thus, their sexual orientation takes on a greater importance than it does for black homosexuals, who already live with an added layer of difference from the dominant group by virtue of their race. For black homosexuals, sexual orientation can often be just another example of their otherness, making them less inclined to view this aspect of their identity as central to who they are. Black lesbians add another layer of difference from the cultural standard by virtue of their gender. The resulting absence of images of openly lesbian and gay African Americans leads all the affected communities to misunderstand, misidentify, and underrepresent the black lesbian and gay community. Therefore, white homosexuals, black heterosexuals, and even black homosexuals come to see the gay community as primarily white.

Partly because of such conflicting identities, many black lesbians and gays feel excluded from the white gay community and underutilized by the black straight community. The sense of difference and exclusion from the gay community strikes so profoundly that it occurs even in the use of self-identifying terms. Black gay minister Rainey Cheeks says, "I do not use the term 'queer,' and most black people that I know do not use the terminology 'queer.' " Similarly, Dr. Ron Simmons, former professor at Howard University, explains, "I can appreciate the issue over whether or not we should call ourselves 'gay' as African people because basically it is a white cultural term that white people created." The fact that well-respected openly gay

African Americans express such disconnection with a gay identity reveals the chasm between black homosexuals and the gay community. Some black homosexuals also express concerns about their relationship with the black community at large, but these concerns usually do not seem to create the same distance between them and the black community as that between them and the gay community. Many black homosexuals seem to want nothing more than to be full members of the black community, and many already consider themselves to be so. Far fewer black homosexuals seem eager to identify solely with what they perceive to be a predominantly white gay community. Notwithstanding their desire to be full participants in the struggles of African Americans, a number of black lesbians and gay men feel they must work harder than other blacks just to prove that their allegiances lie with the black community and not with other communities. But while some black lesbians and gays identify exclusively with the black community and some have trouble with both communities, still others find themselves stretched to the limit. Eric Washington, a black gay journalist in New York, describes himself as constantly "between two worlds," the gay world and the black world. "It's not like I'm nowhere," he says. "It's more like I'm everywhere."

As a result of their differences from the white gay community, black lesbians and gay men often feel they have more to contribute to the black community. Charlene Cothran, the editor of *Venus* magazine, a monthly black lesbian and gay publication, describes the feeling she experienced as a member of a mostly white gay contingent in the 1995 Martin Luther King Day Parade in Atlanta. "I just didn't feel connected to the gay marchers," she said. "I felt like I had a stronger connection with these other groups that were going down the street without me." That connection is understandable. Black lesbians and gay men come from black families, and grow up sharing a sense of togetherness in their difference. The bond that connects them as black people is not severed merely because they add a new layer to their identity as lesbians and gay men.

A few black lesbians and gays identify so strongly with the African-American community that they chide other black homosexuals who they believe are too gay-identified. Cleo Manago, the founder of Black Men's Xchange, in Northern California, is one of these. He describes himself as "an advocate and activist for the Black collective, same-gender-loving people and humanity." He shuns the term "gay," which he considers a creation of white Eurocentrists.

For many black homosexuals, being black and gay involves shuttling back and forth between two identities and searching to make peace between them. Even those who do not mention such conflict seem unknowingly beset by it. For example, some black homosexuals claim to have little or no connection to the overall gay community or gay culture or anything connected with homosexuality. "My sexuality does not define me. It's not a part of who I am," one black gay man protests. But the same man can hardly walk through a shopping mall without gawking at attractive men. His sexuality plays a much more significant role in his life experiences than he will admit, and the failure to appreciate this role results from his own identity conflict, albeit unacknowledged.

For other black homosexuals, the most prominent part of their identity may change depending on the company they keep. "Among many of my gay white friends, white male friends especially, I would say my being gay is more to the front than my being black is," says R. Paul Richard, a lawyer at the Equal Employment Opportunity Commission. On the other hand, Richard adds, "with straight black friends, the usual point of connection is our shared blackness. With gay black friends, in many ways, it's dependent upon how comfortable they feel with open expressions of their sexuality." The black homosexuals who do admit some identity with the gay community often find themselves the subject of criticism by other black gays like Manago, who objects to black gay leadership "cultivated by a white [gay] community that only rhetorically acknowledges African-American lives; sending subliminal messages of disrespect, further disenchanting the community."

On the other hand, some black lesbians and gay men identify primarily with the white gay community. Some are fed up with the homophobia they have experienced from the black community or the closetedness of the black homosexual community. Others were raised in white suburbs with white children at white schools, and they feel perfectly comfortable in a predominantly white environment. There are many reasons why black lesbians and gay men identify with the white gay community, but not all of them are self-hating.

Other black lesbians and gay men feel disrespected by some part of the black community, including the black homosexual community. Some black lesbians, who felt betrayed by the black community's support of Louis Farrakhan's Million Man March, told me they have given up on the *straight* black community. Meanwhile, some black gay men have abandoned the black *gay* community, including several who said that they would never date other black men because they don't trust them or because black men don't have enough going for them. "Black men have too many issues," one black gay man said. Still others have felt betrayed by both the white gay community and the black gay community. Sergeant Perry Watkins, the first openly gay man to be allowed to serve in the military, is one of these. He feels he was ignored and neglected by the movement to lift the ban on gays in the military, and his bitterness toward the white gay community is equaled by his bitterness toward the black gay community, both of which he sees as responsible.

Increasing numbers of black lesbians and gay men seem to be comfortably negotiating their way through the various communities to which they belong. They relate to the black community, the white gay community, and the black gay community somewhat differently, but in ways they feel are genuine to their full identities. Of all the generations of black lesbians and gay men that preceded us, ours is the first group to live their lives so openly and proudly, asserting a new identity that challenges the narrow confines of the traditionally white gay community and the stereotypically straight black community. Borrowing here and there from parts of our many different identities, we are creating a unique black lesbian and gay identity, remarkable not for its uniformity but, rather, for its diversity. Each of us, in a different way, is learning to live not simply as man or woman, black or white, gay or straight, but with all the parts of our being as one. We have few role models to guide us, so instead we are "making ourselves from scratch," as black gay writer Joseph Beam has said. Each of us is carving her or his own identity into the elaborate woodwork of history.

Wherever we fit on the continuum of black lesbian and gay identities, nearly all of us share one experience in common—the experience of discovering our sexual orientation. The understanding of one's race occurs fairly early in life, but the discovery of one's sexual orientation often happens in adolescence, or well into adulthood, sometimes after heterosexual marriage and children, sometimes even after retirement. For many black homosexuals, the self-discovery is like finding one more river to cross in the journey to freedom. Our earliest memories often reflect our understanding of our difference from those in power. We've known from childhood that we are male or female and black, but only later in life have most of us realized and accepted that we are also different because of the people we love. For many of us, it has taken years to understand the venom of racism and sexism and to develop healthy antidotes to counter those poisons in our lives. The realization that we are also homosexual brings new challenges. We can no longer concentrate our energies on fighting racism and sexism alone without recognizing that we will also be oppressed by homophobia and heterosexism. But there are also new opportunities presented, including the chance to find a supportive community of people who understand what we are experiencing. Using the same skills we have developed as African Americans, we learn as lesbians and gay men to wade through the murky waters to a better understanding of the world around us and our role in it.

Despite its often late discovery, sexuality can be as significant a part of one's identity as one's race. The motto of the Washington, D.C., Coalition of Black Lesbians, Gay Men and Bisexuals captures the sentiment with the phrase "As proud of our blackness as of our gayness." Because of this duality, questions about loyalty to the overall black community constantly face many blacks who are openly lesbian or gay. "Are you black first or gay first? Which is more important to you?" The question itself reflects a cramped understanding of multiple identities, because even if someone identifies primarily with one community or another, she can still proudly embrace the other parts of her identity. You can be primarily black-identified and still be proud to be a woman or a lesbian or a Hispanic. You cannot truly love yourself if you are permitted to love only a part of yourself. Dr. Marjorie Hill, a black psychologist in New York, puts it this way: "I don't get up in the morning and say, 'Hmm, I feel like an African American. I get up in the morning as Marjorie, and Marjorie happens to be a lesbian, she happens to be African American, she happens to be female, she happens to be five eleven and can bench-press 320 pounds. I get up with all of me, and I take all of me throughout the day as I live my life." To choose between various parts of our identity is like choosing between parts of our body. Which is most important, the left breast or the right, an arm or a leg? All the parts of our body, like all the parts of our identity, help to shape who we are and how we experience the world.

Given their multiple layers of identity, black lesbians and gays do not enjoy the luxury of focusing their energy solely on one oppression in their lives. Unlike black straight men dealing with racism, white straight women fighting sexism, and white gay men combating homophobia, black lesbians and gays face the same challenges these others face, complicated by the additional factor of sexual orientation or race.

To navigate their way through this maze of difference requires unique diplomacy and patience. For example, many black lesbians and gays struggle with the question of whether and how to be out and to whom. They are suspicious of the calls to come out from the lips of white gay men, who benefit from the privileges of race and gender. They are sometimes reluctant to express their gay identity as proudly as they express their racial identity, in part because they fear that in times of upheaval they may be abandoned by a white gay movement that can more easily retreat into assimilation than they can as members of a visible minority group. Shut out from the white gay community, black homosexuals often find little more acceptance in the black community. Therefore, many of them are not readily identifiable, having carefully closeted themselves or having integrated themselves into black straight society, where most black lesbians and gays live.

To find one another, black homosexuals have mastered a highly sophisticated secret language of body signals, facial expressions, and code words and developed elaborate mating dances designed to determine the sexual orientation of others. For example, on a trip to St. Louis with my boyfriend John, I attended a reception at a straight black nightclub. While I mingled, John got into a discussion with three men. None of them wore wedding bands, and one of them, Calvin, spent the evening trying to make a pass at the woman standing next to him. When I joined the group, I struck up a conversation with Vernon, a tall older man whose every word seemed pregnant with multiple meanings. Several times that night, he snooped around and asked me what types of things I liked to do, and several times I mentioned that I liked to go out dancing. "Who do you go out with?" he asked.

"Well, sometimes I hang out with John and sometimes I just like to go dance by myself," I said. "What about you?"

"I don't really like to dance."

"Oh! What do you like to do?"

"Different things," he said.

Time and again, I tried to tug at his veil of secrecy in order to unravel the mystery of his sexual orientation, but each time he seemed to clutch it more tightly to himself.

"I'm a quiet person, a homebody," he told me. "I don't really go out much."

Despite his declarations of quietness, Vernon invited John and me to join him and his buddies for a night on the town. I should have expected his response when I asked what they planned to do.

"I don't know," Vernon said. "We're gonna hang out, unless you have something in mind."

"Where do you go to hang out?" I asked.

"Oh, here, there, everywhere," he said, dragging out each word as he spoke.

I decided to play his game by being just as coy. "What types of places are here, what types of places are there, and what types of places are everywhere," I asked, mimicking his speech pattern.

"You know, just places," he said.

"Actually, I *don't* know. I haven't lived in St. Louis for fourteen years," I reminded him, "and when I was here I was too young to know any places to go out."

"We like to have *fun* when we go out," his friend Fred interjected, and both Vernon and Fred broke out in laughter.

Feigning ignorance, I said "I don't get it" and got no response.

Fred asked, "What are your plans for tonight?"

"I think John and I are going to get something to eat," I told him.

"And then what?"

"And then, I don't know, do you have any suggestions?"

"What do you usually do for fun when you're in D.C.?"

"Well, we go out to clubs sometimes, but we spend a lot of time at home just entertaining ourselves." That was the big hint. I thought, If these guys can't tell that John and I are gay by now, then they'll never pick up on it without our saying it.

Yet the discussion went on and on, with none of us offering enough information about ourselves to confirm that we were gay. We were a group of adults acting like children playing doctor. "I'll show you my secret if you show me yours," we might as well have said. As the three St. Louisans joked among themselves and looked at one another with stereotypically dramatic head and eye gestures, John and I began to confirm our suspicions that they were gay but were not yet ready to acknowledge it.

After pushing the conversation to the line, John and I told them we were ready to leave the reception and head back to our hotel. Then Fred broke the ice. Motioning for me to lean over, he whispered that they planned to go to an "alternative" club. "You mean gay?" I asked. He nodded his head yes. "Sure, those are the only types of clubs we ever go to," I told him.

This experience amounts to a snapshot of everyday life for many black lesbians and gay men. Because we are usually not segregated in the controlled environments of the gay ghettos, we often meet each other in our natural habitats, cautiously feeling out one another like wild animals wary of being attacked. We learn to communicate with the body signals and code words that Craig Washington, a black gay man in Atlanta, calls "closet speak." The process of identity awareness is often more of a struggle for black lesbians and gays than for white lesbians and gays. The gay communities, even in the urban areas with large black concentrations, are usually populated by whites, many of whom have migrated to these areas seeking refuge from their families or their communities. However, most but not all black homosexuals, for economic, social, or family reasons, usually live in the black community and socialize with other black homosexuals in a subset of that community. Several people I interviewed noted the singular importance of the black family for black homosexuals. Linda Villarosa, openly lesbian executive editor of *Essence* magazine, joked, "In the black family, no one throws you out [for being gay]. In fact, they keep you in to torture you and try to change you back." As a result, the same familial and social networks that assist them as black people often do not assist them as homosexuals. As black gay writer E. Lynn Harris explained, "[With] the pride that I take in being black, I feel like I have support. When you bring in the sexuality, there's a lot of African Americans who don't understand it, who have a problem with understanding it, and will never understand it because it's not their experience. So that creates a loneliness within a place you should be able to call home."

For black lesbians and gays, unlike straight blacks, our sexual orientation does not insulate us from the oppression of homophobia, and unlike white lesbians and gays, our skin color does not insulate us from the oppression of racism. We can cocoon ourselves in isolated, artificial environments, but the moment we step out of our protective spaces, we are targets again, the prey of the dominant culture. I was reminded of this difference later that evening during the same trip to St. Louis.

With the ice finally broken, John and I and our three new friends went to one of St. Louis's black gay nightclubs. I was surprised to find the place so well integrated by gender, because so few gay establishments in Washington tend to be as inclusive. Both men and women strippers thrust their pelvises to the beat of the music as they undressed down to their bikinis. John and I stuck out like the new kids on the block. John wore oversized jeans, a flannel shirt, and Timberland boots—a popular uniform for young urban black men in D.C.—while I dressed more conservatively in black jeans and an elbow-length shirt. But when John and I left to go home, we blended into the tableau of the seedy area around the club. Outside the club, no one knew we were gay. All they could tell from looking at us was that we were young black men.

We arrived back at the hotel at 2:30 A.M. and made our way to the elevator, where we waited a few moments until the door opened. Out sprang a black female security guard, who looked at us suspiciously and then took a few tentative steps past us. She turned around once, then twice, as we entered the elevator. "Do ya'll have a room key?" she blurted out.

"Give me a break," I thought, rolling my eyes.

"Wait a minute," said John as he darted out of the elevator. "If we were white, you wouldn't even ask that question."

"Yes I would," she said. "We're supposed to ask that to everybody who comes through here."

"So you're telling me that you ask every single person who comes in here if they have a room key?" I asked.

"Yes, if they come in after midnight."

"I find it hard to believe that you would have asked those white people"—John motioned toward a white couple checking in at the front desk—"for their room key if you had seen them. But because we're black, you ask us."

"It's not like that," she insisted. "My instructions are to ask everybody who looks suspicious."

"Hold on. Just a minute ago you said you stopped everybody, and now you say you only stop people who look suspicious. Which is it? And what makes us suspicious—that we're black?"

"No, I, ah . . ."

"You know, the sad thing is that I expect to be mistreated by white people, but I hate it when it comes from my own people," John added.

"No," she insisted.

John asked to see her supervisor. A few moments later, a middle-aged white man appeared in the lobby and asked what the problem was. "The problem," John said, "is that your security guards are instructed to harass black people, which I find racially offensive."

"Sir, that's not the case. She's obviously not being racist if she's black herself."

"What does that have to do with anything? If you tell your employees to stop suspicious-looking people and then you tell them that black people look suspicious in this hotel, then you're telling them to make racial assumptions."

"Well, she's just doing her job, she's new here, and she is just trying to follow procedures. So, I do need to see your room key."

We scowled, and John answered, "Why? What, you don't believe me either?" As John pulled out the key, he said, "Why else would you need to see my key after we've had this conversation?"

The manager apologized and offered to send a complimentary bottle of wine to our room to make up for the problem. We declined, but the wine arrived the next afternoon. The spirits, however, did little to change the assumptions of the security personnel at the hotel. The next night, we were stopped and interrogated at the same place by a different security guard.

Many black straight people do not understand that black lesbians and gays experience the same discrimination that they do because of their race. Instead, they see homosexuality as a white issue and therefore assume that black lesbians and gays have no connection to the black community or no understanding of what it means to be black. The implication that black homosexuals are not interested in helping the black community undergirds part of the concern that blacks have about homosexuality. Particularly when the black community is facing so many challenges in saving its young people, blacks expect other blacks to be involved in the struggle. But again, they do not realize that black lesbians and gays are already involved, raising children of their own and adopting others. Many black teenagers struggle not only with their race but with their sexual orientation as well. Black openly lesbian and gay role models can help them in ways that straight blacks might not. By teaching these young people to respect themselves and become healthy, functioning members of society, black lesbians and gays are able to impart fundamental survival skills to them. In addition, by providing healthy outlets for the expression of their individuality, they can assist these young people to grow up and become involved in the life of the black community.

Kerrington Osborne is one such role model. He knew when he was in high school that he was different from some of his peers, and he recalls seeing a book his mother was reading about homosexuality. "She's reading that because of you," his younger brother told him at the time. Growing up black in a middle-class family, Kerrington heard dozens of white people say to him, "You're not like other black people." Years spent working to become the all-American boy left him confused and out of place. He remembers, "According to these white people, I'm not like other black people, but then some of the [black] kids in junior high [said], 'You're not black enough.' He tried various ploys to fit in, including attempting to talk more black. "I spent a lot of time feeling like I needed to fit into this conception of what other people were telling me it was like to be African American. But fortunately I had my family, who said, Look in the mirror, baby. What do you see?"

Still, he avoided coming out of the closet and avoided some people he suspected were homosexual out of concern that he might be perceived as gay as well. The experience of struggling with his racial identity, however, paved the way for finding his sexual orientation. "I spent [so much] time working on breaking the stereotype and accepting myself for who I am in terms of my race that by the time I got to dealing with my sexuality, it was easy in a way," Kerrington says. His parents made it easier still. He first came out to his mother, a family counselor, who was very supportive. His mother then told his father, and the next day his father spoke to him. His parents understood so quickly that they immediately began to seek out more information about gay children, and within a month they formed a chapter of a support group called Parents and Friends of Lesbians and Gays.

Partly as a result of his positive coming of age as a black

gay man, Kerrington not only has accepted his homosexuality but is a father as well. He spends his days and nights like any other parent, taking care of his three-year-old son, Alexander. He handles the feeding, the bathing, the changing of diapers (except when he must leave his son with the babysitter). A glow appears in his eyes when the conversation moves to his first love, Alexander. "Being a father is incredible," he says. "It is something that I have wanted to do for a very long time. And to be honest, I would say it was one of the factors delaying my coming out of the closet."

When he was still wrestling with his sexual orientation, he found himself looking at other people's children and thinking to himself, I am witnessing something that I will never be a part of. Eventually, he decided to initiate the adoption process. Because of the high demand for infants, some thought a single gay male would never have a chance to adopt one. But Kerrington succeeded. Even though he is gay, Kerrington is part of a family of two, helping to save the life of a young black boy and to steer him in the right direction.

Kerrington says that being black and gay often involves a unique experience with discrimination. Unlike heterosexual blacks who experience racism and homosexual whites who experience homophobia, black homosexuals sometimes encounter a prejudice because they are both black and gay. Each layer of difference from the majority increases the likelihood of oppression and devalues the individual's life. For example, in the summer of 1995, when District of Columbia emergency rescue teams arrived at the scene of a car accident, they immediately began treating a victim, Tyra Hunter. A few moments later, one emergency worker reportedly stopped treating the victim when he discovered that Tyra, although dressed as a woman, had male genitalia. Crimes against lesbians and gays are often not taken seriously, according to some police officers, but crimes against gay men of color may be handled even less diligently. For example, when police confronted white serial killer Jeffrey Dahmer outside his house, they were reportedly reassured by

Dahmer that the controversy between him and the younger man with him was merely a lover's quarrel.

Historian Eric Garber shows that black homosexuals from the South, like other black migrants to Harlem in the 1920s and '30s, soon learned that racism, unemployment, and segregation affected black communities of the North. But on top of their experiences with racism, these black lesbian and gay men were also under continual attack from the police and judicial systems for their homosexuality. The same oppression persists today. To be both black and gay means "double jeopardy," says black gay AIDS activist Gregory C. Hutchings. Unlike black homosexuals who experience two types of prejudice, white homosexuals still have the capability to compensate for their sexual orientation. As Hutchings says, "Walking in the door as a white man or a white woman, they're already three steps ahead, before you even say that I'm gay. So they've gotten further down the road than the black man who walks in the door who doesn't even have to say he's straight or gay. He may not get past door one, regardless."

Unlike their sexual orientation, black homosexuals' race is usually easy to recognize, but this is no blessing for those who value their anonymity or who want to avoid poor treatment based on racial stereotypes. When easy recognition translates into an equation that black equals criminal, many black gays find the anonymity of the gay closet to be a luxury.

Even when black homosexuals hide their sexual orientation, they still must face the everyday prejudice of racism. Whether catching a taxicab, renting an apartment, applying for a job, or negotiating a loan, black lesbians and gays continue to carry the burden of their blackness. Ken Reeves, the former mayor of Cambridge, Massachusetts, and an openly gay black man, says, "In my life, it has been much more easy to be gay than it has been to be black." Rather than being double beneficiaries of diversity policies, many black lesbians and gays feel themselves to be double victims of discrimination, with the source of the discrimination often too cloudy to pinpoint.

Following a conference on black and gay issues held in New York, my host for the weekend found the letters "KKK" scrawled on the hood of his BMW. Was this Klan hatred directed at blacks or homosexuals or both? Adding gender, national origin, disability, and other layers of difference further reduces the precision with which one can identify the source of oppression. As Dr. Marjorie Hill asks, "How do you determine whether a white male subordinate is giving you shade because he doesn't want to report to a woman, he doesn't want to report to a person of color, or he doesn't like gay people?"

The different experiences with prejudice based on gender among black homosexuals are particularly difficult to unravel. "Being an out black lesbian is probably easier than being an out black gay man," speculates Linda Villarosa. She suggests that maleness represents power in society, and to the extent that the lesbian image suggests maleness and the gay male image suggests effeminacy, the lesbian is more associated with power than the gay man is. "I gain a little, whereas the black gay man loses some," Villarosa says. The amount of power is still insignificant, but it is power nevertheless. On the other hand, black writer bell hooks, in her book *Talking Back* (1989), describes her experiences differently. Because of economic advantages, homosexual men with money were part of what hooks calls "the materially privileged ruling black group and were accorded the regard and respect given that group. They were influential people in the community. This was not the case with any women."

Because of the differences in the way men and women are socialized, it may be easier for closeted black women to disguise their homosexuality than for black men. Although women learn to appreciate intimacy and friendship, men are conditioned to be more distant with one another. Black cultural attributes may expand the gulf of these gender differences. Black women, for example, sometimes refer to one another as "girlfriends," while black men are socialized to wear supermacho facades and avoid affection.

Black homosexuals, like their white counterparts, also discriminate against one another based on gender. But this is somewhat predictable given the inclination of homosexuals to seek out people of the same gender for companionship. When practiced by women, the exclusion is even more understandable because of the dominant role of men in society and the often-expressed need for some women to find safe spaces away from them. But sometimes political functions can reflect the bias as well. In one city I visited, an organization of black gay men invited black women to participate in a Friday night discussion session on relationships. When one of the black gay men commented that women in business tend to "vacillate" and that women generally are "indecisive," nearly all the women in the meeting hall stood up and walked out. Homosexuality does not shield black gay men from practicing sexism any more than it shields white lesbians and gays from practicing racism.

For both men and women of African descent, the fact that they are less likely to consider themselves "out" and a part of the gay community does not mean they have greater difficulty dealing with the oppression related to homosexuality. In fact, many black lesbians and gays may tend to deal with this oppression more easily than do white homosexuals who may not have experienced discrimination prior to coming out. Black homosexuals, on the other hand, often expect to experience prejudice in their lives because they have struggled with racism years before many of them recognized their sexual orientation. For example, Abner Mason, the national president of the Log Cabin Federation of gay Republicans, says that he has "a much healthier attitude" about how to deal with homophobia than white homosexuals do. "I'm used to the idea that people would discriminate against me for an illogical reason," but he says his white friends are "completely freaked out by that idea because being white they never experienced it in racial terms."

Being black and gay sometimes means having more in common with straight blacks than with white gays. In fact, if there were a motto for the black lesbian and gay community to use with the black community, it might be: "We're just like you. But we're not you." For instance, in dating and relationships, black homosexuals seem to absorb many of the same cultural issues of the black straight community, but in some other ways black lesbian and gay relationships uniquely defy the labels of either the black straight community or the white gay community. Black homosexual relationships share at least one major controversy with black heterosexual relationships: interracial dating. A popular joke among some black homosexuals underscores the issue: A closeted black gay man tells his parents he has both good news and bad news. "First," he says, "I'm dating someone white." "Oh my Lord," says the man's mother. "What's the good news?" "That *is* the good news," he says.

Thirty years after the Supreme Court invalidated state laws restricting interracial marriage, many blacks and whites still do not accept even the thought of dating outside one's race. This sentiment is so deep and basic that it transcends sexual orientation, with many homosexuals of both races carrying the same racial baggage. Not surprisingly, then, gay interracial couples often face the scorn and derision of both racial groups. Several white homosexuals I spoke with told me they had heard other whites criticize those lesbians and gays who crossed racial dating lines, and just as many black homosexuals criticized black lesbians and gays who crossed the lines. Derogatory terms like "snow queen" (a black person who primarily dates whites) and "dinge queen" (a white person who primarily dates blacks) have developed to label these modern day "race traitors."

The problem of interracial dating for blacks is compounded by the number of black lesbian and gay leaders with white partners and lovers. Posing a battery of questions that people ask about these leaders, black gay activist Maurice Franklin says, "Who is the real messenger? Are you just a storefront? Who's delivering the message? Is that white person you're sleeping with telling you what to do?"

The only two major national black lesbian and gay organizations (the National Coalition of Black Lesbians, Gay Men, and Bisexuals and the National Black Gay & Lesbian Leadership Forum) were both started by leaders of the group Black and White Men Together (BWMT). According to one early participant in the Coalition, every one of that organization's founders was involved with a white man. Similarly, the Forum's leadership has long been identified with BWMT. While black lesbians and gay men are free to date whomever they choose, it is nevertheless troubling that so few of our visible leaders are involved with other blacks.

Franklin attributes part of the desire for blacks to date whites to self-esteem issues, and says, "Many of us still think that white is better than black." While he is careful to acknowledge that interracial love is possible, he argues "that there's so many psychological and social factors in this country dealing with race that it's almost impossible to not have any of that baggage in the back of your head when you're selecting someone you want to date." One factor that might influence one's decision is the belief that association with whites will connect the black person to the white person's privilege. This attitude seems to be borne out by some black homosexuals in their aspirations for economic and social mobility. Some white lesbians and gays also recognize the power imbalance. Judith McDaniel, in the *Lesbian Couples Guide (1995),* writes: "If I, as a white woman, am in a relationship with a woman who is black or brown, we are going to have to deal with our power differences every time we go out in the world."

In fact, black lesbians and gay men can experience other people's interracial relationships as disempowering to themselves. Such was the case when, after I spent an evening at a fund-raising dinner ogling an attractive black gay man, he introduced me to his white lover. In addition, there have been countless times when I have pointed out an attractive black man to an interracial couple, only to have the white man agree with my observation and his black partner disagree. My tastes are often more in common with my white friend's than his black partner's.

Another influential factor in interracial dating may be the perception of a limited "pool" of acceptable black homosexual partners. Black gay activist Ric Irick, explaining "the chances of landing a Black boyfriend in the '90s," writes in a 1995 issue of the black gay publication *Malebox,* "The arithmetic is scary." First, AIDS has taken thousands of black men. Second, hundreds of other black men "simply don't 'have their acts together' (and never will)." Third, "countless more Black men say they are just 'not ready' for a relationship (and may never be)."

While a number of black homosexuals seem to have dated whites at some point in their lives, perhaps more intriguing is the pattern among some blacks to date exclusively one race or another—either they date only blacks or they date only non-blacks. Several black homosexuals who date only blacks said they simply found blacks more attractive, while other black homosexuals said they appreciated the comfort level in not having to explain themselves all the time to someone of a different race. Another group of blacks date only blacks partly for political reasons, either as a reflection of their black identity or their opposition to white racism.

Rhonda Smith, a thirty-four-year-old black lesbian from Texas, has been thinking about these issues in her own life. Writing in a February 1996 column in the *Washington Blade,* she says, "The woman I grow old with will probably be African American. She could be a woman of color, but she probably won't be white." Although Smith says she has had two painful relationships with white lesbians and "even more bad times" with black women, she still feels "like an outsider" when she goes to bars or churches with white lesbians and gay men. "Some speak. Most hardly seem to notice when I enter the room," she writes.

Other explanations given for dating only blacks actually amount to explanations of the problems associated with dating whites. Ric Irick cites three questions that some black men consider. First, what will my friends and family think? Second, why would I want a white guy who likes only blacks? Third, does the white person like only blacks because of some stereotype, perhaps about black bodies or penis sizes?

A personal ad in a recent issue of the *Washington Blade* reads, "Very normal Black Male seeks very normal White Male. I'm well-educated & somewhat attractive. I'm the kind of guy you take home to meet your parent(s). You should be the same." Advertisements like this one are not difficult to find in the gay newspapers of most major cities, but perhaps out of fear of criticism, only a handful of the black homosexuals (all of them men) I came in contact with acknowledged that they exclusively preferred whites. Those who did admit this preference often complained that black men could not satisfy them intellectually or emotionally. One black gay man complained that black men were too immature, while another complained that they were too selfish in bed. Even though black themselves, these men freely generalized from their experiences to say that other black gays were not of their caliber. The pattern has changed little over time. Freeman T. Freeman, a fifty-five-year-old black gay clinical social worker in Rochester, New York, recounted his own experiences from twenty and thirty years ago, when "most of the young black men that I met in bars were not interested in other black men as life partners." Black men were not seen as able to provide as much to a relationship as white men could. "We were somehow led to believe that we were all in the same boat of not having a lot to offer each other in terms of getting ahead in life."

Distinctions based on gender also need to be made. While stereotypes suggest that black women couple relatively easily with other women, the same stereotypes indicate that black gay male relationships are notorious for their brevity. Because both male and female homosexuals are indoctrinated by the same antigay, heterosexist culture, we might expect to find equal success rates for black male and female relationships, if self-esteem issues were the primary cause of their failure. But because black gay female relationships appear to outlast black gay male relationships, factors other than self-esteem must be at work. In a society whose gender roles create uncommunicative and insensitive men, we might expect that any male-male relationship would be less likely to succeed than a relationship involving at least one female. Then, because racist elements in society help create dysfunctional black relationships, an added burden would be placed on the couple. The combined effect of maleness and blackness in a relationship might well increase its probability of failure.

Homosexuality, for men and women, can still make relationships much more difficult to sustain. The story of Vera Frazier provides a true-life example. When Vera was still a child in 1930s rural Louisiana, her foster mother told her something that would stick with her for years: "Sex is dirty, filthy, and bad." Vera grew up during the Great Depression as an only child on a farm. Her foster family owned horses, cows, chickens, pigs, and other animals, and she remembers her life was filled with chores. From sunup to sundown in summer, she worked in the fields, packed the water for the chickens, took the cows to pasture, milked the cows, cooked meals, washed dishes, made the beds, cleaned the house, and did anything else that her foster family told her to do. Vera's foster mother tried to instill in her a strong sense of religious, almost puritanical, values about hard work and abstinence from pleasure, even refusing to allow her to play with some of the neighborhood kids for fear that they would corrupt her. Only at school did Vera's life resemble the lives of other children her age, but even there she carried the burden of her foster mother's message. "I was so terrified of doing something that was going to cause disgrace or shame or something that I just thought if a boy talked to me, something bad was going to happen," Vera recalls.

Vera's life was not all drudgery. On weekends after church, her mother allowed her to play with the dolls in her dollhouse, and she also learned to ride horses. But her nearest neighbors lived so far away that she had few friends outside of the school year. By the time she entered middle school, Vera began to experience a change in her life. She and her good friend Norma began to play house, but not just any kind of house. Vera would always play the mama and Norma would always play the papa, the one on top. It was during this time that Vera had her first lesbian experience.

At age sixteen, Vera left Louisiana and Norma to meet her biological mother, who called her to California to live with her. In Los Angeles, the young mother was so embarrassed to have it known she had a sixteen-year-old child that she lied about Vera's age, forcing her to repeat two years of high school. At nineteen, three months before graduation in 1942, Vera married her first husband. Although she had been an A student in school, when it came to relationships, Vera says, "I put the *d* in 'dumb.' " No one had ever told her about sex, birth control, love, or relationships, so she stumbled into her marriage both misinformed and uninformed. Early in the marriage, her husband left for the South Pacific to serve as an Air Force engineer. When he returned after World War II, they had grown further apart than the ocean that had separated them.

Unaware of birth control measures, Vera not only bore two children but became pregnant constantly, sometimes several times a year. Each time, the couple would have to find someone to terminate the pregnancy. "Sometimes it was in somebody's kitchen and they used a kitchen table. Sometimes it was in the restroom in a department store and you just stood up on the toilet seat. Sometimes it was in the restroom at a [night]club," Vera remembers. Four of Vera's friends died during these makeshift abortions, but Vera endured twenty of them, often fighting off death herself. After each abortion, she pleaded with her husband not to make her do it again, not to suffer the consequences of continual sex. Sometimes she held out for months, but eventually she always relented. She had no choice.

Thirteen years after Vera and her husband married, they divorced. Vera vowed not to remarry until her daughter moved out of the house. At that point, she dated women for the first time, including a Japanese woman who died suddenly in the midst of their relationship. Crushed by her friend's death, Vera decided not to continue dating women; eventually, in 1963, she married a man. She describes him as "the nicest, quiet, very handsome, very giving person." They had long, deep conversations before they married, and he placed no sexual demands on her. "In that day, at that age, that just wasn't heard of," Vera recalls. "I had stopped dating men because every time I went out with one, it was like going out with an octopus."

Vera eventually discovered that the man she loved was a closeted homosexual in deep denial. She told him about her own sexual orientation. Later, when they married, Vera's husband proposed "an agreement" in which they would continue to act as a family unit that supported each other and her child, but in which he would be able to go out when he wanted and she would be able to do the same thing. When she agreed, he acted on it but she did not. "The mother's always the one that's left home with the child," Vera says. Finally, her son moved off to college, but two months before her tenth wedding anniversary, her husband died.

Weeks later, Vera came out to her son, announcing that she would probably make a major change in her life and that it would most likely involve a woman. She told her son that she did not want to embarrass him and was concerned how his friends might react to his having a lesbian mother. "If they can't accept you for who you are, then they're not my friends," he replied. Vera's daughter took the news differently, restricting her children from interacting with their grandmother. But the children, who had grown accustomed to spending Christmas and Easter with Vera, pressed their mother as to why they couldn't go to see her anymore. When told that it was because their grandmother was living a homosexual lifestyle, they responded, "So what?" Two of Vera's grandchildren who asked that question later revealed that they, too, were homosexual.

In 1975, forty years after her initial lesbian experience as a child, Vera entered her first long-term relationship with a woman. It lasted nearly nine years. She fell in love again recently and now at seventy-one, is involved in a new same-gender relationship.

What is unique about black lesbian and gay relationships largely involves the dynamics of race in this country. Like white homosexuals, black lesbians and gays struggle with questions of fidelity and longevity in attempting to forge intimate relationships. Unlike white homosexuals, however, black lesbians and gays also often have to deal with additional relationship problems based on race. The role of religion in the black community often plays a part in how black homosexuals see themselves and their interactions with one another. "If your religion, which informs the way you think, tells you that you are wrong, then people that are like you are wrong, then your relationships are wrong. Everything about you is wrong, so you're not going to put any energy into anything and the best thing to do is just hope and pray that you can change somehow," says Dr. Elias Farajaje-Jones, a former professor at Howard University's Divinity School. He argues that religion should instead work on "arming you to name your oppression and to struggle against it and to create a world where you and everyone else can live and feel and be fully themselves."

The relationship quandary takes on unique permutations for dissatisfied lesbians and gays because not only do they sometimes seek different races for relationships, but some abandon hope for a successful homosexual relationship altogether and seek heterosexual companionship instead. Bisexual men and women are the obvious example, but they are not alone. Some homosexuals seem to deceive themselves into thinking that they are not homosexual. Others, frustrated by the lack of success in their same-sex relationships, seem to think that they will find better luck with the opposite sex. It is not unusual for people who are down on their luck to think that the "grass is always greener" on the other side. In the case of relationships, the truth is that a great many of them do not survive—whether heterosexual or homosexual, black or white, married or live-in. This does not mean that most people will never find a suitable mate; it only means that it can take time. But for black homosexuals, struggling with two separate and complicating identities, the temptation for many to give up one in exchange for the hope of bliss is often too great to resist.

Of course, being black and gay is not only about love, sex, and relationships. It can also involve negotiating distinctions between political and social identities. As a result, some black homosexuals start to see their sexual orientation primarily through political lenses, while others see it through social lenses. "Social homosexuals" are so called not because they are the only ones who socialize but, rather, because their identity as homosexuals is manifested primarily in their social rather than their political activities. These homosexuals are more likely to be closeted, although the term strikes many as odd considering they rather openly attend black gay social functions as well as nightclubs and other establishments. They are considered closeted because they often do not come out in contexts outside their social setting—contexts such as their workplaces, their families, and their churches. On the other hand, "political homosexuals" usually do come out in non-social settings—to their employers, their families, and their nongay friends, for example. For political homosexuals, black or white, the personal is often considered political, meaning that the act of coming out is in itself a political step to further the cause of gay liberation.

When black homosexuals speak of being "in the life," they often refer to the social life rather than the political one. Part of being "in the life" for younger homosexuals involves attending house parties and nightclubs. The socializing is easier in cities with larger black populations. In Washington, the black gay capital, it is possible to attend a different black lesbian or gay nightclub each night of the week. But in smaller cities such as Little Rock, there are no black gay nightclubs; all the gay establishments are white. Another part of the life, for those who can afford it, revolves around a yearlong informal social calendar of events in various cities across the country. The highlight of the year occurs during Memorial Day Weekend, when thousands of black lesbians and gays converge on Washington, D.C., for Black Lesbian and Gay Pride Weekend. Its centerpiece event takes place in broad daylight at Howard University's Banneker Field. (Benjamin Banneker, an eighteenth-century scientist who helped design the layout for the city of Washington, is considered by some biographers to have been a homosexual.) In few other cities would thousands of black homosexuals openly congregate in such a public setting. Other important occasions during the year include an annual Independence Day weekend beach party in Los Angeles and a Labor Day retreat in Atlanta. Some events parallel those of the young black heterosexual social scene. At Atlanta's popular "Freaknik," Chicago's Bud Billiken Parade, and Philadelphia's Penn Relays, black homosexuals often stage a number of parties and other social functions that rival the events put on by straight blacks. The most invited, most well-traveled of these socialites become the divas of the social circuit and are known as "A-list" people.

Political homosexuals do not necessarily cloister themselves away from all entertainment, but when many of them do attend social functions, they do so partly for political reasons or to stay in touch with their particular community. As a result, many black political homosexuals find themselves insulated from some of the less sophisticated thoughts of the black gay world. Black lesbian activist Mandy Carter, for example, candidly acknowledges that the people in her circle usually share her fairly enlightened views about racism and homophobia. Although she is a longtime field organizer, she is still surprised when I ask her about black homosexuals who do not support gay rights. "I don't want to put the bar crowd down," she says, "but I think sometimes when you get into the apolitical [groups], that's probably where you'll hear more of that."

Where political and social identities seem most likely to merge is in the proliferating of black gay discussion groups across the country. Mark Johnson, author of an article called "Something to Talk About" in the November/December 1992 issue of *SBC* magazine, writes that these gatherings regularly occur over potluck dinners in private homes in such places as New York, Chicago, Los Angeles, Atlanta, and the San Francisco Bay Area. Sherry Harris, a black lesbian and former member of the Seattle City Council, says, "The problem with the black gay community is that they're about ten years behind the white gay community." This distinction has resulted in a lot of white gay people who see that our salvation is coming out of the closet and being known and letting people know who we are and know that we're not freaks," she says. On the other hand, Harris says members of the black gay community "are still very, very afraid."

Some black lesbians and gays argue that black homosexuals should remain in the closet. A black gay man who identified himself only as Glynn wrote in the February 1996 issue of the black gay magazine *Malebox*, "When was the last time an activist or a queen got you a well-paying job?" Indeed, if you don't have a job or a steady income, the thought of coming out may seem more like masochism than liberation. Glynn also complained that most black gay activists are not positive role models: "It's a lot to ask a regular guy to come out and be subjected to public ridicule and possible physical abuse when the public image of gay men is currently taken over by flamboyant, outrageous queens."

The chasm between black social and political gays is also revealed in the attendance lists for various black and gay conferences and panel discussions throughout the country. There are plenty of conferences to attend. In one month's time during the winter of 1995, I attended three separate gay or gay black conferences, first in Los Angeles, then in Boston, then in New

York. Dr. Farajaje-Jones, an acknowledged participant on the conference scene, laments the divide that has been created: "Often in the sort of black gay elite, people have removed themselves from any danger in the sense that they don't really deal that much anymore on a day-to-day basis face-to-face with the black community," he says. Farajaje-Jones also criticizes the sentiment among some black gay leaders that they do not have time to deal with closeted black homosexuals. "I think that that's something that paralyzes the movement," he says. Noting that some of the distinctions in attitude and identification depend on class status and economics, Farajaje-Jones suggests that black gay leaders should be keenly sensitive to those who attend conferences at great personal sacrifice. But just as importantly, he encourages the leaders from the black political homosexual crowd to take the lessons they learn to the black homosexuals on the streets.

Finally, no discussion about being black and gay in America can ignore the impact of AIDS. Fifteen years ago, the word might never have come up in a discussion about being black and gay. But today, the black community, the gay community, and the black gay community know all too well that the disease has plundered many of their most valuable human resources. The effect of AIDS has disproportionately fallen on communities of color. Although African Americans make up only 12 percent of the nation's population, they account for 39 percent of all new AIDS cases, according to 1994 statistics from the Centers for Disease Control. HIV infection is the leading cause of death for black men between the ages of twenty-five and forty-four and the second leading cause of death for black women in this age group. Fifty-three percent of all infants with AIDS are black. Globally, the statistics are even gloomier. The World Health Organization estimates that two thirds of the 15 million people infected with the HIV virus are Africans and 2 million of the 3 million people who have died from the disease have been Africans as well.

With more and more black people dying, one might expect

the black community and black institutions to be leading the fight against the disease, but instead the response has been underwhelming. The Reverend H. Beecher Hicks of Washington's Metropolitan Baptist Church offers a typical response to the question of whether the black church is doing enough to fight AIDS. It is not doing enough to prevent cigarette smoking and to discourage alcohol abuse, he says, citing a variety of social problems afflicting black people besides AIDS. Hicks cautions that the black church "should not be expected to be the Messiah in relation to those issues." But while lung cancer and liver disease are certainly killing black people as well, no affliction—not even homicide—claims the lives of more young black adults than AIDS, and no affliction is spreading as rapidly as HIV.

Much of the delay behind the black community's response to AIDS follows directly from its unwillingness to address openly certain issues of sexuality. In the District of Columbia, for example, where black gay men make up the largest group of people with AIDS, any serious effort to fight the disease would involve candid discussions about homosexual behavior, a topic that black religious leaders are often unwilling to address except in lofty moral terms. At a town hall meeting on AIDS hosted by Black Entertainment Television, Nation of Islam Minister Dr. Abdul Alim Muhammad suggested that AIDS would not have been a problem if more people had followed the advice of the prophets. But if you don't follow the prophets, use a condom, shot back Rae Lewis-Thornton, a heterosexual black woman living with AIDS. The exchange between the two panelists represents the tension in the black community between moralists and pragmatists. While some pragmatists may themselves be moralists, they at least recognize the folly involved in preaching against behavior without providing tools for people to make wise choices.

As a result of the black community's phobias related to sex, black homosexuals and heterosexuals are dying. Those who have not died out of ignorance—because they were never told what to do—have died out of prejudice—because they were taught that their lives were expendable. When the church teaches that one's very existence is an abomination, it is easy to understand why so many black homosexuals struggle with issues of self-image, sometimes leading them to engage in increasingly risky behavior. Even those not directly affected by the black church's attitude are affected by the black community's failure to address issues related to AIDS straightforwardly. According to Phill Wilson, the former public policy director of AIDS Project Los Angeles, the two most commonly heard comments from HIV-infected youth are that they never expected it to happen to them and that it didn't really matter, because they felt they were going to die anyway from violence or some other malady in their community.

Patricia Fleming, the national AIDS policy director, sees a clear connection among racism, homophobia, and AIDS. Racism and homophobia, she explains, leave people with low self-esteem, which she calls "a co-factor" for AIDS. "People who don't care about themselves and don't value themselves as human beings because they've been taught that they're not as good as other people or they're worthless . . . they internalize that and they treat themselves as though they are all those things," she says. Fleming advocates "a huge effort" to teach young people "that each and everyone one of them is worth something" and "to teach them about their bodies and how they work." But the results of the self-image crisis extend beyond AIDS. As Dr. Farajaje-Jones says, "It's not just a matter of HIV. It's matter of suicide. It's a matter of all kinds of self-abuse with substances, and what have you, in which people engage."

With all that needs to be done to fight AIDS, many black leaders seem fixated on spouting conspiracy theories about the origin of the disease. Citing the Tuskegee syphilis experiments and other government-funded medical projects, including biological warfare, black writers Haki Madhubuti and Frances Cress Welsing suggest something sinister involved. Certainly, for many blacks it would not stretch the imagination to find government complicity behind the rise of AIDS. Without arguing the plausibility of these theories, one can see a dangerous side effect of repeating them: they distract the black community's attention from much-needed action against the epidemic itself. The preoccupation with theories about the unknown reflects an unwillingness to address the known needs of people living with AIDS or those in danger of acquiring the HIV virus through their behavior. While the black community works itself into a fuss about the past, we are steadily losing the future. In a recent study released by the National AIDS Policy Office, the HIV infection rate among white gay men was shown to have increased only 14 percent, but during the same time period studied, the rate for black gay men increased 79 percent. With all the sound and fury about conspiracies and white people's diseases, the message of prevention is still not sinking into the heads of the population most at risk.

As with many crises, the AIDS pandemic has brought out both the best and the worst in the affected communities. Many black gay leaders, for example, became active in the gay movement largely because of AIDS. Some were infected themselves, others watched their friends and lovers become infected, but all have been affected personally in some way. "We've been impacted at such a level—and because of the shrinking dollars and the competition for funds—that we have to be more vocal, and those people who've been more vocal in our community came out primarily because of HIV and AIDS," according to Maurice Franklin. As time progressed, the "work that they've done in HIV and AIDS has transcended HIV and AIDS into other political issues that have to deal with the lesbian and gay community," he adds.

Although many in the black community have struggled to fight the disease, one aspect of homophobia still prejudices the attention given to some AIDS victims. The black community, like other communities, has developed some compassion toward children, heterosexuals, and celebrities infected with the virus. But the concern often evaporates when the victims are homosexuals. Unless the homosexual victims are family members or close friends, the black community—like the white community—often views them differently from the rest. The children are innocent, the heterosexuals are merely unlucky, and the celebrities—regardless of what behavior led to their acquisition of the virus—are courageous role models. This is just another example of many in the black community refusing to acknowledge the presence of homosexuals.

Given the various hues of the black gay experience, what does it mean to be black and gay in America? Many black lesbians and gays ask themselves this question. Lesbian activist Carlene Cheatem, in an open letter to blacks "in the life," writes, "I'm often asked, *how do Black lesbians feel about this or that; what is the Black lesbian and gay commUNITY's position on this or that?*" Cheatem responds, "How do I know?" Her response accepts the diversity of black lesbian, gay, bisexual, and transgendered attitudes, opinions, and lifestyles.

What most of these diverse people seem to share, however, is some experience with oppression. Some are lucky enough to avoid oppressive environments, but many find themselves asking where do they go to be fully accepted? To their families, which do not understand them? To the gay community, which does not represent them? Or to the black community, which seeks to hide them? Some black homosexuals respond to this pressure by compartmentalizing themselves into multiple personas, seeking the comfort of different homes for different needs. But when they define "home" as a place where they can find unconditional love and support, each of these separate homes is often too weak to support the entirety of their beings. Even the black gay community, with its splintered divisions over issues of identification, relationships, and personalities, fails to meet the needs of many black homosexuals. What blacks and gays both need to learn is that black lesbians and gay men do not threaten the unity of either community—they preserve it.

CHAPTER FOUR

Bearing Witness: Faith in the Lives of Black Lesbians and Gays

David, a black gay man in Washington, describes the days before and after his friend Vaughn died of AIDS in the summer of 1995. David remembers Vaughn's mother as being "sweet" when he met her in the hospital, but says her attitude changed when Vaughn passed away. She resisted David's efforts to find a minister to perform the funeral service and instead insisted on her own minister. She also rejected Vaughn's wish that David sing at the funeral. In the middle of the service, the minister called for congregants to come to the altar if they wanted to dedicate their lives to Jesus. Finding that no one answered the call after several repeated requests, the minister told the organist to stop playing and decided to speak candidly to the congregation.

"We all know what Vaughn died of," the minister said. Eyeballing a contingent of a dozen black men sitting together, the minister warned that more people would die if they did not dedicate their lives to Jesus. Leaving the pulpit, he walked to the pews where the men were seated. "Vaughn is gone away to rest now, but his soul will remain here and suffer," the minister told them. Hearing this, a friend of David's rose and quietly walked out the back door. "That's one soul the devil took away," the minister responded, and then continued to harangue the group. "Who in this church is saved? Raise your hands if you've been saved." David raised his hand, and the minister glared at him with disbelief. "How could you be saved?"

"I've accepted the Lord in my life and glorify and praise Him," David responded.

"Son, the Bible says that homosexuality is an abomination in the eyes of the Lord. Vaughn is on his way to Hell, and you will be too if you don't change your ways," the minister told him.

"The Bible says, 'Judge not that ye not be judged,'" David retorted, keeping his composure but all the while shocked that this exchange was occurring in church, at a funeral, with Vaughn's mother sitting there quietly. David and the minister continued their open dialogue, back and forth, until one by one the entire group of men got up and walked out of the church. David "sat there stunned," he recalls. When the casket was removed, "people walked outside like nothing happened." No one even apologized. As David learned that day, religion carries enormous influence over the lives of black people.

The black religious experience—a source of compassion and strength for many African Americans—can be a mixed blessing for black lesbians and gays. As they prepare to go to their final resting place, many of them cannot find peace in their churches. Even well-known black gay writer Essex

Hemphill, who died in November 1995, was eulogized in a church ceremony that minimized his homosexuality and his contribution to the black lesbian and gay community. But the influence of religion on that community extends far beyond funeral ceremonies.

From the earliest days of slavery, the black church has played an integral role in African Americans' longing for salvation. The words of the Negro spirituals testify to the influence of religion, particularly Christianity, in procuring the freedom of a people in bondage: "Nobody knows the trouble I've seen, / Nobody knows but Jesus." In another popular spiritual, developed from the Book of Exodus, we sing: "Go down Moses, / Way down in Egypt land, / Tell old Pharoh, / Let my people go." From slavery onward, many blacks first learned the English language from reading and studying the Bible, even as white society wanted to keep them ignorant by restricting their access to education. As a result, the most informed, articulate, and well-read in the black community became the leaders of the black church. Two of the best-known black men who led slave revolts in the nineteenth century were both heavily influenced by the Bible. One, Nat Turner, felt that God wanted him to capture Southampton County, Virginia, while another, Denmark Vesey, was a minister in the African Methodist Church before his attempted revolt in Charleston, South Carolina.

Even today, leaders in the black community often begin their training in the ministry. The Reverend Martin Luther King, Jr., the Reverend Joseph Lowery, former Atlanta mayor Andrew Young, former congressman Walter Fauntroy, former NAACP executive director Benjamin Hooks, Minister Malcolm X, the Reverend Jesse Jackson, the Reverend Ralph Abernathy, and Minister Louis Farrakhan are but a few modern examples. Black church leaders from the Southern Christian Leadership Conference (SCLC) organized boycotts and demonstrations throughout the civil rights movement of the 1950s and '60s. Unlike many white Americans, blacks have often seen religion and spirituality not so much as a mere set of rules but as a mechanism for liberation in the struggles of their lives and times, which have taken them from slavery to segregation to economic dislocation. Salvation and redemption remain guiding principles in the black church today, even when dealing with the question of homosexuality.

The significance of the church as an institution within the black community is so powerful that many blacks dare not stray from it. As Wardell Payne, editor of the *Directory of African American Religious Bodies,* told the *San Francisco Chronicle* in January 1994, there are nearly fifty thousand black churches in the nation, with a membership of about 20 million people. Young blacks often start going to church because their parents make them go, but later it becomes a significant part of their own lives as well. The need or desire to preserve this bond leads many black homosexuals to maintain their religious ties even when the church may seem unfriendly to them. Its teachings against homophobia do not differ significantly from those of white churches. Nevertheless, because of the influential role the church plays in the black community and its politics, the religious aspect of homophobia seems particularly significant among blacks. Even under these circumstances, it is not so much the church community but, rather, church dogma that ostracizes homosexuals. This distinction helps explain why the black church is alternately cited as the most homo-tolerant and the most homophobic black institution.

Black homosexuals have always been a part of the black community and the black church, according to former Howard University professor Dr. Ron Simmons. Referring to the archetypal black gay man, Simmons says, "You knew he was in church every Sunday. He may even have been playing the organ. You knew he wasn't married. You knew that he was always smiling, so my man was getting something somewhere." Even legends in the black church such as James Cleveland, "the godfather of gospel music," were known to be homosexual. According to the Reverend Rainey Cheeks, "James Cleveland was gay. James Cleveland died of AIDS. Nobody wants to say it."

Cheeks's observation seems to be supported by the comments of Bishop Carl Bean. Recalling his experiences traveling across the country and the segregated South as a gospel music singer, Bean says, "It was gay folk in all those towns in Mississippi, Alabama, Georgia, and the Carolinas who opened their homes to you." He also credits "gay preachers," who opened a "gospel highway" so gospel singers could make a living.

Despite the widespread awareness of homosexuality in the black church, we still find black ministers, deacons, ushers, choir members, music directors, organists, congregations, and homosexuals themselves participating in an elaborate conspiracy of silence and denial. Several of the black ministers I interviewed—even those with reputations for homophobia—acknowledged the presence of large homosexual contingents in their churches, but this fact has not stopped their homophobic preachings, particularly because the lesbian and gay parishioners accept and even participate in the rhetorical gay bashing.

The Reverend James Sykes is one of the best-known opponents of homosexuality in the black church. Born the seventeenth of eighteen children in Plant City, Florida, this otherwise obscure minister has become the darling of the talk show circuit, appearing on *Jerry Springer, Donahue,* and other shows to preach against homosexuality. What makes Sykes so appealing to the talk shows is not that his views represent mainstream black churches but that they appear so extreme. When a black reporter from the Tampa Bay area called Sykes to ask his opinion about an antigay Ku Klux Klan rally in nearby Largo, Florida, his response made the headlines. "If I knew that was the only reason that they were there, I would be there with them," he said. When I asked Sykes about his views in an interview, he boldly defended them: "If I like pork chops and the Klan likes pork chops, nobody has nothing to say. But because the Klan agrees that homosexuality is wrong, and I agree that homosexuality is wrong, then all the sudden I'm sleeping with the Klan."

As pastor of the four-hundred-member St. James A.M.E. Church in Tampa, Sykes acknowledges that "quite a few" of his members are gay, but he maintains that he does not single out homosexuals for condemnation or for special treatment. "I'm not gonna kick you out," he says. "Some of my best friends are gay." But then, like so many other homophobes, Sykes obsesses on a stereotypical image of male homosexuality. "Don't come to me and tell me that they deserve some special rights, because some gay people want to come up and flaunt their sexuality, and you got two men in the same thing and they're sticking their thing up their rump and they got all kind of semen coming out of their mouth. You want a right because you're gay? That's wrong."

I did not need to go all the way to Tampa to find black ministers opposed to homosexuality; I had only to walk down the street. There, at the end of my block, stands a great beacon of black religion—the Metropolitan Baptist Church of Washington, D.C. Sprawling across nearly a full city block, this impressive new facility helped resurrect a once-depressed black neighborhood: the church bought much of the local property, fixed it up, and converted it to new uses. Today, the church claims one of black Washington's best educated middle-class congregations. Among many other notable distinctions is its reputation among black homosexuals as "the place to be."

I visited Metropolitan on the last Sunday of February in 1995, on Communion Sunday. I walked past two ushers whom I recognized as black gay men and up to the balcony, where I took my seat. Looking around, I noticed a number of men whom I had either seen in gay establishments or thought to be gay. One of the few whites in the church that Sunday was a young man wearing an earring who walked in accompanied by a black man whom I thought to be gay. The minister, the Reverend H. Beecher Hicks, preached a sermon called "No Shoes Allowed" and focused on the story of Moses' encounter with the burning bush and on Hezekiah's recovery from a near-death illness. "You can't tell me you love God, who you have not seen, and you don't love me, who you see every day," Hicks said. I took notes on the sermon, and after church I greeted two black gay acquaintances, who invited me to join them for brunch. Four days later, I met Hicks in his office for an interview. He wore a dark suit, with his feet in dress shoes (next to a pair of slippers neatly placed under his desk).

Given my positive experience in the church and its reputation among black gay men, I was not sure what to expect from Hicks. Several people had told me that his views about homosexuality had evolved over time, and I thought this might be the case when I walked passed a Mercedes in the church driveway. The car had a window sticker from Harvard Divinity School, an institution with a progressive reputation. In fact, during the interview he repeatedly sipped from a Harvard coffee mug. Despite my uncertainty as to what he would say, he quickly solved the mystery, describing homosexuality as an "abomination." Citing the first chapter of Romans, Hicks said, "It is the sin, according to Paul, upon which God gave up."

When I asked Hicks about the division among Christians about homosexuality, he said that "those who seek to find a way to legitimize this particular lifestyle will meet with no success." Homosexuality, he said, places the emphasis on the individual's satisfaction and exalts the self over God. But by Hicks's own standard, heterosexuality places the same emphasis on self. If procreation is the only justification for human sexual activity, then many more heterosexuals than homosexuals have violated God's law. Some Baptist ministers recognize this dilemma. The Reverend Peter J. Gomes, a Baptist minister and professor of Christian morals, serves as the chaplain at Harvard University's Memorial Church. "To say that homosexuality is bad because homosexuals are tempted to do morally doubtful things is to say that heterosexuality is bad because heterosexuals are likewise tempted," Gomes wrote in an August 1992 *New York Times* op-ed piece. "For St. Paul, anyone who puts his or her interest ahead of God's is condemned, a verdict that falls equally upon everyone."

"With great respect," Hicks responded, "I would say [the Reverend Gomes is] incorrect." Hicks sees Gomes and himself as coming from the same tradition, but he points out that not all Christians agree. "I don't know that you can reconcile the two [viewpoints]," Hicks admitted.

Hicks and Gomes may not be able to reconcile their differences on homosexuality, but many black homosexuals are eager to reconcile their sexual orientation with their religion. Many continue to worship at churches like Metropolitan even though their ministers preach against homosexuality. Others abandon the church, either longing to make peace with their religion or distancing themselves from it altogether. Some find supportive places of worship, such as the Unity Fellowship Church, whose ministry welcomes black lesbians and gays, and the Metropolitan Community Church, a mostly white gay church. Still others join nongay churches that are not homophobic, including the Unitarian Church.

The Reverend Dr. Hicks said he had made it clear in his church that homosexuality is a sin. Nevertheless, black lesbians and gay men still flock there. According to some black gay activists, the church has the largest black homosexual congregation in Washington. "That is false, that is so false," according to Emory Perkins, who chairs the church's AIDS ministry. In an August 1994 article in the *Washington Blade,* Perkins protested, "Metropolitan Baptist Church is by no means a gay church, the majority are not [gay], of course some are, but sexual orientation is not an issue." Referring to his gay parishioners, Hicks said, "If they don't know [my position], it is because they either can't read or can't hear." When told about their minister's comments, gay members of Metropolitan downplayed Hicks's beliefs, content that he hadn't delivered a homophobic sermon in quite a while. Apparently, the infrequency of the homophobia made it more tolerable for many of the lesbians and gays who worship there. As long as the minister did not beat up on them too often, they could deny there was a problem.

Once or twice a year—sometimes more often, depending on the church—a black minister is expected to deliver his homophobic sermon, says Bishop Bean. "But when that sermon is over, no one walks up to that obvious homosexual and says, 'Get out of here.' " In fact, many of these homosexuals may be playing parts in the conspiracy. As the Reverend Rainey Cheeks tells it, "Let the minister preach one of these gay-bashing sermons and you got the queeniest people in there going, 'Preach! Preach! Come On!' "

Cheeks suggests that the conspiracy is based on economics, and he half-seriously challenges homophobic black ministers of the big churches in big cities to do one of two things. First, if they really disapprove of homosexuality as vehemently as some of them claim to, then they should tell their lesbian, gay, and bisexual members to "get out of my church. Do not come back here. Keep your money. Keep your tithes, your talents, everything. Get out of here!" Cheeks says that homophobic churches are not willing to take this drastic step because "that messes with their money." The second alternative is this: "Tell the whole church, For the next three months put your money in an envelope. If you're gay, lesbian, or bisexual, don't put any money in the envelope. See how much money you collect."

Gay members of black congregations in Washington, D.C., have come to Cheeks on several occasions seeking advice about how to respond to homophobic sermons by their ministers. "I always ask them, 'Why are you coming to me?' I can talk to you. I can explain it to you. But if you don't go back and challenge your own ministers, why are you here in front of me?" Many black homosexuals go to these churches and continue their silence because they have not yet accepted their homosexuality, and they feel guilty about being gay. Cheeks jokingly responds that he might develop a new ministry that will save time, energy, and money for everyone involved. "When you feel guilty, just come to me. I'll smack you. Drop five dollars and you can go home. That way you don't have to listen to long sermons or nothing. And if you're feeling *really* guilty, come and I'll call you a few names and smack you and you can drop twenty dollars."

Dr. Elias Farajaje-Jones, formerly of Howard University's Divinity School, criticizes what he calls the "hypocrisy" of the church. "I'm talking about ministers who engage in all kind of sexual practices yet at the same time preach every Sunday about how this [homosexuality] is so wicked and this is the worst abomination, and the Word says, and the Word says, and the Word says. And these are people that don't read a word of Hebrew, don't read a word of Arabic, don't read a word of Greek," says Farajaje-Jones, who does read Hebrew, Arabic, and Greek. He has spent several years researching the biblical narratives and writings associated with homosexuality in their original languages, and he harshly chastises the ministers who "just get up on Sunday morning, quote the same thing they've been quoting, and they have no idea what the frame of reference is."

Bishop Bean points the finger of blame for black homophobia squarely at the psychology of racism: "All oppressed people try hard in that whole idea of assimilation to prove to the oppressor that they're okay." Bean believes the homophobia of the church contradicts the reality of the community. "If you tear that [assimilation] away and just look at the community, you'll find that the other side of the coin is great acceptance. There is no one in the church who doesn't know who's gay and who's lesbian. Everyone knows." Taking it a step further, Bean says, "There is not a community, black, that I've ever known of where homosexuals were not living. Real, honest-to-God, broken-wristed, twisting sissies don't get thrown out of the black community. That white phenomenon does not happen in our community."

Bean's own experiences growing up in the black church support the complexity of his observations. From his earliest childhood days, he remembers how it influenced who he was as a person. "I was always in love with the church and I was always in love with the teachings of Jesus," he says. "We were taught those teachings in such a way that we saw Him as an advocate for human justice." As a member of the Providence Baptist Church in Baltimore, Bean learned the connection between Christianity and the civil rights movement—both were about liberation. So it was no surprise that Bean would become involved with the NAACP's youth council, run by a churchgoing woman named Lillian Jackson. She taught Bean the value of struggle and instilled in him a sense of social justice as a core part of his identity as a black person.

At age ten, Bean told his church that he wanted to be a minister, and church became a central part of his life. "I loved the church so much that I would leave school as a kid and go by the church in the evenings just to help run the stencils for the church program." Perhaps his earliest lesson in ministry was with his own godfather, who, along with his godmother, raised him from such an early point in his life that he still considers them his father and mother. Although his godfather provided for the family financially, on weekends he would often go out drinking with his buddies, and when he came home, "there would be chaos in our home on Saturday nights," Bean recalls. In quieter moments, when Bean would return home from Sunday School, his godfather would often ask him what he had learned. On one occasion, Bean told him that he had learned a story about a man who wanted to reach Jesus but was afraid to do so because he thought he would be rejected. His godfather was so moved by the story that he decided to go to church with Bean the following Sunday. Then he joined the church, never drank again, and ended up going to church nearly every Sunday thereafter.

Like some other young males in the black church, Bean knew he was gay early on, but he made no effort to hide it. "I never wanted to date the girls. I never wanted to act as if," he says. Everyone, including friends, schoolmates, relatives, and church members, knew he was gay. "And I was totally accepted as a black kid in the hood as a homosexual." But the fact that everyone else knew did not make it easier for his relatives to accept it. When his family realized that he wasn't just going through a phase, they took Bean to see his preacher. The preacher asked, "Carl, what's wrong?" Bean responded, "I don't know," but the preacher prodded him to come out with it. "Give me a piece of paper," Bean said. He took the paper and wrote the word "homosexual" on it and handed it back to the minister. "That's what I thought," the preacher said. But nothing the minister said shook Carl from his sexual orientation or his faith in God.

Bean's godfather had his own strategy for making his son a heterosexual. He brought home baseballs, and baseball gloves, and baseball bats, but it was too late. "I was twirling batons from the age of nine," Bean remembers. "I was not gonna put my batons down." His father even went so far as to buy a pool table for Bean, but the plan backfired. Instead of making his son heterosexual, it gave him an opportunity to invite attractive boys over to his house.

When he saw that kindness failed to change his son, his father's next tactic was intimidation. "You know what *they* do," his father would say to him, suggesting some sort of sinister behavior. His godparents tried to ostracize him because of his homosexual thoughts, separating Bean's eating utensils from the rest of the family's and instructing him to drink out of a tin cup. Bean finally gave up. One day he went into the family's upstairs bathroom and wrote a note to his family: "Mommy and Daddy, I don't know what to do. I don't think you love me anymore, and I don't know how to make you love me. I don't know how to change me." When he finished writing the note, he opened the medicine cabinet, pulled down the bottles of medicine from the shelves, and poured all their contents into his hand. He poured a glass of water, took a sip, and dumped the handful of pills down his throat. He left the note in the bathroom, went to his room, and pushed the dresser in front of the door. When Bean's godfather later wondered why his son wasn't watching TV downstairs, he went upstairs to check on him and found the door shut and blocked. After several tries, he pushed the dresser over, found his son, and rushed him to the hospital just in time for an emergency crew to pump his stomach.

A well-behaved boy, a member of the school honor society, and an active participant in the local church, Bean, except for his homosexuality, might have been everything a parent would want in a son. But the hospital staff suspected something was seriously wrong at home and would not allow him to return to his family after he was treated. Instead, he was put into a psychiatric facility, where a doctor told him she could help him learn to accept who he was and still live out his dreams. In addition, the head nurse, a black woman, told him that she had a brother who was gay. "So I felt that even in that [terrible predicament] God had kind of guided my situation in such a way that I was still being looked out for." The worst part of his hospital experience, he remembers, was being strapped down onto a cold machine and undergoing shock therapy, designed to treat mental illness and homosexuality by running electric currents through the body. When he was released, he left the hospital and moved to live with his natural mother for a year. When his mother died from a botched abortion, Bean had to return home to Baltimore to his godparents, but this time he felt he was in charge of his life. He quit school, started learning by tutor, and ran the streets with his friends until, at sixteen, he decided to move to New York.

His life changed again when he joined the Christian Tabernacle Church in Harlem, where a number of black gays worshipped. Bean joined the choir and started going to church several times a week. Even as a church member, he still frequented gay establishments, and it was at one such establishment in Harlem that an underage Bean found himself harmonizing to a song on the jukebox. Alex Bradford, a black gospel star, overheard Bean's voice at the nightclub and recruited him for a musical group. Bean passed the audition and started rehearsing that same night. He performed in a new show, based on the birth of Jesus, called *Black Nativity,* for which Langston Hughes had written the dialogue. As Bean soon discovered, "the whole gospel field was as gay as you can get," describing the situation as "unbelievable." He continued singing professionally for years and performed in popular shows such as *Your Arms Too Short to Box with God.* But it was in 1975 that he recorded his gay spiritual disco tune, "I Was Born This Way," which climbed the *Billboard* charts.

Bean moved to Los Angeles, joined the ministry in 1982, and soon founded the Unity Fellowship Church, which opened its arms to black gay worshippers. He developed an active AIDS ministry and constructed a new AIDS care center in South Central Los Angeles. He argues that many ministers have misinterpreted the Bible as homophobic and points out that Jesus himself never said a homophobic word, placing his emphasis on love instead. Bean rejects the claim that the black community does not tolerate homosexuals, and says that many churchgoers are tiring of the old-line black homophobic church message. One mother, he notes, has bequeathed her property to Bean's church because when her son was sick no one else, including her family or church, would be involved. "That's a black woman, and a black *church* woman, who made that decision," Bean stresses. In black churches, "the gay people are there, they're in the church. They're not really kicked out of the churches that need their services, but they have to deal with that ridiculous theological battle and internalizing somehow that the very force that created them is not pleased with who they are."

Some black ministers are sensitive to homosexuality even though they are not associated with black gay churches. Father John Payne, the youngest priest at Washington's "mother church for African-American Catholics," is among this group. Born and raised in black Washington, Payne found that his experience with discrimination shaped his view of the church. In an interview, he said he continues to experience racial discrimination in the Augustinian sect of the priesthood by white clergy who ostracize and criticize him. Undeterred, Payne boldly takes issue with his own religion's views on several issues, calling the Catholic Church "racist, sexist, and homophobic." Payne's ministerial home, St. Augustine's Catholic Church, seems to defy many of the labels he affixes to the Church at large. With something of a renegade spirit, St. Augustine's has zealously defended its right to call itself an African-American Catholic Church, despite the protests of some whites who believe the Church should not segregate itself as such.

In the winter of 1995, several months after our interview, Father Payne—the only priest at St. Augustine's to regularly condemn homophobia—announced that he was leaving the church. Perhaps his views were too much even for St. Augustine's, because he had been known to challenge Church dogma from the pulpit during the popular twelve-thirty Mass, ridiculing the sanctimoniousness of the "holier-than-thou" crowd who sit in judgment on other members. The Catholic Church, he told the congregation one Sunday, must embrace all its members, black and white, male and female, rich and poor, and of course, straight and gay. Several months after he announced his departure, Father Payne was still preaching at St. Augustine's.

Payne is not concerned that some Church teachings conflict with his own beliefs, and he argues that the Bible says remarkably little about homosexuality and that what it does say has been misinterpreted by some clerics. Ironically, his church and his religious sect both derive their name from one of the Catholic Church's original homophobes, St. Augustine of Hippo. Born in North Africa, Augustine acknowledged in his *Confessions* that he had been involved in homosexuality as a youth. But later in life, perhaps never able to accept his youthful behavior, he became a principal proponent of the view that all nonprocreative sexual activity is sinful, which remains the view of the Church today. Although many of today's loudest critics of homosexuality neglect to mention this fact, the Church officially disapproves of both heterosexual and homosexual sexual activity. Even for a heterosexual married couple, the only purpose of their sexual intercourse must be to produce offspring. Payne, not surprisingly, disagrees. And like a growing number of African-American ministers, he has begun to rethink the Church's traditional teachings on homosexuality.

Without the benefit of formal religious schooling, many black lesbian and gay parishioners are reaching their own conclusions about God and homosexuality. Some, like Sonja Berry, have reconciled their religious beliefs with their sexual orientation, while others, like Rudy Cook, feel differently. Sonja was born and raised in Pennsylvania. Unlike many women who prefer the term "lesbian," Sonja describes herself as "gay." "I've been attracted to women all my life, as far back as I can remember," she says, "but I guess I never knew you could act on it." When she was a young girl, Sonja's first experience with female intimacy happened when she played house. One person would be the daddy and the other would be the mommy and they would turn the lights off and get under the covers. There was no pretense of cooking, cleaning, or other domestic chores. Playing house simply meant sleeping together and being sexual with each other. The girl with whom Sonja played house turned out to be heterosexual, but as Sonja learned that she herself was homosexual, she tried to maintain the friendship without coming out to her friend.

Later, after a difficult breakup, Sonja told her childhood friend about the relationship by substituting male pronouns when she mentioned her female lover. In the midst of the discussion, Sonja broke down and told her childhood friend that she was gay. "Oh my God," the friend reacted. "I knew something was going on." But then she added, "I'm glad it's over, and you should see this as a sign that that's not the life that you're supposed to lead, and that's God's way of telling you." Sonja was stunned and hurt by her friend's response.

As members of the Church of God in Christ (COGIC),

Sonja's family was very religious. Her father, grandmother, and two uncles were preachers, and her mother sang and played music in the church. Although COGIC's reputation is homophobic, Sonja says she never experienced it because she believed that people in the church leadership were themselves gay. Today she attends a different "Holiness" church, which she acknowledges is homophobic. But like many black homosexuals, she continues to go, saying, "You have to pick and choose what's acceptable to you. I have my own relationship with God. I think He knows, I know that He knows, and I don't believe He has a problem with that." Catching herself, she adds, "I'm hoping that He doesn't have a problem with that."

Rudy Cook has reached a conclusion different from Sonja's. By his own admission, Rudy and his friends were "not like the average teenagers." He grew up in Louisiana as the oldest of seven kids. The son of a black mother and a Creole/Filipino father, the twenty-eight-year-old remembers that instead of going to high school dances and parties with his friends, "we would get together and we would pray all night. We would read the Bible all day and [then] we would get together and fellowship." Rudy's worship services were not only an extracurricular activity; they became part of his schooling. "We would take our Bibles to high school and tell people about the Lord," Rudy remembered during an interview.

When he left Louisiana to attend college in Bakersfield, California, he began experimenting with homosexual activity. He considered himself bisexual, and because of his relatively conservative ideas about monogamy and sex, he gained a reputation as a good "catch." But things changed when he moved to the District of Columbia, the capital of black gay life. He described feeling like a kid in a candy store as he started to go out to gay nightclubs more and more often and became more adventurous in his activities. Eventually, he realized that homosexuals were so pervasive among D.C.'s black men that he did not even need to go out to meet them. "You can just go anywhere," he said. "You can go to a gym and work out, or you can go to a store, or you can just be walking and you can meet someone. Whereas, where I lived [in California and Louisiana], in order to see gay people or to meet other gay men, you would have to go to a club."

While Cook was consumed in the "gay lifestyle," unbeknownst to him one of his fellow high school worshippers had a vision about him. She saw him astray from the Lord and realized that his life was about to change. On Thursday, October 6, 1994, Rudy joined a friend and went to see an evangelist, and for the first time in his life, he recalled, he felt no emotion at church. "Something just told me that it was over." He described himself as having been "spiritually dead," with the feeling that "there was no use for me on the earth anymore." The following Wednesday, his life changed. When tears fell from his eyes while he was walking down the street, he knew that something was going on inside him. He turned home, where he fell to his knees and repented to God. At the very moment he asked God to come into his life, "it felt like someone dumped invisible warm water on the top of my head." His entire body burned like fire and he could not stand up. Rudy had found God and been "saved."

When I interviewed Cook, on an unusually warm Tuesday afternoon in January 1995, he spoke with the conviction of one who felt that because his own life had changed, then other homosexuals could change their lives as well. "God did not create us that way. God created Adam and Eve, and He meant for Adam and Eve to be together and multiply," he explained. He said he no longer had sexual desires for men but was not dating women either—he wanted to concentrate on God at that time. Following our interview, Cook, who had been a casual acquaintance of mine, told me that he had agreed to participate because he wanted to talk to me personally about God. He asked if I was feeling okay and said he sensed that I was going through some difficult times and was in need of the Lord. "I've never felt better," I told him. "I'm a Christian, but

I have a big problem with a lot of these so-called Christian churches condemning their homosexual members." We talked for nearly an hour, discussing the church and homosexuality. I told him that God probably never meant for *him* to be homosexual, but that did not mean other people had had the same experience. "I just don't think you can conclude that because something is right for you, then it must be right for everybody," I said. We continued our conversation, but eventually parted without persuading each other.

When it comes to religion and sexuality, many of us, like Rudy and I, operate on faith. We reach different conclusions about what God wants or expects from us because our faith in God speaks to us differently. Often this faith prevents us from seeing the reason behind what others think or feel. As a result, we merely repeat the religious prohibitions of the church hierarchy and parrot the rhetoric of church dogma. But for those who believe in Christianity, Jesus says that the greatest commandment is this: "Thou shalt love the Lord thy God with all thy heart, and with all thy soul, and with all thy mind." As Jesus explains, the use of one's mind is not an obstacle to faith but an essential element of it. Those who interpret faith to mean the shutting down of one's mind do not fully appreciate how true faith is not blind. However, many of those who justify their homophobia in God's name do so with arguments that contradict logic and common sense and even the very teachings they quote to support those arguments.

As a society, we run into several major problems when we try to apply religious ideas to homosexuality. First, in a country that recognizes a wall of separation between church and state, religion has no place in determining which citizens should be protected from discrimination. Second, many of the religious arguments put forth are based on a misunderstanding or purposeful misreading of the Scriptures, twisting the word of God to suit the political ends of a particular group. Third, the same tired religious arguments used against lesbians and gays today were used against African Americans in days gone by.

The separation of church and state has not always prevented the government from attempting to interject religion into public laws. For example, the trial judge in *Loving v. Virginia* sentenced the Lovings to a year in prison for the crime of interracial marriage and then suspended the sentence on condition that they leave the state and not return for twenty-five years. In his written opinion, the judge stated:

> Almighty God created the races white, black, yellow, malay and red, and he placed them on separate continents. And but for the interference with his arrangement there would be no cause for such marriages. The fact that he separated the races shows that he did not intend for the races to mix.

The U.S. Supreme Court rejected the lower court's biblical argument and described marriage as a basic civil right "fundamental to [human] existence and survival." The Court said that "the freedom to marry, or not marry, a person of another race resides with the individual and cannot be infringed by the State." The Court thus affirmed the principle that basic privacy rights may not be restricted even if the Bible commands such restrictions. But the courts have refused to extend this principle in gay rights cases, and the Supreme Court refused to recognize this principle in deciding the first major gay rights case in our history, *Bowers v. Hardwick.*

As with civil rights cases in the past, Bible-based arguments appear frequently in cases involving lesbians and gays today. In *Doe v. Commonwealth's Attorney for the City of Richmond,* a three-judge federal panel upheld Virginia's antisodomy law by citing its "ancestry going back to Judaic and Christian law." The *Doe* court even quoted a passage from the Book of Leviticus: "If a man also lie with mankind, as he lieth with a woman, both of them have committed an abomination: they shall surely be put to death; their blood shall be upon them." Several states have lifted language almost directly from the Bible in crafting their homosexual sodomy statutes. North Carolina General Statute §14-177 reads: "If any person shall commit the abominable and detestable crime against nature, with mankind or beast, he shall be imprisoned in the State's prison not less than five nor more than sixty years." Section 18.1-212 of the Virginia Code's "Crimes Against Nature" used similar biblical support. The first antisodomy statute in Texas tracked religious language to prohibit the "abominable and detestable crime against nature." All these religious-based public policy actions regarding gays seem to breach the wall of separation between church and state that the courts had already recognized in cases involving blacks.

In addition, many of the religious arguments for antigay bias simply misread the religious texts. Numerous religious scholars who have studied biblical texts disagree with the notion that the Bible, for example, is homophobic. Of the nine biblical citations traditionally invoked to defend homophobia, four (Deuteronomy 23:17, 1 Kings 14:24, 1 Kings 22:46, and 2 Kings 23:7) simply forbid prostitution by men or women; two (Leviticus 18:19–23 and Leviticus 20:10–16) are part of the widely violated Holiness Code, which also prohibits eating raw meat and wearing garments with two different types of yarn; and the other three (Romans 1:26–2:1, 1 Corinthians 6:9–11, and 1 Timothy 1:10) are from St. Paul, who was "against lust and sensuality in anyone, including heterosexuals," according to the Reverend Peter Gomes. Writing for the op-ed page in an August 1992 *New York Times,* Gomes explains that "there is no mention of homosexuality in the four Gospels of the New Testament. The moral teachings of Jesus are not concerned with the subject."

The Book of Leviticus is perhaps most notorious, appearing to describe certain homosexual behavior as an "abomination" worthy of death. But with its detailed regulations for human conduct, Leviticus is less a book about morality than a code of municipal ordinances for the people of the time. Leviticus sets up elaborate procedures for peace offerings, sin offerings, trespass offerings, and guilt offerings to God. Virtually none of these rules are followed by modern religions. Leviticus 11:7–8 prohibits the eating of swine, "Though he divide the hoof, and be clovenfooted, yet he cheweth not the cud." Leviticus 11:10 prohibits eating "all that have not fins and scales in the seas, and in the rivers" because they are an "abomination." Citing the litany of prohibitions established in Leviticus, Bishop Carl Bean asks, "How can you [defend] that list of Leviticus? You're eating pig. You're eating things out of the sea that don't have fins and scales. So you can't have no lobster. You can't have no shrimp. You can't have a whole lot of stuff." Applying the rules to modern reality, Bean adds jokingly, "The black church would close [if] they couldn't sell pig feet, pig ears, pork chops . . ."

Concerning itself with issues of leprosy and methods of laundry, Leviticus is clearly limited to the world known to humans at that time. It set a penalty of death for cursing one's parents, but no one would seriously encourage that such a penalty be applied today against obstreperous children. Yet religious leaders, such as the minister who wrote me at the White House, claim, "If our government does not start executing homosexuals, as God has commanded in His Word, we will hasten our doom." One wonders whether we will hasten our doom if we also fail to execute our rebellious children. The main purpose of Leviticus, as is true with some of the writings of St. Paul, was to keep God's chosen people, the Israelites, different from the Gentiles, according to Dr. Daniel A. Helminiak in his 1994 book *What the Bible Really Says About Homosexuality.*

In Romans 1:24, the King James version of the Bible says, "God also gave them up to uncleanness through the lusts of their own hearts, to dishonour their own bodies between themselves." Even progay Bible scholars who dispute other biblical references to homosexuality concede that this is the one Christian Bible text that actually discusses the issue. But Paul's letter to the Romans must be read in the context of what he was trying to accomplish, Helminiak explains. Paul wrote his letter in preparation for a visit he planned to make to Rome, where he wanted the Christian church to welcome him. But the early Christian church was divided between Jewish converts, who still kept the Jewish law, and Gentiles, who did not. Because Paul had to appeal to both sides without offending either, he criticized the Gentiles for what Helminiak calls their "homogenital practices" and then criticized the Jewish Christians for their formalistic reliance on Jewish law. But even Paul's criticism "makes no ethical condemnation of male-male sex. He merely points out social disapproval of it," according to Helminiak. The interpretation of Paul's letter to mean that God sees homosexuality as "unnatural" is based on a mistranslation of the Greek words *para physin,* which, Helminiak points out, means "unusual" or "peculiar" rather than ungodly.

Helminiak describes the Bible as "indifferent" to homosexuality and explains that modern concepts of it cannot be compared with early discussions of certain same-sex behavior without understanding the context. In addition, citing the selective use of the Bible by ministers to justify antigay discrimination, Helminiak notes that "the same preachers do not advocate slavery even though the whole epistle to Philemon and many other long passages support it . . . They allow women to teach in Sunday school or to speak in church even though 1 Timothy 2:11–14 clearly forbids that." In example after example, the so-called literalists and fundamentalists must pick and choose which biblical passages to interpret literally. But by confusing faith in the Bible with faith in a minister's or a church's interpretation of the Bible, many Christians unquestioningly accept the dogma that they are taught. An eighty-three-year-old black Texas woman, sitting in a living room adorned with photographs of Dr. Martin Luther King, Jr., and the Kennedy brothers, told *The Wall Street Journal* in October 1994, "The Bible speaks against woman with woman and man with man . . . I don't believe the Bible would lie."

Some ministers are so convinced that the Bible is not homophobic that they appear to argue that it actually *supports* gay relationships. The Reverend Rainey Cheeks describes the story of David and Jonathan in the two books of Samuel as "one of the greatest love stories in the Bible." In fact, the story of Jonathan and David's relationship reads almost homoerotically. To quote 1 Samuel 18:1: "[T]he soul of Jonathan was knit with the soul of David, and Jonathan loved him as his own soul." In the same chapter we learn that "Jonathan stripped himself of the robe that was upon him, and gave it to David, and his garments, even to his sword, and to his bow, and to his girdle." Jonathan, later learning of his father Saul's plan to kill David, tells his friend to hide away in a secret place. When Jonathan goes to the hiding place, David "fell on his face to the ground, and bowed himself three times: and they kissed one another, and wept one with another, until David exceeded," according to 1 Samuel 20:41. And David says to Jonathan in 2 Samuel 1:26, "Thy love to me was wonderful, passing the love of women."

Despite arguments for a nonhomophobic reading of the Bible, antigay religious leaders maintain that the Bible prohibits homosexual behavior. Those who have been victimized by religious dogma on other issues might want to question the certainty with which many clerics cling to the mantle of homophobia. Religion, after all, was used to justify the institution of slavery in America and later used to defend racial segregation in schools and public accommodations. Some critics fault the Catholic Church for failing to speak out publicly against the killing of millions of Jews in Nazi Germany and elsewhere; and for hundreds of years, the Church's own Inquisition thrived on forcibly converting Jews and persecuting heretics. In the name of God, the Church sanctioned religious wars that led to any number of unnecessary deaths, and condemned Copernicus for suggesting that the Earth did not occupy the center of the universe. The Vatican took 350 years to acknowledge formally that Galileo was right to claim the Earth orbited the sun. Given the record of human fallibility in deciding God's will, we might think twice before we blindly accept current Church pronouncements about homosexuality.

Many of the modern Christian religious teachings about homosexuality spew out so much venom that they eclipse other, valuable principles in the Bible, including the commandment to love thy neighbor as thyself. The Reverend Van Dayton was the only black pastor to attend a summer 1994 meeting in Niagara Falls of the antigay Christian Coalition. But even Dayton was not satisfied with their message, which ignored the importance of redemption and salvation to African Americans. "Our concerns have been justice, not just morality," he told *The Wall Street Journal.* "Until the Republican Party addresses that, it's no drawing card for minorities." Similarly, Bishop Bean laments the absence of love in the religious right's message. "Every time [the Pharisees] would challenge Jesus about, quote, the law, he would say, 'But a new law I give unto you: L-O-V-E.' "

The use of religion to justify discrimination is, of course, not new. In 1845, Frederick Douglass described how his master converted to Christianity and then "found religious sanction and support for his slave holding cruelty." "I have seen him tie up a lame young woman," wrote Douglass, "and whip her with a heavy cowskin upon her naked shoulders, causing the warm red blood to drip; and in justification of the bloody deed he would quote the passage of Scripture—'He that knoweth the master's will, and doeth it not, shall be beaten with many stripes.' " Recognizing the hypocrisy of using religion in this way, Douglass commented, "The warm defender of the sacredness of the family relation is the same that scatters whole families . . . leaving the hut vacant, and the hearth desolate."

Historian Richard Mohr and others suggest that societal prejudices, and not the Bible, are the problem with homophobia. Comparing today's biblical arguments to those a hundred years ago, Mohn writes, "Slavery didn't stop because people ceased interpreting the Bible as approving of it; rather when civilization gave up on slavery, people ceased using Bible passages to justify it." In a newspaper article, "The Current Position of Gays in America," Mohr continues, "The Bible didn't change, the culture did."

The homophobia in black religion is as much a province of Muslims as it is of Christians. Growing up in a black Islamic family, Julian Keith Tolver was introduced to the Nation of Islam at an early age. His father attended services at the local mosque, his family did not eat pork, and they observed the tenets of Islam in their home. Tolver, at the same time, knew something else about himself: he was attracted to men. These fundamentally distinct identities placed him on two separate, but occasionally crisscrossing, paths in a lifelong journey of confusion and self-understanding.

Although he calls himself a black gay man, Tolver is quick to point out that he does not lead a "homosexual lifestyle," adding, "I'm only a homosexual when I'm having sex with a man." Pointing out a common identity conflict, Tolver says, "Blacks have a different way of actually trying to conduct themselves. We don't tend to put ourselves in any kind of categories. If you go out on the street and ask a brother does he lead a gay lifestyle, he would ask you, 'Well, what is that?' " Tolver also criticizes some black gay activists who insist that he be more "out of the closet." "I don't think I am closeted," he says, " 'cause I go to more gay clubs than most of them." Speculating on the reasons why gay activists consider him closeted, Tolver says, "I guess because I'm not waving a rainbow flag or because I act the way I've always acted." Most people would probably never suspect he was gay just from his appearance. A naturally well-built, conservatively dressed man, with close-cropped hair, a clean-shaven face, and wearing no earrings or other jewelry, he might strike many as the archetypal black Muslim. But, Tolver says, "the way I conduct myself, I think I'm open. I'm open enough for me."

Tolver does acknowledge struggling with the apparent conflicts between homosexuality and Islam, and faults some in the Nation for their views. Although Tolver recognizes that Islam considers homosexual behavior to be a sin, he retorts, "I don't think that my behavior is a sin." Citing the story of Sodom and Gomorrah, Tolver objects to the stereotypical depiction of all homosexuals as "immoral" and unloving. "They talk about [homosexuality] in such a way that makes it seem you're not talking about a human being. That's what I don't like about it," he says. The focus should be on love, whether it's between two men or however it is expressed. As Tolver sees it, though, the popular perception of homosexuals disconnects their emotions from love and reduces them to mere sexual actors. "But I would prefer to have a companion to share my time with as opposed to somebody to have sex with," he says. The negative stereotypes about homosexuals contribute to their own perceptions of self: "If you think a part of you is wicked and sinful, then if you can't accept that part of you, it's hard for you to accept the whole of you." Tolver has had to experience a great deal of personal suffering to reach the point where he can say that.

In 1985, Tolver graduated from college at Indiana University, started graduate school at Norfolk State in Virginia, began his first job working as a prison correctional officer, assumed the role of assistant minister at Norfolk's Mosque 57, and shortly after his identical twin brother had married, married a woman himself. These activities put him on a breakneck pace, working the graveyard shift at the prison, studying and attending classes during the day, ministering for the Nation on weekends, and leaving little time for his wife. Not surprisingly, the marriage lasted two years on paper, but even less time in reality. A year into his marriage, Tolver checked himself into a psychiatric facility, having contemplated suicide. He told the doctors, "I think I'm gay," but they did not deal with his sexual orientation, he says, and neither did he. He told his twin brother, "I think I'm gay," but he, too, did not believe it. When his marriage ended in 1987, Tolver sought out a gay man for advice on how to deal with what he calls "my own issues." By the end of the year, Tolver had his first homosexual experience and became a part of an informal relationship with a man that lasted several months.

Time and again throughout his life, Tolver has bounced back and forth between homosexuality and Islam, confused and unable to reconcile the two. When his gay relationship ended, Tolver felt he had done a great wrong by being involved with a man, and he felt the need to make up for his weakness. He describes his philosophy toward life at the time as, "This is how I am, God, but let me do something on this end to balance that out." After the 1987 experience, he became celibate for three years, and late in the first year, Tolver and the head minister of the Norfolk mosque began making plans for Nation of Islam Minister Louis Farrakhan to visit Norfolk. In January of 1988, Tolver flew to Chicago, where he met with Farrakhan at his home and discussed the plans for the Norfolk speech. Three months later, Farrakhan arrived and spoke to a packed audience at the Norfolk Scope Arena. Tolver's work apparently impressed someone in the Nation, and he developed a positive relationship with Farrakhan.

A few years later, Tolver learned he had full-blown AIDS when his doctor recorded his CD4 count at below the 200 mark. Tolver prayed to Allah and wrote a letter to Farrakhan for guidance. "I felt like I was on my way out," he said later, conceding that much of his physical reaction may have been psychosomatic. Farrakhan referred Tolver to the Abundant Life Clinic in Washington, D.C., run by Dr. Abdul Alim Muhammad. Muhammad, at the time, was developing a new treatment for AIDS that involved herbs, holistics, and a controversial drug called Kemron, a low-dosage form of oral alpha interferon. The problem for Tolver was that the treatment, at $2,500 up front, was too expensive. But a group of friends and brothers from the Nation pooled their resources and raised the funds for Tolver's treatment, enabling him to go to Washington to become a patient of Dr. Muhammad's. Within the first month of a six-month treatment, Tolver's CD4 count rose above the 200 mark to 570, he says. He stopped taking oral alfa interferon and says he hasn't needed it since.

Tolver gives the brothers of the Nation a great deal of credit for supporting him during his difficulty and raising the money for his treatment. In the Nation, he says, the brotherhood is even stronger than a marriage. Although a married brother might have a wife at home, when he goes out to conduct business for the mosque or the Nation, his contact with women is limited. "So all you deal with is the brotherhood. If the minister is speaking in Wyoming somewhere, you travel, you share the same hotel room—one time there was ten of us in the same hotel room—and you help each other out and you're always around each other." The intimacy of the brotherhood may even supplant the need for marriage for some members of the Nation's men's group, the Fruit of Islam. Tolver tells of meeting "quite a few" homosexuals in the Nation and remembers an incident in 1993 where a well-known and well-respected member of the Nation who happened to be gay actually killed himself because he could not face the pressure. Defending Minister Farrakhan from charges of homophobia, Tolver recalls that Farrakhan was "upset" about the suicide "because he felt that some intervention should have come." According to Tolver, Farrakhan himself decided he needed to teach the members to deal with homosexuality with compassion, causing some brothers to question that decision. "But I think he ought to teach on it," Tolver says. "Brothers have a difficult time, whether they're in the Nation or not, especially those who don't self-identify and still continue that kind of behavior."

Reminiscing about the changes he went through in his life, from Islam to marriage to thoughts of suicide to homosexuality to confusion to AIDS, Tolver admits, "It was crazy." But with his immune system stabilized for several years, Tolver, now thirty-two and still HIV-positive, says he has been blessed by Allah and saved by divine intervention. "I know I'm gonna die one day," he says, "but it ain't gonna be from AIDS."

Tolver's physician, Dr. Muhammad, is also the national spokesman for Minister Louis Farrakhan. In an interview, Muhammad said that all major religions consider homosexuality to be a sin. He sounded just like Baptist minister H. Beecher Hicks when he said, "I don't think that what is called the 'gay lifestyle' is representative of traditional family values." The Nation's position on homosexuality, unlike that of some Christian ministers, seems to grow largely out of concern for what is seen as the moral and political responsibility that all blacks owe their community. If everybody practiced the homosexual lifestyle, civilization would no longer exist, Muhammad said. "It has always been in the interest of any civilization and any society to support, uphold, and advocate those activities that advance and promote society and allow it to survive, and to discourage those activities that do the opposite." His argument, however, assumes that the number of homosexuals in society can be regulated by public advocacy or opposition. In fact, despite hundreds of years of public opposition to homosexuality, no evidence suggests that the percentage of homosexuals in the population has ever been affected by it. Neither should we expect that removing the stigma and condemnation associated with homosexuality would result in dramatic increases in that population. More homosexuals would probably be willing to *identify* their sexual orientation, but it would mistake cause for effect to assume that they would actually *become* homosexual because of the absence of discrimination.

Dr. Muhammad was quick to point out in our interview that he does not represent Minister Farrakhan on all issues. One example of their differences may be their attitudes about the punishment for homosexual behavior. "I don't condemn one sin over the other," the doctor said, "but Scripture is very clear about sin." Comparing homosexuals to what he calls other sinners, Muhammad said, "That doesn't make a homosexual worse than a thief, or worse than a murderer, or worse than an adulterer. Because all of these are condemned more or less equally in Scripture." While Farrakhan and Muhammad agree on the description, they appear to disagree on the prescription. Muhammad voiced his support for equal rights for all human beings and said he opposed discrimination and "hateful acts" practiced against anyone. Farrakhan, on the other hand, has, at times, seemed to condone violence directed at homosexuals. In a May 20, 1990, speech in Oakland, California, Farrakhan spoke of the need to "sacrifice the individual for the preservation of a nation." He told men they had better "hide" their effeminate behavior and reminded them the "penalty" for homosexual activity in the Holy Land is "death."

Some Islamic scholars have taken issue with Farrakhan's suggestion that Islamic civilization and religion have always been antihomosexual. Professor As'ad AbuKhalil of California State University maintains that, historically, Islamic culture has been more accepting of both heterosexual and homosexual sexuality than has Christianity. In a fall 1993 article in the *Arab Studies Journal,* "A Note on the Study of Homosexuality in the Arab/Islamic Civilization," AbuKhalil explains that "Muslim men and women also talked explicitly about heterosexual matters in mosques and during the Hajj, which is something inconceivable today." In *surat Al-Baqarah,* ayat 223, the Koran says, "Your women are your tilth: go then into your tilth in any way you wish." While some Sunni theologians did not interpret this text to allow certain sexual activities such as heterosexual anal intercourse, others did, and most Shiite jurisprudents, according to AbuKhalil, read the text to allow both vaginal and anal intercourse.

The Koran includes a number of specific social and familial proscriptions, but "has very little to say about homosexuality," according to AbuKhalil. When it does refer to homosexuality, the language used is mild compared to other references in the book dealing with ethical behavior. "Originally, Islam did not have the same harsh Biblical judgment about homosexuality as

Christianity," AbuKhalil writes. Hostility toward homosexuals, he maintains, "was produced by the Christian West." Muslims have been trying since the nineteenth century "to live up to the Western moral code," which led Islamic thinkers to conform their sexual and moral values to Christian codes of conduct. But while homosexuals were condemned in much of medieval Europe, they were rulers and ministers in Islamic countries. AbuKhalil mentions one, the caliph Al-Amin, whose passion for eunuchs was so strong that his mother found several women with short hair and dressed them up as boys with tight jackets and girdles. Another caliph devoted his poetry to his male lover. While some homosexuals were killed, as Farrakhan has maintained, these cases were "rare," according to Abu-Khalil.

Regardless of the prevalence of homosexuals in Islamic culture or the frequency of their punishment, Farrakhan crosses the line by suggesting that homosexuals deserve death. As Dr. Ron Simmons asks in his essay on black homophobia, "Why encourage more death in the African-American community? Too many black men are being killed daily." Some are already being brutalized because of their sexual orientation. In July 1992, for example, two men leaving a popular black gay bar in Washington, D.C., were shot by two black teenagers. As human rights activist Cary Alan Johnson recounted in his testimony to the Congressional Black Caucus, "The victims were left on the street and nearly bled to death."

We must be careful not to confuse "the blood of Calvary with the Kool-Aid of homophobia," says Harvard professor Cornel West in the 1996 documentary film *All God's Children*. Many black lesbians and gay men are bearing witness to this distinction, carving out an existence that respects their religion, their race, and their sexual orientation without subjugating any of them. Their lives testify to the reality that their multiple identities can peacefully coexist. They know, as Bishop Carl Bean explains, that "God is love and love is for everyone."

CHAPTER FIVE

Black Homophobia

Despite the growing number of black congregations that value their lesbian and gay members, religion is often the most frequently cited factor in black homophobia. Malik, for example, considers himself a good Christian. Malik's parents, however, have been so influenced by their minister that they have challenged his faith. "You cannot be homosexual and be a Christian," they told him. A few weeks after I met Malik, he began moving out of his parents' suburban Maryland home and into an apartment of his own in Washington, D.C. During the first of two trips to help him move his belongings, I met his mother, who greeted me graciously.

By the time of my next trip, however, Malik had admitted to her that I, too, was gay. When I arrived the second time, I was banned from entering the house. I waited for thirty minutes outside in the car while Malik, inside, packed his belongings on his own and argued with his family. "God doesn't want homosexuals in his Kingdom," Malik's mother insisted.

Around the time Malik was moving out, he had been temporarily hospitalized with a fractured jaw after being jumped by a group of young men in his neighborhood. There were seven of them, he said. All black males. I volunteered to take Malik to the oral surgeon for his appointment later that week. I picked him up at the subway and we drove up Georgia Avenue in Northwest D.C. for what seemed like an eternity. We arrived on time, took the elevator to the fourth floor of the professional building, and walked through the hallway to the doctor's office. On the next door was the nameplate of a more famous doctor, Frances Cress Welsing, M.D.

Dr. Welsing wrote the controversial book *The Isis Papers* (1991), in which she argues, among other things, that descendants of Africa are not predisposed to homosexuality. A black gay man had turned me on to her book during the summer of 1991, and I strongly disagreed with her conclusions. When I saw her name on the door, I felt as if fate had delivered me to that spot, so I knocked. No one answered. I had only a vague idea of what I would have said to her if she had answered, but I think Malik would have been Exhibit A. I would have pointed to him, with his jaw wired shut from his operation, and said, "Black men are attacking and killing other black men like Malik for no good reason, and you have the nerve to suggest that homosexuality is the problem with black manhood." In her book, Welsing claims, "The dearth of adult Black males in the homes, schools and neighborhoods leaves Black male children no alternative models." They enter prison and "finally, they have sexual intercourse with men." I would have pointed to Malik and said, "Here is a black man with a strong black father who is still married to Malik's mother. Malik went to black schools, lived in black neighborhoods, and has never been in prison. But he is a homosexual nevertheless." In another passage in *The Isis Papers,* Welsing argues that racist programming has led black men to act like women, and that "braided and curled hair, the earrings and bracelets, the midriff tops, the cinch waisted pants, the flowered underwear, the high-heeled shoes with platforms and the pocketbooks are all behavioral answers." Again, I would have pointed to Malik, who has never had his ears pierced, as he stood there wearing a baseball cap, button-down shirt, brown denim jacket, khaki pants, and Timberland mountain boots, and I would have said, "Is this black man trying to be a woman?"

Frances Cress Welsing is not the only black intellectual to associate homosexuality with the black community's decline: Amiri Baraka, Eldridge Cleaver, Nathan Hare, Robert Staples, Haki Madhubuti, and Molefi Asante all view homosexuality negatively. Some black political leaders such as Minister Louis Farrakhan and his deputy Khalid Abdul Muhammad have also spoken critically of homosexuality. But in the black community, " 'homophobia' is not so much a fear of 'homosexuals' but a fear that homosexuality will become pervasive in the community," according to Dr. Ron Simmons, a black gay man and former Howard University professor.

Homophobic black intellectuals tend to view homosexuality in the black community either as an outgrowth of white racism or as a by-product of the breakdown of the black family. Of those who see racism in black homosexuality, Amiri Baraka may be the most controversial. In his 1965 book *American Sexual Reference: Black Male,* Baraka claims, "Most American white men are trained to be fags." His evidence to support this assertion ranges from the stereotypical ("their faces are weak") to the circular (their eyes are "silk blue faggot eyes") to the outdated ("can you, for a second, imagine the average middle class white man able to do somebody harm?"). Like so many other black intellectuals of his time, Baraka sees masculinity in terms of raw physical strength and condemns what he sees as the "softness" of white men and black homosexuals. Baraka's supermacho mythology, however, overlooks the many black heterosexual men who would be considered "soft" by his own standard and, for that matter, the black male homosexuals and black females who are unstereotypically strong.

Baraka's rantings make for popular rhetoric, but they do little to advance the cause of black people, male or female. He rails against "weak" white men, whom he sees as so fearful of "real" manly conflict that "even their wars move to the stage where whole populations can be destroyed by *pushing a button . . .*" In perpetuating his atavistic notion of manhood, Baraka never pauses to reconsider the social value of armed conflict. Instead, he whines that white men win their fights without "physical work." He does not deconstruct the violence in white society and never stops to examine whether physical strength actually is or should be the measure of power in our society. Baraka does not want to challenge white society's violent culture; he merely wants to emulate an earlier form of it. But with the advent of modern technology, including the development not only of sophisticated weaponry but of the global economy, even Baraka would have to admit that his hand-to-hand combat mythology has become meaningless. As Michele Wallace—in her book *Black Macho and the Myth of the Superwoman* (1978), has noted about the black male revolutionaries of the 1960s, "A big Afro, a rifle, and a penis in good working order were not enough to lick the white man's world after all."

Wallace and others have suggested that something else might be going on inside Amiri Baraka other than black macho fanaticism. Self-hatred may play a role in Baraka's views, Wallace suggests, pointing out that he deserted his white wife and children and "all of a sudden" began advocating death to all whites. Similarly, black lesbian writer Cheryl Clarke labels Baraka an "irreversible homophobe" and wonders if "he protests too much." Baraka's first wife, Hettie Jones, later conceded as much when she wrote in her autobiography that her husband "once confessed to me some homosexual feelings, though never any specific experiences."

Born Everett LeRoy Jones, Baraka spent his youth as a successful poet in the white world. He lived in Greenwich Village, associated with noted homosexual writer Allen Ginsberg, and was described by white friends as "the nicest man you ever met." According to Dr. Ron Simmons, Jones hid his homosexual desires throughout his teens and his college experience at Howard University, where he saw gay men harassed and ridiculed. He changed his name to LeRoi but dropped out of Howard in his junior year because of bad grades and joined the Air Force. Simmons contends that Jones's 1966 book, *The System of Dante's Hell,* is an autobiographical account of his early homosexual experiences. "Understanding Baraka's life turns our anger toward him to sympathy; indeed, pity," Simmons writes in an essay published in *Brother to Brother* (1991), a black gay anthology edited by Essey Hemphill.

If Baraka has been involved in homosexuality, self-hatred could explain his homophobia, but it does not explain the homophobia of other black intellectuals. Some are, no doubt, misinformed about the origins of homosexuality in the black community. For example, Molefi Asante, in his book *Afrocentricity: The Theory of Social Change* (1980), and Robert Staples, in his *Black Masculinity: The Black Man's Role in American Society* (1982), both suggest that the increasing imprisonment of black men has caused a proliferation of homosexuality. But neither writer's theory explains the spread of homosexuality in the nonprison black population. Of the hundreds of black lesbians and gay men I interviewed, only one had ever served a day in prison.

Eldridge Cleaver's popular book *Soul on Ice* (1969) accuses black homosexuals of acquiescing in a "racial death-wish . . . bending over and touching their toes for the white man." By assuming a stereotypical sexual couple—"passive" black man and an "active" white man—Cleaver underscores the widespread ignorance about the practice of homosexuality in the black community. He disregards other sexual relations, including those between an "active" black man and a "passive" white man or between two black men, and he ignores relations between black lesbians altogether. Contrary to the black revolutionary's stereotype, many of the black homosexuals I interviewed were involved primarily or exclusively with other blacks. But even those who were involved with nonblacks often expressed revolutionary views about black liberation; they viewed themselves as part of the struggle, not as part of the problem.

Other black intellectuals such as Nathan and Julia Hare view homosexuality as the by-product of "family disintegration" and a "decaying and decadent society." In their book *The Endangered Black Family: Coping with the Unisexualization and Coming Extinction of the Black Race* (1984), the Hares assume rather dismissively that "homosexuality does not promote black family stability and that it historically has been a product largely of the Europeanized society." Citing historical examples of family breakdown in ancient Greece and Rome, the Hares explain homosexuality as the result of rampant "gender confusion" in the population. But their analysis fails to deconstruct the rigid gender roles and family structure they espouse. Adherence to the Western concept of the nuclear family, for instance, may overlook the social utility of the extended family in African and ethnic American cultures. Like so many other black intellectuals and self-described revolutionaries, they neglect to challenge basic tenets of the Western culture they claim to despise.

Writer Haki Madhubuti, in his book *Black Men: Obsolete, Single, Dangerous?* (1990), initially describes himself almost apologetically as having been one of many "misinformed confirmed heterosexuals . . . convinced that AIDS was a white middle-class homosexual disease that, at worse, would only touch Black homosexuals." But later in his book, Madhubuti seems to fall back into the same trap he earlier lamented when he describes his association with the late Max Robinson, the first black person to anchor a major television network news broadcast. According to Madhubuti, Robinson wanted people to know that he "did not contract [AIDS] through the assumed avenues of drug use or homosexual activity. Max was a woman's man to the bone . . ." But Madhubuti's disclaimer about Robinson's sexual orientation only perpetuates the stigma attached to those who do contract the HIV virus through homosexual activity. Although he exhorts his readers to "be understanding of those that are ill," his own words reflect only a limited understanding of the experiences of many African Americans living with AIDS. Instead, Madhubuti contributes to the perception that homosexuality, like drug abuse, is a cause for shame.

Historian Barbara Tuchman taught us that every successful revolution eventually puts on the robes of the tyrant it deposed. The Black Power revolution is no exception to Tuchman's rule. Many black intellectuals selectively target elements of white society for critique, but challenging only racism, they appear to accept heterosexism, homophobia, sexism, and violence. As black gay activist Phill Wilson explains, "For African-American society, so much of its survival is based on this construct of being able to master the principles of the larger society, and all of America is about assimilating and being the same, and part of that sameness is the types of people that we hate." Similarly, the failure to examine sexist and heterosexist institutions of white society leads some black women such as Cheryl Clarke to conclude that black macho intellectuals "have absorbed the homophobia of their patriarchal slavemasters." Clarke finds it "ironic" that the Black Power movement could transform the consciousness of an entire generation toward black self-determination and, at the same time, "fail so miserably in understanding the sexual politics of the movement and of black people across the board."

Although Clarke and others believe that the homophobia in the black community has "a markedly male imprint," black women are often homophobic too. In addition to Drs. Frances

Cress Welsing and Julia Hare, pseudointellectuals like Shahra-zad Ali and social commentators like Sister Souljah show their homophobia in less sophisticated fashion. In her book *No Disrespect* (1994), Sister Souljah describes the hurt she felt when she discovered that a romantic interest of hers was actually struggling with his homosexuality, after which she saw him as an emasculated "husk of a man."

Ali, however, is perhaps the most ridiculous of all the black homophobic writers. In her book *The Blackman's Guide to Understanding the Blackwoman* (1989), she writes, "When [the black woman] . . . becomes viciously insulting it is time for the Blackman to soundly slap her in the mouth." The discussion of homosexuality in her follow-up book, *The Blackwoman's Guide to Understanding the Blackman* (1992), shows little more intelligence. She claims to have conducted interviews with, and made evaluations of, black homosexual men and found: (1) they become homosexual because of unsuccessful relationships with females, (2) 95 percent of them grew up in homes with either no father or a weak father, (3) "they feel no special connection or responsibility to other Blacks," (4) "they can cook, sew and bake and are determined to be a better woman than all the women they know," and (5) they do not understand that "homosexuality is a decision."

My own interviews with black gay men contradict Ali's claims. First, although some of these black gay men had had unsuccessful relationships with women, many felt they were unsuccessful precisely because they had not yet dealt with their homosexuality. Sister Souljah's boyfriend Nate, for instance, grew apart from her because he could not reconcile his preexisting and still lingering homosexual desires. When she asked him why he had lied to her, Nate responded that he had lied to himself and lied to God, so why should she be surprised that he would lie to her. Ali seems to confuse cause and effect by assuming that men like Nate become homosexual because of their unsuccessful relationships rather than realizing that they are already homosexual and that their unreconciled homosexual desires often contribute to the failure of their relationships.

Ali's other claims also muddy the waters of cause and effect. While some black gay men I interviewed grew up in families with no fathers, many grew up in intact families with a strong father. Some, including myself, were even raised primarily by our fathers. Ali's approach works backward from the conclusion that a particular person is homosexual to find any dysfunctional characteristic in that person which might have caused his homosexuality. But because all people have dysfunctional elements in their personalities and families, Ali's theory fails to explain why everyone with these dysfunctions does not become homosexual. She also cannot explain why all homosexuals do not share the dysfunctional characteristics she associates with homosexuality.

Ali's third finding, that black gay men feel little "connection or responsibility" to the black community suffers from the same logical flaw. She does not take into consideration the fact that many of them may feel disconnected precisely because they have been ostracized and condemned by people within their community. In effect, Ali's theory blames the victim for being angry. Of the hundreds of black lesbians and gay men I interviewed, only one indicated he had no communal responsibility to black people. Despite the ostracism by their friends, condemnation by their churches, and denunciation by Black Power intellectuals, many of these black gay men and women were self-described Afrocentrists. In fact, they often seemed far more disconnected from the white community than from the black community. Many of them lived in the black community, and few of them seemed willing to abandon it altogether.

As for Ali's fourth claim, I confess that I did not inquire into the culinary skills of most of the people I interviewed, but it did seem that only a tiny fraction of the black gay men I spoke with said they wanted to be women. Some could cook and bake and sew, but just as many probably could not. Given the unpopularity of my own dishes at our annual family

Thanksgiving dinner, I can only conclude that I was not blessed with this gay cooking skill.

Finally, Ali's claim that black gay men do not "understand" that homosexuality is a "decision" is based on a premise that defies proof. Several of the black homosexual women and men interviewed said they would never have chosen to be homosexual, even though they had achieved peace with their homosexuality. Bill Alexander, a forty-eight-year-old black gay man in Los Angeles, told me, "Who would actually wake up and say, 'Gee, I think I'm gonna be gay today and go through the ridicule and the harrassment'? Who would ask for that unless they're masochistic or something?" Once they had acknowledged to themselves that they were homosexual, many black lesbians and gay men recalled, the only "decision" they made was not to hate themselves because of their sexual orientation.

Any discussion of homophobia in the black community must also address the specific topic of antilesbianism. As a measure of pervasive gender-based differences, black men and women sometimes view lesbianism through different lenses. Black homophobic men, for example, view it either as something to be despised or as something to be ignored, often depending on whether they feel threatened by particular lesbians or by lesbianism in general.

Alice Walker's novel *The Color Purple* (1982), inspired a great deal of controversy when the film adaptation was released. Although much of the controversy focused on the film's perceived negative portrayal of black men, some critics such as Tony Brown objected to the relationship between Celie and Shug, two female characters. Writing in a syndicated editorial, the host of the television show *Tony Brown's Journal* declared, "No lesbian relationship can take the place of a positive love relationship between black women and black men." Brown symbolizes the antilesbian strand of homophobia that sees women-women relationships as threatening to the ever-important black family.

Some black women have noted a certain hypocrisy in the attitudes of the black community toward lesbians. Feminist writer bell hooks, for example, describes a "double standard" in the community where she grew up. "Black male homosexuals were often known, were talked about, were seen positively, and played important roles in community life, whereas lesbians were talked about solely in negative terms." In hooks's community, lesbianism threatened the social structure of the family because lesbians were not seen as childbearers, which was the primary mode by which women defined their womanness. Other black women have contributed to the gender distinction themselves, as Maya Angelou did in her autobiographical *I Know Why the Caged Bird Sings* (1970). Angelou describes her early feelings about lesbianism as looking into "the mysterious world of the pervert" but at the same time "ruling out the jolly [male] sissies" from her condemnation.

Some black men ignore lesbians altogether or, worse, exclude them from the category of women. Again, Amiri Baraka stands out. In a bizarre poem in his *Preface to a Twenty Volume Suicide Note* (1961), Baraka suggests that cartoon character Charlie Brown has been sexually involved with his dog, Snoopy, but reserves his greater disgust for the character Lucy. Baraka suggests that bestiality is a definite improvement over "that filthy little lesbian." Other writers, such as Calvin Hernton, seem to view lesbians as confused players in a racist plot. In his *Sex and Racism in America* (1965), Hernton states that "even the Negro lesbian is a 'man.'" Similarly, Muhammad Ali, responding to a question about the Equal Rights Amendment, was quoted as follows in New York's *Amsterdam News* in January 1978: "Some professions shouldn't be open to women, because they can't handle certain jobs, like construction work. Lesbians, maybe, but not women."

Some black women have equaled or surpassed the antilesbian homophobia of their brothers. Shahrazad Ali describes the black lesbian as jealous of "normal looking" black women, as a figure to be "pitied" and in need of "a special exorcism."

On the other hand, Sister Souljah acknowledges that many lesbians defy stereotypes, but she seems to understand lesbianism primarily through her experience with a college roommate whose "embrace of a lesbian life was due more to inner weakness and her victimization as a black woman than out of any genetic compulsion." Souljah accuses her roommate of being selfish, and concludes that "homosexuality, while perhaps offering some individuals relief from their pain, was nevertheless a way of avoiding our people's need to build strong, life-giving, and enduring family structures—structures rooted in our original African culture." Both Souljah and Ali perpetuate stereotypes about lesbians without critically examining the experience of the black lesbian in the black community.

Writer Barbara Smith objects to the suggestion that black lesbians have not contributed to the black community, and points to the hundreds of battered women's shelters serving black women across the country as one example of their work. She also recognizes connections between their work in the lesbian feminist community and in the African-American community. Some younger women believe that older lesbians "weren't about anything except for eating granola and dressing badly," she says. "They don't know that to be out in the sixties and the seventies, you had to be a damn warrior. Whatever we had on, we were fierce. We were trying to create a context in which people who were not white, not straight, not male, and not rich, could actually survive."

Some black feminists show their heterosexism by omission of the topic of lesbianism in their writings. However, many of the black feminists who have criticized others have been criticized themselves. Much of the disagreement appeared in Smith's groundbreaking 1983 black feminist anthology, *Home Girls*. Lesbian writer Cheryl Clarke hypothesizes that black women's homophobia develops because some of them are "afraid of risking the displeasure of their homophobic brothers." In an essay on homophobia in the black community, Clarke criticizes Michele Wallace's *Black Macho* (1978), noting that "The Myth of the Superwoman," one of the book's two essays, omits any mention of black lesbians. Wallace also comes under fire from Linda Powell and bell hooks. In her *Ain't I a Woman?* (1981), the latter criticizes Wallace's book as "neither an important feminist work nor an important work about black women." But hooks then is criticized by Cheryl Clarke for purposefully ignoring the existence of black lesbians and their contributions to the black feminist movement. "Hooks does not even mention the word lesbian in her book," Clarke complains. In the same anthology, Ann Allen Shockley chides the black community for ignoring black lesbians only a few pages before Jewelle Gomez criticizes one of Shockley's books for "trivializing" black lesbians and their sexuality. If nothing else, this spirited debate should put to rest any notion of a monolithic population of black women or black feminists.

Unfortunately, homophobia in black America is not confined to the writings and speeches of black intellectuals. In the black community at large, homophobia and heterosexism reach all demographic groups, men and women, heterosexuals and homosexuals, the young and the old, the famous and the unknown. The views may differ from one group to another, but in all of them, homophobia and heterosexism are frequently seen not as prejudices but as survival skills for the black race or the black individual.

I mention both homophobia and heterosexism here because both play a role in the activities of everyday people, with heterosexism often occurring in ways too subtle to be detected. I observed this phenomenon when I walked into the office of the Nation of Islam's Washington, D.C., health care facility, the Abundant Life Clinic. I was greeted by a tall, attractive black woman who introduced herself as Sister Sheila. I told her my name and explained that I was there to meet with the clinic's director, Dr. Abdul Alim Muhammad. I had a long list of questions I wanted to ask him about the Nation's positions on homosexuality and AIDS, so I sat down on a sofa in the waiting room and reviewed my notes in preparation for our interview.

Eventually, I looked up from my notebook and saw Sister Sheila gazing in my direction with a closed-mouth smile on her face. I smiled back politely, but before I could burrow back into my notebook, she asked me if I was from Washington. "No," I responded, "I'm from St. Louis."

"I didn't think so," she said. "I can tell by your shoes."

I glanced down at my shoes—a pair of strapped black Kenneth Coles that I had actually bought in Washington—and left it at that.

"I can see a lot about you," she said. "I like watching people. I have a talent for picking up things about them."

"Oh really, what can you tell about me?"

"Well," she said, "you're not married."

"You could figure that out by looking at my fingers," I shot back.

"No, these days you never know, because a lot of men don't even wear their wedding rings. Or if they do, they take them off when they're out."

"Well, that's true. What else can you see about me?"

"I see you're not married but you have a sweetheart."

"Nope," I chimed in immediately.

"Really? Because I see you with a real pretty girlfriend," she said.

I did not respond, and I thought for a moment about whether I wanted to tell her more about myself than she might want to know. Perhaps sensing my unease, she changed the subject. "So I see you're not a patient. What are you meeting Dr. Muhammad for?"

"I'm interviewing him for a book I'm writing on being black and gay in America."

"Oh."

I sat quietly, watching my words sink in.

"That should be interesting," she said. "So what do you think about gay men?"

I took a deep breath and told her. "As a gay man myself, I don't think you can make any easy generalizations about them. You know, there are lots of different kinds of people out there with a variety of different experiences."

If Sister Sheila showed any outward reaction to my admission, I failed to see it. She merely paused for a moment, then told me that she had not meant to offend me with her question. I assured her that she had not offended me, but I realized how this type of everyday experience illustrates the ways in which society's compulsory heterosexuality quietly coaxes and coerces homosexuals into the closet. Had I answered coyly without acknowledging my homosexuality, Sister Sheila might have held on to the assumption that I was heterosexual merely because I hadn't fit into her stereotype of a gay man.

Sister Sheila was not the only homophobe in that conversation. I was guilty as well. I knew where she was headed when I fielded her first question. But for all my openness about my homosexuality, I hesitated to identify myself when the opportunity first arose. Although I had decided long before not to out myself under every circumstance, I had no exact rule of thumb for when to identify my sexual orientation. When Sister Sheila asked me about a girlfriend, I could have told her then that I was gay, but my own homophobia told me not to. I had already come out to my family, my friends, and my colleagues at work, but I was reluctant to come out to someone I had just met.

If a self-described openly gay man has not overcome his homophobia, it is not hard to imagine other homosexuals struggling with this issue as well. Some just want to avoid the hassle of confrontation. "You sometimes have to decide whether or not you want to deal with that," one black gay man told me. The comment was typical of others I heard, but the speaker in this case was Alan Bell, the openly gay publisher of *BLK,* a magazine for black homosexuals. "When I want to go to the supermarket," he said, "I just want to go there and get my milk and bread and I want to come home. I don't want to have to lecture somebody that I have the right to do this, that, or the other." Admitting that there were times when he might not be affectionate with a male lover in public, Bell said, "I don't necessarily put myself in a position where I have to deal with that [homophobia], or give somebody a look, or tell somebody off."

Homophobia grips everyone in the black community, but it can sometimes show itself differently in men than it does in women. Many ordinary black men, like their counterparts in the Black Power intelligentsia, have expressed concern about homosexuality because of its effects on black manhood. Not thinking to challenge the stereotype, they know that the black man is supposed to be strong and believe that the homosexual man is inherently weak. But even if we accept the often sexist and patriarchal criteria of male strength (physical ability, style of dress, number of children, education, wealth, political power, black consciousness, independence from the white establishment), it would be hard to see why many black gay men would not be included. Unfortunately, because of their fears of retribution or of losing their jobs, many of these "strong" black gay men refuse to be identified publicly, even though they are often well known in the black gay male community. A Los Angeles County deputy sheriff, one of the White House Honor Guard (who protect the President), a Philadelphia TV reporter, an Olympic sprinter in Florida, a professional bodybuilder in Atlanta, a married soldier in Texas, and a UPS deliveryman in Washington were only some of the many closeted black gay men I have encountered.

I have spoken with hundreds of black gay men and observed thousands of others, many of whom defied the stereotype of who they were supposed to be. Some were muscular weightlifters and others were thin dancers. Some had fathered children and others had adopted them. Some were married, most were single, and many were divorced. A few were crossdressers, transvestites, and transsexuals. (Some transgendered people did not consider themselves to be gay.) Socioeconomic status spanned the range from wealthy to poor. Some were Afrocentrists and others were ensconced in the white community. But by no means were they all alike.

Dr. Elias Farajaje-Jones, who taught the history and sociology of religions at Howard University, recounted an incident that reveals the depth of the stereotypes. Standing over six feet four inches, with nine years' growth of thick dreadlocks down to his waist and wearing a hooded sweatshirt, Farajaje-Jones might be mistaken for a homophobic reggae artist rather than a homosexual. When he greeted one of his male students by hugging him, the student turned and saw the stunned expression on a friend's face. His friend whispered, "Man, he a fag. What you hug him for?"

"A lot of your homeboys are probably fags too, but you just don't know about it," the student responded.

"But I can't believe he's a fag. I mean he's got them dreads. He wearing a hood. He looks real down," the friend continued.

This story, recounted by Farajaje-Jones, shows that stereotypes persist largely because many black straight men simply do not know, or refuse to believe, that many of their friends, family, and coworkers are gay.

Some black women, on the other hand, seem to suspect male homosexuality everywhere. They see this not so much as a manhood problem but as a numbers problem. "It's so hard to find a good black man these days," the lament begins. "They're either in prison or on drugs or unemployed. And the ones that aren't are gay!" This attitude does not necessarily reflect homophobia, but it does encourage some black gay men to lie about their sexual orientation so they can try to fulfill an unwritten obligation to black women. One explanation for heterosexism among some black women may be found in their traditional attitude about the male-female power structure. By accepting society's bias about male dominance, these women may view black homosexuals as weakening society's perception of black people overall. If outsiders are to judge the entire black community by its men, then some heterosexual black women want stereotypically strong heterosexual black men to represent the race.

Homophobia in the black community cuts across generations as well. Although younger blacks seem more accepting of lesbians and gay men than do older blacks, people in every age group I interviewed expressed some homophobic sentiments, perhaps for different reasons. The young may be trying to stave off speculation about their own sexual identities. As Dr. Ron Simmons explains in his essay on black homophobia, "In the black community, a male is often forced to denounce homosexuality in order to avoid suspicion." A song from the rap group the Disposable Heroes of Hiphoprisy shows how these denunciations can create a "language of violence." The song describes a teenager taunted from the first day of school as a "faggot" and "sissy" and explains that the taunters were trying to prove to each other that they were not gay. Eventually, one of the bullies ends up in prison and finds himself the subject of the same taunts.

This culture of homophobia, with its language of violence, may contribute to real acts of mayhem against homosexuals. In October 1994 in the small town of Laurel, Mississippi, a sixteen-year-old black boy shot and killed two older white gay men. Arrested four days after the bodies were found, the boy admitted to the shooting, but claimed in his defense that he believed the two men might be HIV-positive. The boy's defense raises troubling questions as to why a sixteen-year-old black male with a gun would get into a car with two unarmed white gay men. We do not know for sure, but the boy could have wanted to join the two men, only to become conflicted about his decision.

Widespread homosexual experimentation by young people helps explain some of the homophobia among them. They may fear being labeled faggots themselves unless they forcefully, even violently, oppose homosexuality. For example, a black woman in Chicago described to me an unacknowledged gay subculture in Chicago's black male gangs. Several of the gang members had girlfriends, she said, but "fooled around with men on the side." None of these young gang members, however, considered themselves to be gay.

Homophobia sometimes takes a different form among older blacks. They often express a preference for a simpler day when the world was not complicated by such things as androgyny and open expressions of sexuality. Older blacks are also more likely than younger ones to be religious, and most black religions still view homosexuality as an abomination. Of course, not all older blacks are outwardly homophobic, and some who were homophobic (like my grandmother) have started to change or question their views after discovering or finally acknowledging homosexuals in their own families.

Prominent and well-respected black public figures tend to view homosexuality in one of two ways. Either they avoid the topic out of fear that they will be labeled gay and their careers will be ruined, or they embrace the gay community and its causes because they are comfortable with both their careers and their sexual orientation. Not all the public figures rumored to be gay are gay, but the label of homosexuality can be so poisonous that even the famous, wealthy, and powerful fear for their reputations. For instance, the Langston Hughes estate successfully blocked filmmaker Isaac Julien from showing his unedited Hughes film in the United States. The family feared that the documentary, which quoted Hughes's own writings, would portray the poet as homosexual or bisexual. Similarly, according to *The Advocate* magazine, members of Barbara Jordan's family appeared to object to a posthumous report that outed her only a month after she died in January 1996.

Still living African-American public figures face similar pressures. Legends such as Michael Jackson—one of the wealthiest men of any race in the music industry—zealously and indignantly defend against any suggestion that they might be homosexual. In interviews, Jackson has strongly denied that he is gay, and his mother, Katherine, has flatly rejected the possibility, claiming in a December 1993 interview on TV's *Hard Copy* that "you can tell when a person is gay." According to Katherine Jackson, "Sometimes you look at a person's face and you say, 'Oh my God, that guy is gay.' " But then she insisted, "Michael is not gay." Her comment relies heavily on a stereotype about gay behavior and appearances, but the irony is that her son, to many people, perfectly fits the stereotype she perpetuates. Thus, when Michael Jackson married and then divorced Lisa Marie Presley, more than a few eyebrows were raised by skeptical blacks and others. If you live by the stereotype, you may die by the stereotype.

Rumors about the sexual orientation of Whitney Houston, Luther Vandross, Teddy Pendergrass, Carl Lewis, and other black celebrities have swirled in the media for years—often to be quickly denied by the celebrities themselves. Houston responded passionately when an *Entertainment Weekly* reporter asked if she had read a *People* magazine cover story that repeated rumors suggesting her marriage to singer Bobby Brown to be a "sham" to hide a lesbian relationship. "Oh my God, oh my God, oh my God," Houston reportedly replied. "I am not a lesbian. I wish they'd stop saying it. I have a daughter, for God's sake. What do they mean by this? They write this shit and one day I'm gonna have to talk to my daughter." It is unclear whether the reference to her daughter was meant to prove that Houston is not a lesbian or to demonstrate the harm the rumors had done to her family. Either way, her response was disturbing, perpetuating the popular perception that lesbianism is a cause for shame. The real threat to Houston's daughter is not that her mother might be a lesbian but that a child is unable to grow up in society where she is free to be herself.

In the course of my interviews, I came across the names of many other black public figures who I was told were homosexuals. Some were musicians, others were politicians and journalists, several were athletes, and quite a few were actors and actresses. Others may tell of sexual encounters with celebrities, but only the celebrities themselves can confirm or deny their actual *orientation*. Moreover, if those black public figures who are lesbian or gay feel so uncomfortable with their sexual orientation that they feel the need to hide it, outing them would only perpetuate the stereotype that being lesbian or gay is shameful. It might titillate us and satisfy our curiosity, but it would not show the homosexuals who lead happy, healthy lives. The hundreds of average black women and men who are not celebrities but who are homosexual better illustrate the reality of black lesbians and gay men.

The comments of Chicago Bulls player Dennis Rodman provide some insight into the dilemma faced by black public figures. In a interview in the February 1996 issue of *Inside Sports,* Rodman says, "If I was gay, I would tell the world I'm gay. But being in sports, the people looking at me would say, 'He shouldn't be there; he's a high risk for AIDS.' " Rodman ventures into unchartered territory for superstar professional athletes when he speculates that "a lot of people in the world have views about being with someone of the same sex, but they won't express it. There's no way you can say you didn't ever think about it, because when asked, 'Have you been with another man?' most [men] answer, 'God no, it's disgusting.' Well, how do you know it's disgusting if you've never thought about it?" Unlike other professional athletes, Rodman admits that he frequently goes to gay bars and has gay friends, who occasionally kiss him on the cheek. Such nonsexual male intimacy is not unheard of among some black heterosexual athletes, including Magic Johnson and Isiah Thomas, who reconciled a famous dispute by publicly holding hands and cheek-kissing at the fifth game of the 1988 NBA Championships.

When asked if other athletes ever thanked him for publicly expressing his views on controversial issues such as homosexuality, Rodman responds, "Of course. A lot of people who really didn't respect me now respect me for speaking my mind, for speaking about what people are afraid to do. A lot of people are afraid to express what they think . . . Just the other day, a guy came to me and said, 'God, you have a lot of guts to do what you do and say the things you say.'"

Rodman is one of the few professional athletes to speak about homosexuality, and the fact that he is black is significant. Although he is considered to be somewhat peculiar, his popularity among sports fans, black and white, is still high because of his incredible talent. But the mere discussion of homosexuality, a taboo topic in sports, represents a breakthrough in the way some view their heroes. If a white person had made these comments, it might have been easier for the black community to ignore it as a "white thang."

Regardless of the sexual orientation of celebrities, homophobia forces many ordinary black gay people into the closet, a high price to pay for those struggling for acceptance within the larger black community. As Dr. Ron Simmons puts it, "We don't say we're gay, thus our families and the community do not realize the significant contributions we make as gay and lesbian members of the family and the community." Most troubling, however, are the occasions when closeted homosexuals attack "out" lesbians and gays, who, by their openness, threaten the conspiracy of silence. Noting this problem, the writer Reginald Jackson, in an "open letter to a brother," writes, "It is downright tragic to think that the brother giving me a dirty look is a fellow black gay man."

Homophobia extends its tentacles to every corner of black society. Not only does it infiltrate the rhetoric of intellectuals, public figures, and ordinary people, but it also pervades the church and other institutions and rears its head at important events, and in the popular culture.

Every summer, the Bud Billiken Parade (the nation's largest African-American parade) makes its way down Martin Luther King Drive from 35th Street to 51st Street, through the heart of Chicago's black South Side. Plans for the 1993 parade were shaping up as usual. After reading a solicitation for participants printed in the *Chicago Defender* newspaper, a black

Chicago woman named Karen Hutt typed an application form
for a group of black lesbians and gay men. At the place where
the group was supposed to enter its name, she typed "The Ad
Hoc Committee of Proud Black Lesbians and Gays" and sent
the application by registered mail on the first of June.

More than a month after submitting the application, Hutt
received notice from Michael Brown, the parade coordinator,
that the group's application had been rejected because of
"time, space and manpower constraints." Hutt and her friends
were not convinced. While they complained publicly about the
discrimination, they secretly submitted another application under the false name "Diverse Black Role Models" and purposefully misspelled a number of words so it would not look as
literate as the first application. Within a few days, they were
notified that the application had been accepted, and they were
granted a spot in the parade. "We had them in a classic lie,"
Hutt said later. But the group decided to hold off mentioning
the disparate treatment until the right moment; they continued
to talk publicly about a gay contingent in the parade. The radio
talk show switchboards lit up with callers complaining that
gays would "ruin" the parade because it was a "family" event.
Some said they feared that men would be "wearing dresses"
down King Drive. Others speculated that "white people must
be behind this" as part of a ploy to divide the black community. But Hutt and the other group members stuck to their
script. "Our line was real simple," she recalled. "We're part of
the black family. We belong here too."

Days before the parade was scheduled to begin, while the
public still believed that the gay group would not be able to
march, the group scheduled a press conference in front of the
office of the parade's sponsor, the *Chicago Defender*. Dramatically pointing their fingers across the street, the group members revealed their evidence to the media, hoping this would
pressure the parade organizers to allow them to participate. It
did not. But with increased attention focused on the incident,

)c Committee hired a lawyer to sue the newspaper.
, a mediator was brought in and helped settle the
owing the group to march.

At the same time the Ad Hoc Committee was winning its case, another group of black gays was fighting a different battle halfway across the country. A performance ensemble called the Postmodern African American Homosexuals, better known as Pomo Afro Homos, applied for participation in the third biennial National Black Theater Festival in Winston-Salem, North Carolina. The award-winning group, which had played to sold-out audiences across the country, wanted to perform its show *Fierce Love: Stories from Black Gay Life,* but its application was rejected. Responding to the litany of possible explanations for its rejection, the group said in a statement, "We did not miss the application deadline. We did not score too low in a peer panel process. We are not 'unknowns.' " The group even expressed its willingness to make special accommodations. "We offered to perform at noon or midnight, on another company's stage, in a cabaret or conference room with 'adults only' plastered all over it . . ." But none of these concessions affected the outcome of the dispute. Instead, the festival went ahead as scheduled during the first week of August 1993—without the Pomo Afro Homos.

Later that month, 250 miles away, yet another controversy would develop involving black lesbians and gays fighting to be included in an event sponsored by the black community. The 1993 March on Washington for Jobs and Justice marked the thirtieth anniversary of the historic 1963 march during which Dr. King delivered his "I Have a Dream" speech. Black lesbians and gays demanded the right to participate, and the organizers agreed to the request. But on the afternoon of August 28, 1993, as the lengthy speeches put the activities behind schedule, the march organizers had an idea: to save time, they decided to eliminate the lesbian and gay speakers. Tired and hot after a long afternoon in the draining sun, Phill Wilson, living with AIDS, almost agreed to the proposal. But after a moment's reflection, he and his cohorts rejected it. The scenario seemed all too familiar; ten years before, noted lesbian writer Audre Lorde had to fight just to be able to speak at the twentieth-anniversary March on Washington. Wilson had come all the way from Los Angeles so that black homosexuals would be represented, and they were determined to see him speak. When the organizers saw that the gay group would not relent, they placed Wilson at the end of the long program. As the day drew to a close and Wilson was finally announced onstage, only a small sliver of the huge crowd that had gathered that morning remained on the Mall. But Wilson's mere presence broke the thirty-year silence of the black civil rights establishment, which had excluded another black gay man, Bayard Rustin, from a more open and significant role in the first March on Washington.

These three incidents, all in August 1993—the community parade in Chicago, the theater festival in North Carolina, and the thirtieth-anniversary March on Washington—symbolize just how far black people have come, and how far we still have to go, in dealing with homophobia.

The homophobia in black institutions is not limited to special events. In Washington, D.C., for example, the president of the local chapter of the NAACP, Morris Shearin, refused to accept a contribution from the local black gay organization. Accepting such money would endorse an "immoral" lifestyle and give "special treatment" to homosexuals, he said. Like many black civil rights leaders, Shearin grew out of the religious tradition in the black community. He serves as pastor of the Israel Baptist Church, and in December 1994 was elected to lead the NAACP chapter. His comments are typical, and surprising only because of his stature in a civil rights organization in Washington, in the midst of what many consider a black gay mecca. Washington, with an overwhelmingly black population, has elected gay-friendly city council members, school board members, and mayors. Current mayor Marion Barry and former mayor Sharon Pratt Kelly both campaigned heavily for the black gay community's support. And no city has more black gay social establishments than Washington does. But despite the NAACP chapter's $51,000 debt, Shearin rejected the offer of the D.C. Coalition of Black Lesbians, Gay Men, and Bisexuals to hold a fund-raiser. "We accept money from anyone who wants to buy a membership in the NAACP," Shearin told the *Washington Blade.* "But I am not going to show any special treatment to any group."

When a financially ailing civil rights organization refuses to accept money from black lesbians and gays, it is little wonder that some of them feel estranged from their community. The pop psychology theories of some black writers only explain the distance that sometimes separates black homosexuals from the rest of the black community, but fail to see that many of these lesbians and gay men are driven out of the community or out of organizations by the actions of intolerant black heterosexuals.

Tom Morgan could have become just another victim of the homophobia in black organizations. A forty-three-year-old journalist from St. Louis, Morgan has been a reporter for the *New York Times,* the *Miami Herald,* and the *Washington Post,* where he gained rare experience for a black man. His great-great-grandfather, Captain Charleston Hunt Tandy, led the fight against Jim Crow segregation on the streetcars of St. Louis. "I grew up understanding that there were people who put their lives on the line for the civil rights struggle," Morgan says. Later he became involved with the National Association of Black Journalists (NABJ) and spent six years as its treasurer. Then he decided to run for NABJ president. With his impeccable credentials, his commitment to the struggle, and his family history, Morgan appeared on paper to be an impressive candidate.

Some NABJ members opposed Morgan's candidacy because they felt he would harm the organization. A gay president would present the wrong image, they said. But "no one raised any issues of sexuality when I handled the organization's finances for six years," Morgan says. Ultimately, he and his campaign advisers decided they would not raise the issue of his sexual orientation and instead would let the opposition raise the issue. "We made the strategic gamble that the whispering led by the opposition would become so negative that it would turn a lot of people off." Morgan's gamble paid off and in 1989 he was elected as the first openly gay president of the NABJ.

Other black lesbians and gay men have also been attacked after coming out in black organizations. Dr. Timothy Moragne, a black psychologist at Nova University in Fort Lauderdale, Florida, felt the pressure of his community while he served as acting president of the Association of Black Psychologists. Moragne's crime was writing an article in the association's newsletter, *The Psych Discourse,* that described the experience of watching a relative die of AIDS. Soon afterward, members of the association began calling for Moragne's resignation and pressuring him to step down, he says.

Of all the black institutions that perpetuate heterosexism and promote homophobia, black popular culture may be the worst offender. For example, nineteen-year-old Jamaican musician Buju Banton hit the popular music charts with his song "Boom Bye Bye," in which he threatens "faggots" with a "bullet in the head." Banton stands out as much for his apparent advocacy of violence as for his homophobia. Many other black musicians are similarly homophobic. Popular rapper Tone Loc in one of his songs protests the suggestion that he would be involved with men: "This is the eighties / And I'm down with the ladies." Snoop Doggy Dogg criticizes someone's mother as "a Frisco dyke," the rap group Brand Nubian boasts that they can "fuck up a faggot," and a song from the Lench Mob protests that "I don't play that fucking gay shit." Likewise, Chuck D, Ice-T, Ice Cube, Queen Latifah, Shabba Ranks, and numerous other black musicians have all contributed to the homophobia, both in their music and in their politics.

Black films add to the problem. Popular movies such as *School Daze* and *Beverly Hills Cop* feature homophobic characters and stereotypical homosexuals. Even the popular and politically correct film *Waiting to Exhale* casts its two black gay male characters in standard fashion, one as a hairdresser and the other wearing a large earring. Hollywood still hasn't learned that most black gay men don't fit into these stereotypes. In John Singleton's *Higher Learning,* one of the few black feature films to address homosexuality seriously, the lesbian and gay characters are white, thus perpetuating the myth that homosexuality does not exist in the black community. But despite the film's racial limitation, Singleton deserves credit for doing what few other black filmmakers have done—depicting homosexuals as human beings rather than as stereotypes.

The message may not be sinking in. Dr. Elias Farajaje-Jones saw Singleton's film at a predominantly black theater, where the audience hissed and booed at the romantic scene involving two women. Similarly, when I saw the film at a different black theater, several audience members spoke aloud at the movie. One woman even kept up a running monologue loud enough for the entire audience to hear: "Oh no. She's not gonna kiss that woman! No, she didn't kiss that girl! Oh, I see, she didn't really kiss. I was about to say. Wait, wait, or did she? I don't understand." On the other hand, black lesbian activist Sabrina Sojourner told me that when she saw the film, some audience members rumbled in their seats, but one man actually screamed "Yes!" If a single scene with two white women could generate so much energy, one could only imagine what would have happened had the two characters both been black. When I watched the scene in *Waiting to Exhale* as the gay father comes out to his ex-wife, the black audience at the theater in Atlanta's Lennox Square Mall applauded the character's courage.

Black comedy and black comedians provide their own spin on the homophobia. Eddie Murphy has become notorious in the gay community for his "faggot" jokes, but other, lesser-known black comedians are just as homophobic. *Russell Simmons' Def Comedy Jam,* a popular late-night television show, frequently wins laughs at the expense of homosexuals. (Ironically, Simmons has been relatively supportive of the gay community and of AIDS-related causes.) Black comedians at scores of comedy clubs and bars across the country daily make names for themselves using material that disparages homosexuals. Even black television shows like *In Living Color* have gained notoriety by depicting stereotypical homosexuals in their comedy skits.

At the same time that homophobia pervades black popular culture, several well-known black artists have begun to challenge that culture by presenting themselves as open lesbians and gay men. Danitra Vance broke through the sexual orientation barrier on *Saturday Night Live* to become the first out black lesbian in television comedy. Singer Me'Shell Ndegé-Ocello's songs continue to soar to the top of the charts, although she openly acknowledges that she is a lesbian. And lesbian writer and editor Linda Villarosa has helped bring a whole new outlook to black women as the executive editor of *Essence* magazine. However, as Villarosa and Sabrina Sojourner recount a 1990 incident, the road has sometimes been rocky.

In the fall of 1990, the National Black Gay & Lesbian Leadership Forum began placing buys in the media to advertise its upcoming annual conference, to be held the following February. The group sent its ad copy to *Essence* magazine in New York for a December run. The advertising director wrote back rejecting the group's copy. Convinced that this was a blatant case of sexual orientation discrimination, the group decided to take action. At a press conference, the Forum announced its intention to sue *Essence,* the nation's premier black women's publication. Soon after the announcement, a *Washington Post* reporter placed a call to Harvard University's School of Public Health in Cambridge, where Linda Villarosa picked up the phone. She was serving as a fellow at Harvard and commuting to New York weekly to work at *Essence.* One of the projects she was working on was a "coming out" story in which she and her mother would announce to the world that she was a lesbian with a supportive parent. "Have you seen this wire-service story?" the reporter asked. Villarosa had not seen the story. "What is going on at your magazine?" the reporter continued. Villarosa had no idea what was going on, and the reporter volunteered to fax her the story. Not long after she hung up, Villarosa received another call. "I saw the piece in *USA Today,"* the caller said. "I didn't know that *Essence* was so homophobic."

At the same time Villarosa was dealing with the news, the Black Gay & Lesbian Leadership Forum was coming under attack from voices in the black community. "How could you?" they asked. *Essence* was a proud symbol of black women and of black media, so the thought of suing the magazine felt like a betrayal to some African Americans; it was more evidence that lesbians and gays did not support black institutions, they claimed.

When she finally received a copy of the article, Villarosa was stunned. "I think I was shocked that I could be working with people—even though I was 'out' on the staff—that would make this poor, really stupid choice." The following Monday in New York, *Essence* editor-in-chief Susan Taylor called Villarosa into her office. "I just want you to know this is absolutely wrong," Taylor said. As with many publications, the editor-in-chief of *Essence* has no direct responsibility over the advertising and business sides of the publication.

"But I'm so humiliated," Villarosa said.

"*I'm* so humiliated," Taylor responded. Later, after Taylor visited the business office to discuss the matter, the publication agreed to accept the Forum's advertisement for free for two months. According to Villarosa, the negative press generated by the Forum's lawsuit and the pressure from the editorial side of the magazine turned the issue around. The lesson of that incident, she says, was the importance of "coming together, being strong enough to stand up against an institution [*Es-*

sence] that many people grew up with" and putting black lesbians and gay men out front in the effort.

Such incidents have no doubt contributed to the popular perception that black people are virulently antihomosexual. As conservative professor Richard Mohr writes in San Jose's *Out-Now* newspaper, "Though most members of the Congressional Black Caucus are cosponsors of the federal gay rights bill, on gay issues they do not represent their constituents. Louis Farrakhan does." Mohr cites unrepresentative examples to prove that most blacks are homophobic. "Even the NAACP's magazine *Crisis* admits that blacks in general are more homophobic than whites," he writes, but since when did *Crisis* magazine become black America's official spokesperson?

Mohr may represent popular opinion, but he is out of step with the establishment of the white lesbian and gay community. In fact, the view that blacks are more homophobic than others was more frequently expressed by the black people I interviewed than by the whites. I attribute this result partly to the fact that many of the white homosexuals I spoke with may not have wanted to disclose their complete views about black homophobia, either because of political correctness or because of a fear of retribution. One prominent white gay man I interviewed told me that blacks were definitely not more homophobic than whites, but a white gay writer who had interviewed him for a different piece was told the opposite, off the record. On the other hand, since many black lesbians and gay men live within the black community, they may have experienced homophobia more profoundly from blacks than from whites.

But for all the examples of antigay sentiment among blacks, we cannot conclude that blacks are more homophobic than whites. Black lesbian Cheryl Clarke writes, "I sometimes become impatient with the accusations of homophobia hurled at the black community by many gay men and lesbians, as if the whole black community were more homophobic than the heterosexist culture we live in . . . Since no one has bothered to study the black community's attitudes on homosexuals, homosexuality, or homosexual lifestyles, it is not accurate to attribute homophobia to the mass of black people." When we do study black attitudes on homosexuality, we might reach a very different conclusion.

In fact, the significant figures spouting homophobia throughout American history, people such as Joe McCarthy, J. Edgar Hoover, Anita Bryant, Pat Buchanan, Robert Dornan, and Jesse Helms, have not been black. Even the religious leaders who have led the fight against gay rights have been white. While a number of black ministers view homosexuality as an abomination, few of them—perhaps because they realize the black community has more important concerns than dividing itself over the issue of sexual orientation—have been on the front lines of this debate. Despite recent efforts by the religious right to recruit black ministers into the antigay rights fold, the most visible spokespeople—the Reverends Lon Mabon and Lou Sheldon and televangelists Pat Robertson and Jerry Falwell—are white. On the other hand, prominent black religious leaders such as the Reverend Jesse Jackson and Dr. Joseph Lowery have supported gay rights.

When we consider cultural and ethnic community events, we find plenty of examples of white homophobia as well. For several years running, the streets of New York and Boston have become the venues for ugly battles over gay participation in the St. Patrick's Day parades. Some antigay protesters proudly wave signs stating that "fags" are condemned to hell. Even New York's Salute to Israel Parade was disrupted in 1993 by a debate over whether a lesbian and gay synagogue could participate. These examples, across several different cultures, indicate that homophobia is neither black nor white, but American.

In early 1993, CNN, *USA Today,* and the Gallup Poll combined their resources to conduct a public opinion survey about the President's controversial plan to lift the ban on gays in the military. Fifty percent of the respondents disapproved of the

President's plan, while only 43 percent approved. Buried deep in the poll results, and curiously underreported at that time, was a significantly higher disapproval rate by whites (51 percent) than by blacks (44 percent). In fact, the majority of blacks who expressed an opinion about the issue approved of allowing gays in the military. While the 7-percentage-point difference may not indicate conclusively that blacks are less homophobic than whites, later polls make the point more convincingly. After the initial controversy had subsided, a follow-up Gallup Poll found that the racial variance had widened considerably. By April 1993, 61 percent of blacks favored ending the ban, while only 42 percent of whites held that view.

Since the plan to lift the ban on gays in the military was so closely associated with President Clinton, whom most blacks had supported in the 1992 election, the poll could have indicated a racial preference based primarily on party identification. But when Gallup asked respondents about other gay issues not associated with the Clinton administration, the racial variance remained. Eighty-five percent of blacks and only 79 percent of whites felt that "homosexuals should have equal rights in terms of job opportunities." Fifty-eight percent of whites and only 38 percent of blacks felt that leaders of the homosexual rights movement were "pushing too fast" in pursuing their goals. On the question of whether homosexuals were asking for "special rights" or equal rights, only 31 percent of blacks felt that homosexuals wanted special rights, but whites were nearly evenly divided on the issue, with 45 percent of them saying they thought homosexuals wanted special rights.

Some black gay activists have speculated that blacks are no more homophobic than whites but that many blacks are concerned about the gay community, with its white image, taking advantage of civil rights laws designed to remedy discrimination against blacks. Blacks "may be less willing to have the rights of gays and lesbians be a part of their agenda," speculates H. Alexander Robinson, a black gay man who is president of the board of the National Task Force on AIDS Prevention. But despite the widespread perception that blacks were self-ishly guarding the mantle of civil rights, the April 1993 Gallup Poll found that 61 percent of blacks and only 44 percent of whites favored extending civil rights laws that protected blacks to include homosexuals.

Complicating the analysis of the poll results were the re-sponses by blacks to the last two questions of the survey. When asked what causes homosexuality, 34 percent of whites and only 14 percent of blacks agreed with many gay activists that people were "born homosexual." According to the Gallup analysis, "Besides gender, the most important factor influenc-ing people's attitudes is their opinion about what causes homo-sexuality." Those who felt that people are born homosexual displayed what Gallup called "the most tolerant attitudes." But racially, this was clearly not the case, as blacks were more likely to support gay rights even though a plurality of blacks (42 percent) felt that homosexuality was simply "the way that some people prefer to live." The lack of correlation between black tolerance of homosexuality and black opinion on its origin sug-gests that the causes of homosexuality seem less relevant to blacks than to others. In other words, blacks seem to support gay rights not because homosexuals have no choice about their orientation but because it is the right thing to do.

The last question in the April 1993 survey asked whether homosexuals should "stay in the closet" rather than openly reveal their sexual orientation. Here again the results con-founded the expectations. Only 29 percent of blacks surveyed said that homosexuals should remain in the closet, while 65 percent disagreed with this statement. Many black homosexu-als, including those who feel that blacks are no more homophobic than whites, have told me that the black commu-nity does not object to homosexuality as much as it objects to *open* expressions of it. The comments of black gay writer E. Lynn Harris are typical. The author of two best-selling novels involving a closeted black bisexual character, Harris says, "I think the black community as a whole would rather have you not say it." Citing well-known black entertainers and athletes, Harris explains, "People may know that they're gay but they're not out there saying it. They get the recognition. They get on TV and they talk about looking for that someone special and everybody's fine because that makes [the public] feel comfortable." However, the Gallup Poll suggests that the fears of these closeted public figures may be unfounded.

Other polls support the conclusion that blacks, on average, may actually be less homophobic than whites. For example, a poll conducted February 9–11, 1993, by the *New York Times* and CBS News found that 53 percent of blacks supported guarantees of equal rights for lesbians and gays, while only 40 percent of whites favored such guarantees. Public opinion, of course, changes over time, but even earlier polls have not supported the claim that blacks are more homophobic than whites. A Gallup Poll conducted in June 1992, for example, found that 50 percent of blacks and only 37 percent of whites felt that "homosexuality should be considered an acceptable alternative lifestyle." The one issue where blacks expressed more conservative views on homosexuality than the general public was on the question of legalization of homosexual relations, where blacks were nearly evenly split between those who opposed legalization (49 percent) and those who favored legalization or had no opinion (51 percent).

Other evidence also suggests that blacks may be less homophobic than whites. Although they do not want the lesbian and gay movement to appropriate the symbols of the civil rights movement, black political leaders still have been among the most supportive elements in the gay rights movement. The positions of the Congressional Black Caucus (CBC) may provide the clearest contrast of black and white attitudes about sexual orientation. The CBC and its members solidly supported the two defining gay rights legislative issues that arose in the first two years of the Clinton administration. In the gays-in-the-military debate, CBC members not only supported lifting the ban, they led the fight for it in some cases. House Armed Services Committee Chairman Ron Dellums, for example, held hearings to counter other hearings held by Senator Sam Nunn, a conservative Democrat who opposed lifting the ban. Dellums considered the question "a fundamental civil rights issue" and said the ban was based on "ignorance, fear, bigotry, and oppression." When gay rights leaders proposed legislation the following year that would have outlawed sexual orientation discrimination in employement, CBC members were again out front. In several states where white politicians feared supporting a gay rights bill, black politicians defended gay rights. In conservative Louisiana, Representative William Jefferson, a CBC member, was the only member of the state's congressional delegation to support the Employment Non-Discrimination Act. Likewise, in Missouri, CBC member Bill Clay was that state's only representative, Democrat or Republican, to support the bill. The two lone supporters of the bill in Georgia, Representatives John Lewis and Cynthia McKinney, are both black as well.

Voting records dating back fifteen years reveal the strong support of the CBC for lesbian and gay rights issues. In 1981, it voted unanimously to allow the Legal Services Corporation to use federal funds in cases dealing with gay rights, even though the majority of the House of Representatives voted against the proposal. In 1989, when right-wing congressman Bill Dannemeyer won a 279–134 vote to exempt religious institutions from laws prohibiting discrimination based on sexual orientation, all but one CBC member voted against Dannemeyer. Again in 1993, thirty-six of the thirty-eight CBC members voted against an amendment to prohibit the District of Columbia from spending money to implement its domestic partners ordinance. The amendment passed anyway.

Of the demographic groups in the House of Representatives, "none," says openly gay Congressman Barney Frank, "comes as close to being as progay as the Congressional Black Caucus." Frank extrapolates from this support to conclude that blacks are no more homophobic than whites. Dismissing the possibility that legislators might not represent the opinion of their constituents, Frank, admittedly biased, says legislators usually "are pretty good indicators" of public sentiment. Praising progay CBC members, Frank says, "I don't think they could survive if there was broad homophobia." Examples from local politics, where black elected officials are closer to their constituents than members of Congress tend to be, support Frank's position. The past and present black mayors of New York, Los Angeles, Atlanta, and Washington, D.C., have supported gay rights, and even black mayors in cities with no reputation for tolerance have supported gay rights. For example, I was surprised to find Freeman Boseley, Jr., the black mayor of St. Louis, greeting me at a gay rights fund-raiser when I returned home to that city in 1993. Although some black politicians may support gay rights partly because of their political need to appeal to the white gay population in those cities, the black community has not punished these leaders for their progay positions. In Washington, D.C., Marion Barry began his political comeback by running against, and easily defeating, a homophobic city council member in overwhelmingly black Anacostia. "He didn't beat her because he was progay," Frank says, "but if, in fact, homophobia were as strong as it appeared among the African-American population, Marion Barry could not have devastated Wilhemena Rolark by that kind of margin in a virtually all-black ward."

Black civil rights leaders may have their fingers on the public pulse regarding gay rights issues. Former NAACP executive director Benjamin Chavis, for one, is known for keeping in touch with the people on the street in the black community. But Chavis encountered resistance from some old-line black ministers in the NAACP who questioned the wisdom of his decision to link the civil rights organization with the gay rights struggle. Nevertheless, Chavis ventured into the District of Columbia on April 25, 1993, and told the participants in the National March on Washington for Lesbian, Gay, and Bi Equal

Rights and Liberation that he stood with them in their struggle. The Reverend Jesse Jackson, one of the first black civil rights leaders to openly embrace the gay rights cause when he welcomed homosexuals into his Rainbow Coalition, also addressed the gathering. "Discrimination is discrimination," he said. "We're not talking about behavior; we're talking about status."

Other prominent civil rights leaders such as Coretta Scott King and Dr. Joseph Lowery have strongly supported gay rights. At a press conference on June 30, 1993, standing at the Atlanta gravesite of Dr. Martin Luther King, Jr., his widow, Coretta, reminded the gathering that "many gays and lesbians supported the African-American freedom struggle, and I am not going to turn my back on their movement for freedom and dignity." Recalling her husband's words that he had "worked too long and hard against segregated public accommodations to end up segregating my moral concern," Mrs. King said that "freedom and justice cannot be parceled out in pieces to suit political convenience." Lowery was equally forceful, ridiculing the argument against gays in the military and asking that civil rights not be granted "based on the whimsical likes and dislikes of other citizens."

Despite the 1960s Black Power movement's reputation, even Black Panther leader Huey Newton warned against homophobia in the black community. "We must gain security in ourselves and therefore have respect and feelings for all oppressed people . . . homosexuals are not given freedom and liberty by anyone in the society," he said at the time. "Maybe they might be the most oppressed people in the society." Two decades after Newton's manifesto, many African Americans have as much to learn about lesbians and gays as white society has to learn about blacks.

Although homosexuality appears to have existed throughout black history in Africa and in the diaspora, the recognition of homosexuality as a distinct concept or identity is relatively new. In his 1979 article "Sexual Matters: Rethinking Sexuality in History," Robert Padgug explains: " 'Homosexual' and 'heterosexual' *behavior* may be universal; homosexual and heterosexual *identity* and *consciousness* are modern realities." Therefore, we should not expect to find historical examples where black or white people knew themselves to be homosexual, even though they may have engaged in homosexual activity.

Some 1960s Black Power advocates and some modern Afrocentrists have rewritten history, misstating or ignoring the role of lesbians and gay men along the way. As the Reverend James Sykes, a black minister, told me, "If [white slave traders] felt that there were any gay people over in Africa, why would they want to bring them over here to go in the fields where they can't do the work? Why would they have some limp-wristed people coming over [instead of] people who are going to be men?" This minister maintained that homosexuality among blacks began in America. Like many other outspoken blacks opposed to homosexuality, he speaks with a definitive-sounding voice but with no understanding of the vast evidence to the contrary.

Former Amnesty International official Cary Alan Johnson, a black gay man, testified to the Congressional Black Caucus in April 1993 that "substantial evidence" suggests that homosexuality existed in precolonial African societies. According to Johnson, African homosexuals played "important spiritual roles" in the Zulu, Zande, and Hausa cultures. Similarly, black lesbian writer Audre Lorde has cited the "close, although highly complex and involved, relationships" between African cowives and between the Amazon warriors of ancient Dahomey (now Benin) to bolster her claim that "Black women have always bonded together in support of each other." Lorde cited a 1970 book by Iris Andreski that quoted a ninety-two-year-old Ibibio-Efik woman from Nigeria as saying, "I had a woman friend to whom I revealed my secrets . . . We acted as husband and wife." Andreski further explains that on the west coast of Africa, the Fon of Dahomey have twelve different types of marriage, including one known as "giving the goat to the buck," where a woman of independent means marries another woman. Other scholars, such as Dr. Ron Simmons, have also suggested that homosexuality in Africa goes back to precolonial times.

In fact, modern anthropological evidence suggests the existence of homosexuality in virtually all human cultures, including those of Africa. Here again we must remember that although homosexuality was not thought of as an identity concept prior to this century, homosexual practices—including same-sex pairing, transvestism, sodomy, and even marriage—were widespread throughout black civilization. Scholars such as Warren Johansson, Geoff Puterbaugh, Stephen Murray, and Melville Herskovits have documented the reports of various sexual practices and family structures in black cultures. For example, Portuguese sources indicate that homosexuality was common among the people of Angola at the time when colonists were scouting for slaves. Members of Nubian and Zulu cultures were known to assume alternative gender roles, women taking on important duties and men engaging in transvestite homosexuality. In 1937, Herskovits found that homosexuality was practiced by adolescents in Dahomey, and that some same-sex pairings persisted for life. S. F. Nadel reported having found "widespread homosexuality and transvestiticism" among the Otoro people in Sudan, as well as among the Moro, Nyima, and Tira. In his book *The Nuba* (1947), Nadel also documented marriages of Krongo *londo* and Masakin *tubele*. In a different example, he revealed that attractive prepubescent boys served as pages to the chiefs of the Mossi people and assumed some female gender roles, including their style of dress. In Mombasssa, Kenya, a dance known as *lelemama* served to identify and recruit married women into the lesbian subculture. As an Ovimbundu in Angola acknowledged, "There are men who want men and women who want women." Speaking to an ethnographer, the Ovimbundu told how some women had even constructed artificial penises for use with other women.

Even today, myths about homosexuality in Africa persist, and African countries bring differing perspectives to the debate. Zimbabwean President Robert Mugabe set off a controversy in August 1995 when he banned the Gay and Lesbian Association of Zimbabwe from an international book fair in his country, telling the book fair audience that lesbians and gays are "sodomists and sexual perverts" (according to the *New York Times)*. Mugabe said he was "extremely outraged" that gay rights advocates lived in Zimbabwe and compared them to drug addicts and people who practice bestiality. Like so many other homophobes, Mugabe revealed his limited understanding of sexual orientation, saying, "I hope the time never comes when we want to reverse nature and men bear children." Never mind that gay rights advocates don't even mention this odd thought. If Mugabe aims to stir up the passions of the ignorant with his sensational rhetoric, he has succeeded. In contrast, the black-majority government of South Africa has supported equal rights for lesbians and gays, and the new South African Constitution was the first in the world to prohibit sexual orientation discrimination.

Despite Mugabe's efforts to conceal the truth, homosexuality does exist in Africa. In southwestern Kenya and northwestern Tanzania, the Kuria people observe ancient lesbian rituals that permit women to marry each other. While not necessarily lesbians, these women are part of an intricate and unique African tribal system that allows women to raise families without having to live with men, according to *London Voice* reporter Sophie Reed. In a March 15, 1994, article, Reed profiled sixty-year-old Sabina Mangiti and her family. Mangiti has three younger wives who, among other roles, act as surrogate mothers to produce children for her. She acts as head of the household, providing for and disciplining the children, who are her property. Among the Kuria people, this widespread custom of female families has survived throughout the centuries in a system that recognizes marriage and families as part of an economic ordering. The head of the household, either a man or a woman, must pay the bride's family for the woman. Mangiti, for instance, paid twenty-seven cows to her first wife's family as the price of marriage. It is an ancient tradition that Mangiti says "must go on" because without it many women would not have children or families, and those, she says, "are the most important things of all."

The myth that homosexuality was unknown in Africa was promoted early on in Edward Gibbon's *The Decline and Fall of the Roman Empire,* published between 1776 and 1788. Expressing his own religious-based views in his assessment, Gibbon wrote, "I believe and hope that the negroes in their own country were exempt from this moral pestilence." Such European views may have created reality rather than describing it. Following the rise of colonialism, "people everywhere suddenly desired to be modern, Western, and European," according to Puterbaugh. "European superstitions about homosexuality were swallowed entire, and adopted as if they had always been in force." Early American Negroes, eager to distance themselves from their reputation among white society as "savages," may have latched on to the mythology as well. By doing this, they adopted sexual and cultural values that legitimized the Western puritanical concept of family, thereby denying the tradition of extended families and more flexible communal relationships in non-Western cultures. In our own day, Black Power activists, and later Afrocentrists, have followed this line of reasoning to conclude that homosexuality was thrust upon black civilization by a morally bankrupt white culture. In reality, human nature suggests that a full panoply of sexual practices probably existed in both cultures, but it was homophobia, and not homosexuality, that was white society's legacy.

While none of these theories decisively proves the existence of homosexuality in precolonial Africa, they all cast doubt on the credibility of Afrocentric claims that homosexuality never existed in Africa, particularly since the study of homosexuality in these cultures has only recently begun and societal biases make discovery of this information difficult.

Neither, based on the limited evidence available, can we conclude that homosexuality did not exist among African slaves. Given the reputation for sexual abuse among white male slaveholders, the proposition that homosexuality existed among slaves may be less controversial than the suggestion that it existed in Africa. The history of sexual abuse reinforces the perception that homosexuality was a white creation thrust upon unsuspecting slaves. The suggestion that it existed among blacks even before their involvement of white slaveholders is more controversial, even though slave narratives such as Esteban Montejo's *Autobiography of a Runaway Slave* (1968) support this conclusion. Montejo, a heterosexual black slave, writes about a generational gap among male slaves, in which the older slaves acted as sexual rulemakers, prohibiting men under twenty-five years of age from having sex with women. According to Montejo, "Some men did not suffer much, being used to this life. Others had sex between themselves and did not want to know anything of women. This was their life—sodomy." Montejo's narrative describes a system of household management that recognized roles for both masculine and effeminate male homosexuals in relationships. The effeminate member of the couple acted as a wife and performed household chores such as laundry, cooking, and farming a plot of land, while the more masculine spouse tended to affairs outside of the home, including distributing the couple's products to farmers.

The issue of homosexuality apparently crystallized the gulf between the attitudes of some younger and older male slaves. Although Montejo himself adopts a libertarian attitude that homosexuality "never bothered me," he concludes that it may not have existed in Africa because "the old men hated it." But it is also possible that the older men's views reflected the diminished sense of power that flowed to them if they could not regulate the sexual interactions of some of the younger men. The older men were denied power because the age limit on interaction with women did not preclude homosexuals from engaging in sexual activity.

Other evidence of homosexuality in American slave culture may be difficult to ascertain. Slavemasters knew nothing of the slaves' "secret life," former slave Robert Smalls told the members of the American Freedman's Inquiry Commission in 1863. He observed, "One life they show the masters and another life they don't show," as Paul Escott documented in his 1985 essay "The Art and Science of Reading WPA Slave Narratives." At the time when many of these narratives were complied, in the 1930s, segregated white society still discouraged blacks from speaking critically of whites, so the presence of white interviewers inevitably prevented candor from many of those who were interrogated. Despite some variations among the narratives, most of the interviews followed a suggested set of questions. According to Escott, the topics included work, food, clothing, religion, resistance, illness, the Civil War and Reconstruction. Homosexuality was obviously not on the agenda.

While we know too little about precolonial Africa and antebellum slavery to draw definitive conclusions about the extent of homosexuality in these cultures, more recent historical examples—from the Harlem Renaissance to the civil rights movement—provide a paper trail that validates the often influential role of black lesbians and gay men.

Historian Eric Garber has noted that the attitudes of the blacks who had migrated to Harlem in the 1920s and '30s were best reflected in the blues. "Homosexuality was clearly part of this world," Garber writes. George Hanna, for example, recorded a 1930 tune called "Boy in the Boat," in which he sang, "When you see two women walking hand in hand, just shake your head and try to understand." In a popular song called "Sissy Man Blues," the male singer pleaded, "If you can't bring me a woman, bring me a sissy man." Although the music ridiculed some homosexuals for their cross-gender behavior, such people were not shunned or hated, according to Garber.

Other historical evidence supports the prevalence of homosexuals but leads us to doubt the extent of homophobia among blacks, at least in Harlem. Homosexual performers, writers, artists, and their patrons not only survived but flourished in the black community as part of the group that Zora Neale Hurston referred to as "the Niggerati." Bessie Smith, Mabel Hampton, Wallace Thurman, Alexander Gumby, Bruce Nugent, Porter Grainger, Hall Johnson, Phil Black, Frankie "Half Pint" Jaxon, George Hanna, Claude McKay, Countee Cullen, and Alain Locke were among their numbers. Langston Hughes may also have been involved in homosexuality, according to biographer Arnold Rampersad, although Hughes's estate has zealously defended the poet's legacy against such claims.

In 1926, writing under the pseudonym Richard Bruce, Nugent penned a homoerotic article for the premier issue of a controversial Harlem Renaissance publication called *FIRE!!* Sandwiched between writings by Hughes and Hurston, Nugent's elliptical prose describes how "Alex knew he had never seen a more perfect being, his body was all symmetry and music, and Alex called him Beauty. [L]ong they lay, blowing smoke and exchanging thoughts, and Alex swallowed with difficulty, he felt a glow of tremor, and they talked and slept." Nugent's story also told how Langston and others "knew there was something in Alex." In an interview years later in an oral history called *You Must Remember This* (1989), Nugent commented on the rumors that he and Langston had been lovers:

> "Langston had a physical appearance that was everything I liked at the time. He looked Latin, and he looked like me complexion-wise. Yes, I had quite a crush on Langston. Years later, I discovered Langston had a very strange kind of unnecessary envy of me, that I seemed to be so free and easy sexually, and apparently he wasn't. We kind of had a crush on each other."

The homosexuality of the time was not limited to elite writers, performers, and artists. Black drag balls, the forerunners of the balls depicted in Jennie Livingston's 1990 documentary film *Paris Is Burning,* were also the rage during the 1930s and '40s. These sometimes huge events actually may have predated the Harlem Renaissance. As far back as the turn of the century, the black gay community in Washington, D.C., was known to hold an annual ball attended by many male government employees in drag, according to an account reported by Ward Hauser. During the same period, huge black gay dances were also said to be held in St. Louis. The homosexual nightlife trend continued well past the end of the Harlem Renaissance. By the 1940s *Ebony* magazine had written about a popular Harlem nightspot called Lucky's Rendevouz, saying "Male couples are so commonplace . . . that no one looks twice at them."

The practices and attitudes of the black community during these years would not seem to indicate that blacks were any more homophobic than whites at the time. Some black homosexuals, no doubt, joined the military in the 1940s to represent their country in World War II, but by the 1950s and '60s, the civil rights movement had become the defining aspect of black existence for many African Americans.

Bayard Rustin, the illegitimate son of a West Indian immigrant, was among those black gay civil rights activists. Born in Pennsylvania in 1912, Rustin became a lifelong organizer for progressive causes. He joined the Young Communist League in the 1930s, spent more than two years in jail for his refusal to serve in World War II, served as director of the War Resisters League and race relations director of the Fellowship of Reconciliation (FOR). On January 21, 1953, the day after Dwight Eisenhower was sworn in as President, Rustin was arrested in the back of a parked car in Pasadena, California, while performing sodomy on two white men. All three were convicted on morals charges and sentenced to thirty days in jail. Rustin resigned his position with FOR the following day. He completed his jail sentence determined to redeem himself, but as Taylor Branch describes him in his book *Parting the Waters* (1988), "unemployed, a bastard, a Negro, an ex-Communist, an ex-con, and a homosexual, [Rustin] was a misfit by any social standard." Still, he later became a close associate and an assistant of A. Philip Randolph, cofounder of the Leadership Conference on Civil Rights and perhaps the most noted black leader of the time.

Two years later, on December 1, 1955, Mrs. Rosa Parks refused to give up her seat when Montgomery, Alabama, bus driver J. F. Blake ordered her and three other blacks to clear their entire row for a single white male passenger. Parks was arrested for violating Montgomery's bus segregation ordinance. Days later, local residents had begun planning a protest that would eventually grow into an elaborate carpool system and a black bus boycott involving the NAACP and Dr. Martin Luther King, Jr., of the Southern Christian Leadership Conference (SCLC).

Two books, Branch's *Parting the Waters* and David Garrow's *Bearing the Cross* (1988), provide a description of Rustin's involvement in the civil rights movement. Rustin arrived in Montgomery on Tuesday, February 21, 1956, just as a local grand jury handed down indictments against one hundred Montgomery residents for boycotting the city's buses. For various reasons, Rustin made a number of adversaries, including FOR official John Swomley, who was concerned about associating the movement with "Bayard's personal problem." Rustin's involvement in the boycott had been debated even before he left New York, and only eight days after he arrived, he received a phone call from Randolph advising him to leave. Rustin left, but soon worked his way to become an invaluable adviser to Dr. King, receiving a salary of $25 to $50 a week as King's executive assistant. While King was preparing to leave Montgomery in 1959 to take greater control over the SCLC in Atlanta, he plotted to hire Rustin as his public relations person. Expecting opposition to his choice, King did not mention Rustin's name when he told the SCLC that it needed a professional publicist. Later, using an article from *Jet* magazine that criticized the SCLC, King walked into a meeting with a list of proposals to improve the group's image. One proposal was to hire Rustin, who King assured them would "quietly resign" if a problem arose. Some SCLC members vehemently opposed Rustin's selection for moral reasons, but for King, Rustin's homosexuality "didn't bother him," according to Henry C. Bunton in *A Dreamer of Dreams: An Autobiography.*

King became so dependent on Rustin that, at times, he declined to make important decisions without him. While Rustin was overseas on a political trip to Ghana in 1959, King said to adviser Stanley Levison, "Please keep me informed about Bayard's possible return. We really need his services as soon as possible." Despite the controversy surrounding Rustin, King adopted a number of his ideas and recommendations, including the development of a "corps of persons" for a nonviolent direct action movement. But by the summer of 1960, the long-feared "problem" with Rustin finally arose. Congressman Adam Clayton Powell, perhaps feeling pressure to deflect attention from his own ethics controversy, sent the message that King should call off plans he had made with Randolph to picket the Democratic National Convention in Los Angeles or he would announce that King was having an affair with Bayard Rustin. Randolph attempted to counter-blackmail Powell by threatening to disclose the initial threat to the press, but ultimately he, King, and NAACP executive secretary Roy Wilkins did lead about five thousand marchers through the streets of Los Angeles the day before the convention began. Acknowledging that Rustin's homosexuality might continue to be a liability, King finally gave in to pressure and appointed an SCLC committee that decided to break off relations with Rustin. Hurt by the impersonal nature of the decision, Rustin became estranged from King for several years.

Rustin's reputation would negatively affect him at least two more times, once when he was disinvited to a Student National

Coordinating Committee convention in Atlanta after AFL-CIO officials threatened to cancel its funding, and later in a controversy involving the March on Washington. The idea for the march had been formally proposed by Rustin and two associates in a January 1963 memo to Randolph. On July 2, the six black leaders who would serve as march cochairmen met at New York's Roosevelt Hotel. Taylor Branch and David Garrow provide differing accounts of what took place that day. According to Branch, at some point before the meeting, Wilkins personally telephoned Rustin to tell him he would oppose Rustin's role as organizer of the march because of his past communism, war resistance, and arrest record for homosexuality. Wilkins then barred Rustin and several others from the meeting, saying he had come for a chiefs-only discussion. Randolph led the meeting, Wilkins predictably objected to Rustin's role, and someone proposed a compromise in which Randolph would serve as march director; this Wilkins willingly accepted. According to Garrow, on the other hand, Rustin was not excluded but actually led the meeting. Both accounts agree that King and James Farmer of the Congress of Racial Equality spoke up in favor of Rustin. Wilkins eventually relented, and Randolph immediately announced that he was selecting Rustin as his deputy.

Rustin then continued to coordinate the march with the D.C. police, the White House, and other officials. He had previously moved into a building on 130th Street in Harlem owned by the Friendship Baptist Church and announced the march in a huge banner hung outside the third-floor window. Rustin arranged the march in such excruciating detail that he even planned what to do if one of the two thousand buses coming into Washington should be terrorized, and he notified the speakers that they would be ungraciously pulled off the stage if they exceeded their seven-minute time limit.

As the date for the march grew closer, King told a friend in a telephone conversation that he hoped Rustin would not take a drink before the event and "grab one little brother." An FBI wiretap recorded the conversation, prompting an investigation into Rustin's sexual history, and J. Edgar Hoover passed on the information to South Carolina senator Strom Thurmond. The following day, August 13, Thurmond rose on the Senate floor and accused Rustin of sexual perversion, vagrancy, and lewdness, and inserted a copy of Rustin's police booking slip into the *Congressional Record*. But rather than embarrassing the march organizers, Thurmond succeeded in emboldening them, as his strident criticism actually turned off many moderates.

On August 28, 1963, the march proceeded successfully. King delivered the most widely broadcast speech of his life, and as the crowd slowly quieted down after the cheers and applause, Rustin walked to the podium and read the list of goals for the march. The audience thundered its support. When the march concluded, the leaders went to the White House for a cordial meeting with President Kennedy. Two months later, Kennedy's brother Robert, the U.S. Attorney General, approved the FBI's request to wiretap the homes and offices of King and Rustin.

When King asked Rustin to come to Montgomery, he said he felt "a greater political threat from his own colleagues, especially the preachers," than from the local whites. Both King's widow, Coretta, and King's heir and current SCLC president, Dr. Joseph Lowery, insist that King was right to battle for Rustin. "Martin wanted Bayard Rustin to organize the march because he was the best qualified to do it," Lowery said in 1993. The example set by King and Rustin should not lead modern observers to focus only on their separation and miss the larger point—that each of these men struggled mightily against powerful white and black homophobic social taboos of their time. As Taylor Branch quotes Rustin in a confrontation with Wilkins over Rustin's participation in the 1963 March on Washington, "What happens depends on you people who are the main leaders. If you stand up and have some courage, it will do no damage."

During the same period in which Rustin helped organize

the civil rights movement, another black gay man, James Baldwin, was also active in the struggle. In May 1963, Baldwin and other civil rights activists took part in an angry meeting with Robert Kennedy, pressing the Attorney General to get the Administration more involved in civil rights. Born in the middle of the Harlem Renaissance in New York, Baldwin published *Giovanni's Room,* a homosexual love story, in 1956. Then, in the same year as the March on Washington, he released *The Fire Next Time,* which confronted racial issues that were sweeping the country. Long concerned about the absence of racial equality in America, Baldwin had suggested a results-oriented approach in his 1955 *Notes of a Native Son:* "no matter . . . how many hard, honest struggles have been carried on to improve the position of the Negro people, their position has not, in fact, changed so far as most of them are concerned."

While it would be a stretch to suggest that Rustin's and Baldwin's homosexuality was widely accepted in the black community, their contributions to that community have always been widely appreciated. What white people tend to miss is that the black community has always been supportive of its own members, perhaps most so when outsiders are critical. Not surprisingly, blacks tend to rally around other blacks, even when they might disagree with the people they defend. When African Americans rallied around O. J. Simpson, Clarence Thomas, and Marion Barry, they were supporting not only the individuals but the causes they represented. In different ways, Simpson, Thomas, and Barry represent the persecution of black men by white society. Blacks who disrespected O. J. Simpson for marrying a white woman could still support him when the state prosecuted him. Blacks who despised the right-wing views of Clarence Thomas nevertheless came to his rescue during his controversial confirmation hearings. Thomas himself took advantage of the black community's forgiveness by playing the race card and pleading that his hearings were "a high-tech lynching for an uppity Negro." As law professor Derrick

Bell has explained, black people have always lived with contradictions in their lives. Many accepted Christianity although its early proponents used the religion to defend slavery. Many blacks have strongly criticized America as a racist nation but would never leave the country, even if they could. This history of contradictions helps explain often conflicting views about black lesbians and gay men and about their role in black society.

The October 1995 Million Man March organized by Minister Louis Farrakhan illustrates the depth of internal contradiction among blacks. While many blacks supported the march, many did so without necessarily supporting Minister Farrakhan. Some were very troubled by Farrakhan's participation in the march and refused to be associated with the event, but others chose to take part even though they distanced themselves from the minister. Two hundred black gay men (myself included) and a handful of lesbians were among the latter group, and we participated in an openly gay contingent in the march. Carrying placards that read BLACK BY BIRTH/GAY BY GOD/ PROUD BY CHOICE, we proceeded south on 9th Street in Northwest Washington on a thirty-minute procession to the Million Man March rally on the Mall. A few passers-by hurriedly moved out of the way, two people driving their cars along adjoining streets honked their horns in support, and a number of pedestrians stopped and stared. Sensing no negative reaction, our group grew increasingly ambitious and empowered. We began to chant, "We're black! We're gay! We wouldn't have it any other way!" Still, no one in the crowd of people reacted adversely.

As we moved through the throngs of black men assembled on the Mall, the chant changed: "Gay Men (woof!) of African Descent (descent!)!" Either intimidated or impressed, the thousands of faces turned toward our group with expressions of disbelief. The crowd parted like the Red Sea, and the gay contingent marched for several city blocks toward the front of the rally. Only one of the thousands of black men along the route expressed disapproval. The lesson of that experience is that when we black lesbians and gays believe in ourselves enough to come out of the closet about who we are, our community not only accepts us, they respect us more.

What the group did not achieve was its goal of having an openly gay man and a person living openly with AIDS speak from the podium that day. Repeated requests to the march organizers fell on deaf ears, even though AIDS is the leading cause of death for black men between the ages of twenty-five and forty-four and is spreading rapidly among black gay men while it declines in some other populations. Still, the Reverend George Stallings became controversial for many of the gay marchers. For several years the *Washington Afro-American* had been reporting Stallings's involvement in homosexuality, and he was well known in the gay community for opening up his home to social events for gay men. But three months before the Million Man March, Stallings slipped into his own homophobia when he defended Minister Farrakhan from critics. Stallings said, "What do you want, some milquetoast sissy faggot to lead you into the promised land?" Many in the black gay community were shocked and outraged that someone they considered an ally would betray them with such remarks.

Much like Rustin and Baldwin, a number of prominent blacks on the national stage and in our local communities are known or thought to be gay, but many blacks do not seem to mind, or pretend not to notice, unless the issue becomes embarrassing. A number of blacks suggest that as long as other people keep "their business" to themselves, they do not care to get involved. Likewise, some blacks express concerns that other people would be "putting my business in the streets." Similarly, Malcolm X, in several of his speeches, said that the black community should avoid airing its dirty laundry for the white public to see. Instead, he suggested that various people get together and work it out privately. In differing ways, all these comments indicate a wall of separation between a public and private identity or consciousness which blacks are generally expected to respect. This peculiar method of self-deception might be considered a form of "cognitive dissonance" because it allows blacks to pretend that the reality they know exists does not actually exist.

If blacks are no more homophobic than whites, something must explain why so many people, including black homosexuals themselves, continue to believe the opposite. An allegory about mirrors may explain. Imagine yourself as a black gay security guard assigned to help monitor the conduct of two groups in two separate rooms. Sitting in front of a huge two-way mirror, you can see the white gays who occupy the room on the left and the heterosexual blacks who occupy the room on the right. But the people in the two rooms see only mirrors that reflect images of themselves. They do not see you in the third room unless you open the door and enter the room they occupy. The situation is further complicated by your visible race and invisible sexual orientation. When you enter the room with the gays, everyone in the room knows you're black, but when you enter the room with the blacks, the occupants will not necessarily know you are gay. You can see part of yourself in whatever room you enter, but you cannot find your full reflection in either room. Moreover, once you enter either room, you lose sight of the people in the other room and lose the ability to monitor their conduct. So the same people who act kindly toward you when you are in their room may be less gracious when they suspect you are in the room with the other group. Since the gays will always know if the black guard is in their room and the blacks usually don't know for sure who's gay, the gays will be more likely to mind their words around you. Therefore, you might incorrectly assume that the room filled with blacks has more prejudice in it than the room filled with gays does.

Another factor, namely expectations, may help explain the public perception of black homophobia. Any student of politics is familiar with the power of expectations to shape public opinion. I witnessed this phenomenon while working on my first presidential campaign. In 1988, Massachusetts Democrat Michael Dukakis was widely expected to win the nation's first presidential primary in neighboring New Hampshire. The Dukakis campaign tried, with partial success, to drive down these expectations by suggesting that a strong multicandidate field made it unlikely that Dukakis would win as convincingly as some in the media thought necessary. The campaign also focused a great deal of energy on creating more realistic expectations about its chances in Iowa, the first caucus state. If Dukakis placed in the top three, it would be a victory, the campaign claimed. He did, and it was. When Dukakis actually won New Hampshire's primary by a healthy margin, he further redeemed himself by meeting the expectation there. By losing in Iowa, he had actually won, but winning in New Hampshire would have been a loss had he not won big.

When we think about black attitudes toward homosexuality, we think in terms of experiences that tell us we should *expect* blacks to support gay rights because they, of all people, should know the importance of equality and the pain of discrimination. Therefore, when blacks express the same homophobic views as whites, who do not share a history of oppression, then black opinion defies expectation. In the media, only the unexpected—however it is determined—is newsworthy. If the President signs a bill into law as scheduled, no one may notice; but if he trips and falls on the way to the bill signing, every TV network will put the footage on the nightly news. Similarly, when blacks support gay rights—as the polls indicate—no one may notice; however, when Colin Powell opposes gays in the military or Louis Farrakhan suggests gays deserve death, the public looks up and pays attention.

Black methods of expression may be another issue complicating the public perception of black homophobia. Several black people I interviewed told me that although they did not believe blacks were more homophobic than whites, they did feel blacks expressed their homophobia differently. Blacks were said to be louder or more outwardly expressive, while whites were said to be more polite or, in some cases, "politically correct." The vocal nature of black homophobia may also have led to greater attention focused on black homophobes. Another explanation may involve the way black homosexuals experience the pain of homophobia that originates from their own community. "Black gays and lesbians often experience homophobia more profoundly when it happens in the black community than they experience it in the white community or when white gays and lesbians experience it within the white community," says Phill Wilson. Because African-American homosexuals see the black community as a sanctuary or safe space from white society, "we have to give up the only tools of survival we have" when black lesbians and gays experience homophobia from other blacks, Wilson explains. As black gay activist Maurice Franklin has told the *Atlanta Journal-Constitution,* "We expect everyone else to reject us. That's part of the skin we have as African Americans. [But] it hurts when it's your own community."

Karen Hutt, the organizer of the lesbian and gay contingent in Chicago's Bud Billiken Parade, reports that things changed dramatically after her group's successful confrontation with the parade organizers. "I cried almost the whole way down the parade route," Hutt remembers. "It was very moving to see people who look like my grandma out there clapping for me. It was really coming home." The following year, the group again marched without incident. "We're like all buddies now with the *Defender.* They've done four or five different really good articles about black gays and lesbians. And they've been really great. It's really a turnaround."

The lesson, she says, is that we need to challenge not only our community but ourselves. "This is where black gays and lesbians got on my damn nerves. When we marched down King Drive, everybody thought we were going to get shot." At first, black homosexuals showed "little faith" in the black community and its civility, Hutt says. Then, pointing to controversies surrounding gay participation in St. Patrick's Day Parades in New York and Boston, Hutt throws her own zinger: "It's only white people who go nuts around these things."

CHAPTER SIX

Gay Racism

Shortly after I quit my job at the White House, an official of the Washington, D.C., chapter of the National Lesbian and Gay Journalists Association (NLGJA) asked me to speak to the group about my experiences as a gay man in the Administration. I declined the invitation by explaining that I really did not want to talk about the Administration at that point. I wanted instead to branch out into black gay issues and get away from politics for a while. When the official learned that I was writing this book, he asked if I would be interested in discussing the themes of the book instead, and I tentatively agreed. But after consulting with the leadership of the organization, he called back and left a message on my answering machine that the group was not as interested in the topic of the book as it was in my work experiences. Unless I could tell them something they "don't already know" about race and sexual orientation, the group did not want me to speak, the message said. I decided not to return the phone call.

After talking to another official of the NLGJA, I learned later that the D.C. chapter had only one active black member at the time. It struck me then that if they knew as much about race and sexual orientation as they suggested, they would have been more successful at recruiting black lesbian and gay writers for the organization. In the previous two years I had spent in Washington, I had met at least three black gay journalists on my own, and I had not been looking for them. What made the absence of blacks in the NLGJA so shocking, though, was that the Washington chapter represents a city whose overall population and gay community are overwhelmingly black.

Washington's NLGJA chapter is not the only gay organization with little or no representation of people of color, something I found as I walked around the offices of the nation's two largest national lesbian and gay organizations, the Human Rights Campaign (HRC) and the National Gay and Lesbian Task Force (NGLTF). Both organizations were very helpful to me in my research, and representatives of both groups voluntarily took me on tours of their offices when I arrived to interview their staff. Yet as I walked from conference room to cubicle to office, I noticed a disturbing pattern—nearly everyone I met (again in overwhelmingly black D.C.) was white.

In fairness, I should state that most of Washington's major national organizations that are not gay are also primarily white in their leadership and professional employees. But most of these other organizations do not claim to be committed to civil rights, as gay organizations do. Perhaps because of this stated objective, gay organizations ought to be held to a higher standard than the other groups. But regardless of the standard we use to evaluate gay groups, it should come as no surprise that black people—both gay and straight—view homosexuality as something associated with whiteness. Both blacks and whites will continue to believe that very few blacks are homosexual so long as the primary images of homosexuals seen in the media and in gay organizations are white.

Much of the connection between gay and white results from gay racism toward nonwhites. This prejudice takes on many forms, but the most common complaints involve blacks or other nonwhites who feel they are excluded, exploited, or patronized by the dominant white gay community.

Although racism has become more difficult to practice openly, subtle forms of disparate treatment of blacks and whites still persist. Today, the exclusion of African Americans often works through messages that convey, intentionally or not, the sentiment that blacks are not wanted. Two black gay men told how they had gone to a popular white gay bar called J.R.'s in Washington to get change for a phone call. The bartender scowled at them and said, "We don't make change here." Just his tone was enough to convey to them that they were not welcome at the bar. In another incident, John King, a black gay law student at American University, explained how members of his white lesbian and gay campus organization said they wanted to get more blacks to join but that the activities the group planned were all very white-oriented. The favorite pastime was called "Bar Review," a takeoff on the study courses offered for the Bar Exam. This particular Bar Review merely involved going from bar to bar to drink, which is something that a lot of the black students don't do, according to King. When asked why he had not taken a more active role in the organization, King explained, "Everything was just so white. There was nothing that appealed to me." In fact, there are cultural differences in the ways that black lesbians and gays and white lesbians and gays socialize. While drinking and dancing tend to be key elements in both groups' activities, dancing tends to be more important in black lesbian and gay social settings than in white ones, King said. On the other hand, the "video cruise bars," the popular where men gather to drink, watch videos, and ' men, appear to attract disproportionately more blacks.

The social exclusion of blacks is the most c ... and most common form of gay racism practiced by the white community. White lesbian and gay nightclubs have been notorious either for requiring multiple forms of identification for blacks to be admitted or for not admitting them altogether. As a result of the exclusion, black lesbians and gay men have created their own social settings and nightclubs. One black gay man in New York told me how the Paradise Garage, a popular black gay nightclub in the 1970s, was begun because the Flamingo Club, another gay bar at the time, would not admit most blacks. Stories of discrimination and exclusion are quite common among older black homosexuals, but racism persists even today. For example, a white gay man from Dallas candidly acknowledged that the white gay clubs in that town still regularly manage to exclude potential black patrons. In other cities, from Atlanta to Washington to Philadelphia to San Francisco, black lesbians and gay men described how they had been excluded from white gay social settings.

Sometimes the complaints focus on the disparate treatment of blacks and whites at gay clubs on different nights. In cities with large black populations such as Washington, nightclubs often have a special night for blacks. But at one such club, Tracks, local newspaper advertisements for various events had been geared exclusively toward Saturday's white nights instead of Sunday's black nights. One of the club's owners reportedly told a group of black men who complained about the advertising policy, "Black gay men don't read"—this according to Mark Johnson, a correspondent for *SBC* magazine. Among the other complaints: blacks on Sunday nights were forced to walk through a metal detector and be frisked, while whites on Saturday nights were not asked to do this. On Saturday nights, drinks were served in glasses; on Sunday nights, plastic was ᴄ instead. Saturday night's patrons also enjoyed valet parking, but Tracks offered no such opportunity for Sunday's blacks. After several rounds of negotiations with black gay activists, Tracks began to change some of these policies in 1993 and 1994.

Public ostracism contrasts with private sexual exploitation of blacks, particularly of black men. "WM SEEKING MUSCULAR black dude," began a recent personal ad in a gay newspaper. One can only speculate why the white male wanted to find a "black dude" to satisfy his sexual desires. Several black gay men I spoke with complained that white men often wanted only blacks because they expected them to have large penises. "It's like they [white men] only see you as a walking sexual organ," said one black gay man in Los Angeles. Others suggested that white men sometimes wanted to play out some sort of sexual slave fantasy, either dominating a black man in a master-servant relationship or being dominated by one in a masochistic and guilt-alleviating morality play.

Like its heterosexual counterpart, the white gay media usually projects Eurocentric images of beauty that transmit messages of inferiority to blacks and others who do not fit into the white stereotype. The beauty of black women is often denied by the media unless the women closely resemble white women or share some common features. "When you look through the media, lesbian or straight, there are not many images that look like me," says one black lesbian in Washington. The beauty of black men, however, is reflected almost solely through white gay appreciation of the black man's body or genitalia, objectifying black men only as sexual objects rather than as human beings with emotions and the capacity to think. Robert Mapplethorpe's *Black Book* (1986) may be the most notorious example of such objectification. Although Mapplethorpe's camera often captured images of beauty, with black men it frequently captured only their penises. Mapplethorpe's "Man in the Polyester Suit," for example, depicts a black man wearing a suit with the zipper open, exposing a huge penis. Other photos depict black men's bodies but do not show their heads, the only part of the body capable of emotion, thought, and communication. But Mapplethorpe is only the most recent example of such white gay exploitation of blacks. White gay writer and photographer Carl Van Vechten took pictures of nearly all the major figures of the Harlem Renaissance in the 1920s and '30s. Van Vechten was most notorious for his 1926 novel *Nigger Heaven,* which outraged black Harlem, according to historian Eric Garber in an article titled "A Spectacle in Color: The Lesbian and Gay Subculture of Jazz Age Harlem." Like Mapplethorpe, Van Vechten also took scores of photographs of nude black men for his collection. Again, the men were often not represented as thinkers but rather as sexual objects, partly for the amusement of whites.

The popular gay images of black women are particularly troubling. One example reflecting the exploitation of African Americans is that of the black nanny. She is usually very large, dark-skinned, and often wearing slave garb, such as an Aunt Jemima–style scarf over her head. The image is found frequently on the greeting cards in the gay novelty shops and the supposedly enlightened gay bookstores. While no one takes these images seriously, using them at all perpetuates a sense of difference between blacks and whites that no doubt, in some way, infects the thinking of homosexuals in other, more serious contexts. The other popular image is that of the black diva, like Diana Ross or Patti LaBelle. These women are glorified because of their theatrics or performing ability, but their acceptance into the white gay culture exposes a contradiction, since most black women are still neglected or disrespected by the same culture.

Gay racism extends to the political level as well, as illustrated by the experience of black gay soldier Perry Watkins. Watkins grew up in the 1950s in the sleepy town of Joplin, Missouri, the same city that gave birth to Langston Hughes, the poet laureate of the Harlem Renaissance. In a time and place where homosexuals were thought not to exist, Watkins had lived as one since childhood. He remembers feeling attracted to men long before other kids even knew they had sexual organs. He is the only person in his family he knows to be gay. In hindsight, he says, he grew up openly gay.

Drafted into the military during the Vietnam War, Watkins was by then well out of the proverbial closet. He created a reputation for himself as a grand diva of the drag show circuit in the military. But despite his flamboyant style, he was promoted seven times in his fifteen years of service.

In 1981, under the Reagan administration's newly aggressive antihomosexual military policy, Watkins was "separated" from the military. He objected, and took his case all the way to the United States Supreme Court. The Court ruled in his favor, pointing out that the military knew Watkins was homosexual but allowed him to reenlist and even promoted him over the course of a dozen years. The Court reasoned that if he had not been a threat to unit cohesion and morale before, the military could not argue that he had suddenly become a threat just because its policy had become more aggressive. Watkins became the only openly gay man in history whom the High Court permitted to serve in the military.

But despite this distinction, Watkins was skipped over by the tacticians of the gay movement who plotted to overturn the military's ban on homosexuals during the early months of the Clinton administration. Tom Stoddard, a white gay lawyer, directed the Campaign for Military Service (CMS), an umbrella group that combined the resources of several preexisting gay organizations. In an interview, he delicately tiptoed around the question of Watkin's role in the effort. "Perry, I know Perry, and I like him very much and I greatly respect his history," Stoddard began. "But there was a public relations problem with Perry, to be blunt about it." Stoddard had read about Watkins and felt that his story was "effective," but David Smith, the communications director for CMS, warned Stoddard, "You know, there's a problem with Perry. He wears a nose ring. It's going to be a problem for him to be a spokesperson because people are going to react to the nose ring." As he recounted the story, Stoddard commented, "I must say, although I believe in diversity, I also know the power of public relations." Stoddard agreed to the communications director's recommendation that Watkins not be a spokesperson for the movement. If anyone had asked Watkins to take out his nose ring, he would have accused them of racism, the CMS communications director explained. The official also claimed that Watkins was asked to participate in CMS events, including a nationwide bus tour called "Tour of Duty" to dramatize the impact of the gay ban, but the group could not work out the trip with Watkins's schedule.

As a result of Watkins's exclusion, the primary images of gay service members that emerged were nonblack: José Zuniga, Tracy Thorne, Joseph Steffan, and Margarethe Cammemeyer. Watkins was so disenchanted by the experience with the gay movement that he even refused to be formally interviewed when I called him. But he then continued to talk for twenty minutes *on the record* about why he would not talk to me. Describing himself as "angry, pissed, [and] hurt," Watkins said, "Sometimes the loudest voice we have is the one that's not heard." He complained bitterly about his treatment by the white gay community, and left no praise for the black gay community either, which he said stood by and watched as the white gay leadership neglected him.

Most of his criticism was directed at the gay community's decision to celebrate new poster children such as Margarethe Cammemeyer. A colonel and chief nurse in a National Guard unit in Washington State, Cammemeyer was discharged from the military after acknowledging that she was a lesbian during a promotion review. As Watkins explained, the decision to elevate Cammemeyer suggested that any white person who comes out of the closet is as noteworthy as a black person who has endured and thrived in the military for years. Noting that Cammemeyer, in her fifties, only recently acknowledged her homosexuality to herself, Watkins commented that the decision to focus on her said "we'll go with a woman who lied for twenty-six years before we go with" a black man who had to live the struggle nearly every day of his life.

Watkins believes he survived in Joplin, Missouri, for the same reason he survived in the military—he was able to create an alternative family in each environment, no matter how hostile it might have seemed. The irony, he said, is that he performed drag for fifteen years in the military and became an acknowledged part of that society, only to find himself ostracized by the gay community that should have welcomed him.

Regardless of the appropriateness of the decision not to use Watkins, no other black gay military figures filled his shoes and no one assumed a role as significant as those played by the white celebrities of the season. Although minorities, mostly blacks, make up 29.2 percent of active-duty personnel in the four armed services, the images seen in the effort to lift the ban were mostly of whites. But according to a 1994 Pentagon report cited in the *New York Times,* 30 percent of Army enlistees the previous year had been black, nearly triple the percentage of eighteen-to-forty-four-year-old blacks in the civilian population. Moreover, "the fact that black women are kicked out of the military for homosexuality at twice the rate of white men was left out of the discourse in both the straight media and the continually racist gay and lesbian press," according to author Sarah Schulman in a June 1994 article in *10 Percent* magazine.

The absence of black images in the campaign to lift the ban reflects the common criticism of paternalism toward black homosexuals. Blacks complain either of being patronized by whites who do not take them or their ideas seriously or of having their ideas devalued and neglected by whites who think they know what is best. As an American University law student, John King spent a summer working for a gay organization and was disturbed when some white lesbians and gays were surprised to find him so openly gay. "It must be really hard for you to be gay as a black person," they told him. His response: "What is it? Only white males can be open? Only white males can be comfortable with their sexuality? I really do think if I were white they wouldn't be as impressed by it." In fact, a number of young white lesbians and gay men did work on the same project, apparently without drawing the same level of surprise about their participation. The white lesbians and gays may have intended their comments to be encouraging, but King interpreted the comments as condescending.

One black gay man involved in the effort to pass a national gay rights bill objected to a gay organization's questionnaire, which, he said, did not address African Americans' concerns. "Is this a concern of the black community or is this your concern?" the author of the questionnaire asked him pointedly. The black gay man felt the question devalued his opinion by suggesting that it would be relevant only if he had taken a poll to prove that most blacks did share his concern. The author of the questionnaire apparently viewed the man's role in the discussion as something of a token, merely to represent the opinions of black people, and even then he was only expected to say what the group wanted to hear.

The patronizing of blacks by the white gay mainstream also occurs in the lack of support for black leaders and causes. Ken Reeves, a black gay man and the former mayor of Cambridge, Massachusetts, told me how the gay political establishment in his state initially shunned his election efforts. When Reeves first ran for office in 1985, rent control was a defining campaign issue. An openly gay white candidate opposed rent control, while Reeves, who was not as openly gay as his opponent, favored it. When he went to one of the local gay political organizations seeking an endorsement, Reeves told them it would be a mistake to confuse housing policy with sexual politics. "In the city of Cambridge," he recalled, "the majority of voters wanted rent control and I supported that policy. And I don't quite see how someone's sexual orientation when they didn't support the policy was going to make [them] a good person for them to consider." Reeves described an incident during that meeting. A white audience member stood up and shouted, "How dare you come here and try to tell us what to think! We are more oppressed than any people on earth." Reeves lost the endorsement but won the election.

In 1989, when Reeves ran for reelection, a gay organization made plans to find a more openly gay candidate to support because they did not perceive Reeves as sufficiently "out." Reeves won again. Not until he gave a speech clearly identifying himself as gay did the group grudgingly support him. But in the following election, rather than work for Reeves, the group told him they were too busy working for another candidate and that they did not have time for his candidacy. According to Reeves, when he ran for election as an openly gay mayor, the group voted to stay neutral because they said they were more loyal to the heterosexual former mayor, even though she was not seeking reelection. "My sense is that I don't represent their image of something," Reeves suggested to me, attributing their resistance to his being "both black and gay and determined to be it in a way that's authentic to me."

The patronizing attitude of some gay organizations appears also in the issue of AIDS funding. In Washington, D.C., most AIDS cases occur in the African-American population, but the largest recipient of government AIDS-related funds is a predominantly white-run organization, the Whitman-Walker Clinic. The disparity between the demographics of the community and the direction of the funding leaves some wondering if white paternalistic views are determining the fate of blacks living with AIDS. The Whitman-Walker Clinic was founded in the early 1970s as a health service provider for homosexuals. Until recently, the clinic's leadership has been white. When the AIDS epidemic hit, the clinic responded quickly, writing grant proposals and obtaining city contracts to provide education, treatment, and care for people living with the HIV virus and AIDS. From the beginning, no black organizations could provide the same level of quality AIDS-related services that the clinic offered. So each year the city would open up its bidding process and each year Whitman-Walker would again win the contract. Each year, that is, until 1993, when a black organization called United Response to Black America's Needs (UR-BAN) began a successful challenge to Whitman-Walker for a portion of the District's funds for community outreach. A black consulting firm, URBAN advocates for African-American community-based organizations.

Suggesting that the white clinic should not be the prototype for black AIDS service providers, the president of UR-BAN, Alonzo Fair, says, "They create a barrier for blacks that is impossible to get over. The fact that they are a lesbian and gay clinic is a barrier to blacks. When blacks walk in there they're [in] late-stage HIV infection. No early intervention at all is going on in the black community. Not at all," he repeats for emphasis. A former employee of Whitman-Walker, Fair describes the fearful way blacks would approach the clinic as an example of the problem for blacks. "I would see blacks literally pull their hat down, jump out of the car, and run into the clinic to get a test." Reflecting on his public feud with Caitlin Ryan, the city official who administered the funding decision-making process, Fair charges her with assisting in the "systematic racism" he finds in the funding disparity between black and white AIDS service organizations.

However, racism is only "a simplistic explanation for what is happening here in D.C.," responds H. Alexander Robinson, president of the board of directors of the National Task Force on AIDS Prevention, who is also a black gay man living with HIV. He is not responding directly to Fair, but to the assumption that race is behind all funding decisions. Yet Robinson is not willing to let the white gay community off the hook and fears that funding dollars may be "hijacked" by white gay organizations. Robinson takes Fair's argument one step further when he says AIDS service providers should not discriminate based on race *or* sexual orientation. Not only should blacks not be discriminated against by gay clinics, but gays of any color should not be discriminated against by black clinics, Robinson argues. His comment appears to refer to a controversy suggesting that the predominantly black Abundant Life Clinic (a client of URBAN) is homophobic because of its ties to the Nation of Islam.

Not all the racism in the gay community is practiced by whites. Some white homosexuals I spoke with said they were made to feel uncomfortable in black social settings by black gays who sneered or scowled at them. Their feeling of discomfort is all the better for both black and white homosexuals, say some black gays. They argue that white homosexuals should have to learn what black people, gay or straight, experience every day in all-white settings. In the words of one black lesbian: "Every time I walk into a room, when I go to work, when I turn on the TV, I see white. Why shouldn't white people get to know how it feels for a change?"

On a different level, Alexander Robinson offers several possible explanations for the antiwhite sentiment expressed by blacks. In black gay social contexts, "white gay men are seen as predatory because they are there for sexual reasons." Some black lesbians and gays subscribe to the typical I-don't-like-white-people attitude that many blacks feel, Robinson says. Finally, Robinson explains that because many black homosexuals do not identify as gay or are in denial, the presence of whites in social settings acts as a "reminder" that they are among homosexuals. As black lesbian activist Mandy Carter puts it, "I know that there are people in the black community who it wouldn't bother not to see another white person as long as they live, and I know that there are people in the white community who wouldn't care if they saw another person of color as long as they live." She stops, and then, in halting fragments, says, "I think—bottom line—even though we're queer, we can still be racist."

So strong is the tug of racial identification in our culture that it shapes much of who we are and often transcends our other identities, including our sexual orientation. When black people see white lesbians and gays, what many of them see are not brothers and sisters in a movement but, instead, just a different collection of whites, regardless of their sexual orientation. They attach to them all the same baggage they attach to heterosexual white people, including white privilege. Not surprisingly, then, many blacks, both straight and gay, distrust the gay rights movement's leaders and objectives. Many blacks say they fear that formal protection of gay rights will entrench white gay privilege without addressing deeper societal problems, such as racism. Dr. Ron Simmons, for example, says, "White gay males still benefit from white privilege." While expressing distaste for comparison of oppressions, Simmons nevertheless strongly challenges white gay men who claim to need the same protections afforded African Americans. "When you get white gay men saying, 'I'm just as oppressed as you are,' that's bullshit," he says. White gay men enjoy the luxury of being in a position of relative power over black people, gay or straight, according to Simmons.

Similarly, black gay author James Baldwin once told *The Village Voice,* "I think white gay people feel cheated because they were born, in principle, into a society in which they were supposed to be safe. Their reaction seems to me in direct proportion to the sense of feeling cheated of the advantages which accrue to white people in a white society." Baldwin's sentiments seem to reflect the sense among many black lesbians and gays that white gay men, but for their homosexuality, would be quietly enjoying their white male privilege. They speak out only because they feel their privilege is threatened. Unlike blacks, who are seldom raised to think that they are part of a privileged class, white gay men are surprised when they experience prejudice. They become outraged and vocal and consequently lead the fight for gay rights.

The popular view of gay rights as the exclusive property of a particular group reflects not only the dominance of white gay men in the gay movement but also the gay movement's collective failure to address concerns of nongay minorities. If gay leaders were more vocal in their support of affirmative action or race-based civil rights legislation, blacks themselves might be more supportive of gay rights. Some white gays, like Andrew Sullivan, the former editor of *The New Republic* magazine, argue that the gay movement has hitched its wagon to the wrong star and should instead distance itself from the black civil rights struggle. Conservative writer Richard Mohr is even more critical of black-gay coalitions. Citing electoral results and opinion polls, Mohr claims that minorities tend to be "more homophobic than their Anglo middle-class urban counterparts." He borders on racism when he argues in a March 1996 article in *OutNow*, "If it takes twice as much energy to get a black person up to speed on gay issues as it does a white person, then it is doubly inefficient to expend limited gay political resources to solicit the black person's allegiances." Mohr also perpetuates inaccurate stereotypes about black homophobia when he argues that "on average the white person both is more easily converted and has more power with which then to make a difference." With leaders like Mohr in the gay community, it is no surprise that many blacks distrust white lesbians and gays.

Historically, the lesbian and gay movement has not always been supportive of coalitions with the black community and its organizations. In October 1970, after Black Panther leader Huey Newton wrote a conciliatory open letter "to form a working coalition with the Gay liberation" movement, *The Advocate* rejected the offer. Noting the homophobia of the Panthers, the editors of the magazine said the "overwhelming majority of gays, we believe, do not want to destroy this nation and replace it with—well, what are you going to replace it with?"

Given the comments of some gay leaders who oppose coalitions, many blacks are wary of other gay leaders who favor them. Some blacks also disapprove of the white gay community's attempts to appropriate everything that is black without understanding what it means to be black. They see the white gay community as stealing black fashion, music, style, and wit without knowing how black culture has developed. Moreover, many blacks believe that the gay rights movement should re-frain from drawing some comparisons to the black civil rights movement.

As black syndicated columnist Julianne Malveaux wrote in a January 1994 issue of *California Voice,* "Frankly, I don't think the gay community cares whether there are tensions between themselves and African Americans, as long as they amass as much power as they can through city commissions, department leaderships, and other positions. They have no sense of balance or fairness, but they are always crying fairness and ripping off our heroes and movements."

Despite concerns about white gay exploitation, many blacks still demand that the white lesbian and gay community address concerns facing the black community. Dr. Ron Sim-mons typifies the sentiment: "You support people who support you." Many white lesbians and gays apparently miss the con-nection. As the *Washington Blade* reported in February 1996, white gay men interviewed in Norfolk, Virginia, reacted non-chalantly to the news that a serial killer in the area had stran-gled eleven gay men, most of whom were transients and four of whom were black. "We don't have anything to do with people like that," said one white gay man at a gay nightclub. Another responded, "I don't know anybody who knew any of them." Black gay men, on the other hand, "were very much con-cerned," according to the *Blade.* "I don't agree with those who say this is not a gay issue," said Paul Eubanks, a bartender at a black gay club in Norfolk. "It is a gay issue, and in some cases it's a black issue. If the victims were straight white men who worked in so-called respectable jobs, you can be sure they would have solved this by now."

At the doors of white gay nightclubs and other establish-ments, we find the exclusion of African-American lesbians and gay men. Through the lens of white gay photographers Robert Mapplethorpe and Carl Van Vechten, we see the exploitation of black men. In the funding decisions in the battle against AIDS, we find outmoded assumptions about race and sexuality. And in the popular literature, camp, and drag of the white gay male population, we see the gay community's exaggeration of the black image. White gay America is just as prejudiced as the rest of white America, James Baldwin once observed. "The gay world as such is no more prepared to accept black people than anywhere else in society. It's a very hermetically sealed world with very unattractive features, including racism."

As with black homophobia, much of the problem lies in our expectations of oppressed communities. We often expect that oppressed people, including blacks and gays, will not oppress other people. Victims should know better than anyone else the sting of prejudice, we reason. Therefore, just as white lesbians and gays expect blacks to overcome their homophobia, so blacks expect white lesbians and gays to overcome their racism. Perhaps black lesbians and gays experience the disappointment more profoundly because they are often unable to find support for their homosexuality in the black straight community *or* support for their race in the white gay community. The mistake that black homosexuals sometimes make is in assuming that anyone's minority status translates into greater sensitivity about issues beyond their own status.

The black lesbian and gay movement could learn from the black feminist movement's experiences with the white feminist movement. The white-dominated gay and feminist movements—despite their differences from the white, straight male power elite—still benefit from the privilege of race. In her essay "A Black Feminist Critique of Antidiscrimination Law and Politics," Kimberle Crenshaw explains that white feminists "ignore how their own race functions to mitigate some aspects of sexism and, moreover, how it often privileges them over and contributes to the domination of other women."

Before slavery was abolished in the United States, Frederick Douglass recognized that other struggles were connected to the struggle for black liberation. Well before the women's movement took hold in this country, Douglass fought on the front lines as a champion of equal rights for women. In 1848, he traveled to Seneca Falls, New York, for what would become a historic feminist convention. As the delegates debated a controversial resolution to support women's suffrage, Douglass seized the opportunity and spoke in favor of the proposal, providing a political thrust that assured its passage.

Nearly twenty years after Douglass's fateful speech at Seneca Falls, the women's movement found itself divided again. But this time the issue was not women's right to vote but the black man's right to vote. In a December 1865 letter to the editor of the *New York Standard,* white feminist Elizabeth Cady Stanton questioned the idea of extending the franchise to include black men. She asked, "Are we sure that [the black man], once entrenched in all his inalienable rights, may not be an added power to hold us at bay?" Then, in an arguably disingenuous appeal to black women, Stanton asserted that empowering black men with the right to vote made black women's emancipation "but another form of slavery." In fact, she said, "it is better to be the slave of an educated white man, than of a degraded, ignorant black one."

The possibility that the white gay movement might turn on the black community as the early feminist movement turned on the abolition movement causes legitimate concern for some black gay activists. Black homosexuals might ask the same question of the gay movement that Elizabeth Cady Stanton asked about black male suffrage. Are we sure that the white gay man, once entrenched in all his inalienable rights, may not be an added power to hold us at bay? As one black lesbian organizer posed the question, "When the shit hits the fan, whose side are they on?"

In one response to this dilemma, black homosexuals have created their own organizations rather than work through predominantly white lesbian and gay groups. The nation's largest national lesbian and gay organization is the Human Rights Campaign (HRC), and for years Tim McFeeley's name was synonymous with that organization. A few months after he left his position as executive director of HRC, he reflected on the organization's efforts to promote diversity and greater representation of blacks. "I think we've done a good job, and I think it needs to always be examined and the question needs to be raised," McFeeley said. But only moments later, he added, "I think HRC is clearly defined as a white person's organization. HRC will not be as comfortable a place to black gay people as their own."

Even HRC's black staff members have been somewhat disappointed with the organization. Former staffer Mandy Carter, who headed a joint effort between HRC and the National Black Gay & Lesbian Leadership Forum to fight the religious right in the black community, says that HRC "should do a lot more." Wearing pink triangle earrings and sitting in a conference room in HRC's Washington headquarters, Carter sets up her own test for measuring the organization's performance: "When they start getting some [people] of color in the director role, that's the way I'll know whether this group is moving forward." Carter left HRC in November 1995 to lead a grassroots mobilization effort against Senator Jesse Helms's reelection in North Carolina, but she still maintains her ties to the organization and is hopeful that the new executive director, Elizabeth Birch, will improve the organization's diversity. While acknowledging that many black homosexuals distrust white gay organizations, Carter adds, "For me, this is where I want to do my work. I could sit here or either stand outside and point and say you ain't doing whatever, [but] that's not my modus operandi."

For McFeeley, the concerns of the black gay community are "sufficiently different" from those of the white gay community to justify the existence of separate organizations. In fact, his comments echoed the sentiments of several black gay leaders, including Phill Wilson. "I don't think the Balkanization is a problem," Wilson said. "I think, for example, it is a good thing for there to be black lesbian organizations because the skills that those women gain by having a safe space to deal with their women issues and their lesbian issues and their black issues . . . they can then bring to a black gay and lesbian venue."

Wilson's words seem almost indistinguishable from Mc-Feeley's. Listening to a white gay leader make these comments suggests a sense of futility about promoting diversity in white gay organizations. Yet back and forth, I hear Phill Wilson when I listen to Tim McFeeley. "The best thing that HRC could do is to foster and strengthen in any way we can the growth of gay organizations within the African-American community," McFeeley said in January 1995, a nearly identical comment to what Phill Wilson had told me in May 1994.

But while McFeeley supports black lesbian and gay organizations, other lesbians and gays are beginning to raise disturbing questions. Some have asked sarcastically if there should be a National White Gay & Lesbian Leadership Forum to parallel the black organization. "I think that's what the National Gay and Lesbian Task Force is and the Human Rights Campaign," said Wilson. "So I don't know if there should be, but there is." In fact, in numerous professions and fields, black people have created organizations that essentially parallel white organizations from which they have been traditionally excluded, that give them a comfortable and nonoppressive place to address issues of concern to their constituency. Black doctors formed the National Medical Association, black lawyers formed the National Bar Association, and black writers formed the National Association of Black Journalists. As Audre Lorde writes in her book *Sister Outsider* (1984), "Frequently, when speaking with men and white women, I am reminded of how difficult and time-consuming it is to have to reinvent the pencil every time you want to send a message." The question of separatism, she writes, "is by no means simple."

While some lesbians and gays view people-of-color groups dismissively, with sarcastic questions about creating white identity groups, others, like Urvashi Vaid, have raised more serious questions about racial identity politics. Because she sees the various struggles as too connected to be separated, Vaid, in her 1995 book *Virtual Equality,* asks that the gay community seriously address issues concerning people of color. "If gay organizations at the national and state level wrap themselves in the mantle of civil rights language and history, they must take clear stands on the civil rights of blacks, people of color, immigrants, and women," she writes. Calling for gay leaders to take positions on affirmative action, welfare, and economic justice, Vaid rightly concludes that "our use of racial analogies is suspect, coming as it does from a movement deeply splintered over the relevance of racism to the fight against homophobia."

With so many racial divisions in the lesbian and gay community, better relations between blacks and gays will occur only by addressing the black community's concerns honestly. White men, long the leaders of the gay rights movement, must integrate their ranks in order to allay black concerns about promoting white male privilege. Gay leaders and gay organizations must support and be involved in the black civil rights struggle if they are to convince blacks to support civil rights for lesbians and gays. Perhaps most important, white homosexuals must work to eliminate systemic discrimination against black lesbians and gays and recognize the black gay community's unique role as a bridge between the larger gay community and the black community. If the larger gay community really wants the credibility of black support (and some gay leaders do not want this), then the black gay community will be the mechanism for achieving this. If the gay community cannot convince even its black members to support its causes strongly, it will never, on its own, convince the black heterosexual community that gay rights should be a priority.

For a lesbian and gay movement still struggling with where to go and how to get there, these challenges will be daunting. The movement must use its members to play discrete roles in forwarding the race–sexual orientation analogy. White lesbians and gay men need to show their sensitivity to black concerns, while black lesbians and gays must work from the inside to counter the homophobia in the black community.

Already bearing the burden of double discrimination, many black homosexuals believe the white gay leadership should assume responsibility for beginning the dialogue. A comment typical of black lesbian and gay organizers: "I'm ready to work with the white gay community, but first they have to demonstrate they're serious about working with me."

Given the level of distrust between black and white homosexuals, it would be a mistake for white lesbians and gays to act as though their homosexuality somehow inoculated them from such deeply ingrained characteristics of whiteness as racism. When the NLGJA official suggested to me that his group had heard everything it needed to hear about racism, he was indicating an incredibly naive view of the problems within the white gay community. His comments were not entirely surprising, but they were unusual because they were made to someone he could see was black. In the course of conducting interviews, I found that nearly everyone in the politically correct lesbian and gay community knew the right words to say to a black gay man writing about racism and homophobia. But when I was not interviewing, I encountered the everyday biases that one expects but few people admit.

A few white lesbians and gays, like longtime gay rights activist Frank Kameny, have shown their true colors about race relations. In a December 1994 opinion piece in the *Washington Blade,* Kameny argues that the gay rights movement "has always put out the welcome mat" to black gays. "That the invitation has been largely unaccepted until relatively recently is the fault of black Gays not of white Gays," he writes. Kameny ignores the rampant racism in the white gay community and concludes that white heterosexuals "could take lessons from" white homosexuals and that "racism in the white Gay community is miniscule compared with the level of homophobia in the black non-Gay community." Like some other white gay men who focus singlemindedly on gay issues, Kameny asks, "Why should the gay movement take on racism as an equal issue, when the black civil rights movement does not take on homophobia and the concerns of Gay people as being as important as the black civil rights mission?"

In a subsequent issue of the *Blade,* Carol Wayman responds that white lesbians and gay men should not act as "gatekeepers" of the movement. "Instead of trying to fault black Gays, perhaps we white queers should question if we are at the right doors," she writes. Wayman and Barbara Smith suggest that lesbians and gay men become more active in diverse issues involving farm workers, political prisoners, police brutality, racial violence, homelessness, reproductive freedom, and violence against women and children. Writing in a July 1993 article in *The Nation,* Smith says the gay community's unwillingness to address broader issues leads lesbians and gays of color to ask, "Does the gay and lesbian movement want to create a just society for everyone? Or does it only want to eradicate the last little glitch that makes life difficult for privileged (white male) queers?"

The dirty little secret about the homosexual population is that white gay people are just as racist as white straight people. They are not all dyed-in-the-wool, hard-core racists like David Duke. Some, in fact, are quite enlightened. But all white people, whether they be gay or straight, are indoctrinated early on by a racist society that promotes conformity to a narrow norm. Similarly, all black people are indoctrinated in this same racist, homophobic system. To suggest that white gay people are not racist is as ludicrous as suggesting that blacks are not homophobic. Blacks are homophobic and white gays are racist *because* they all develop and live in the same homophobic, racist society. Nevertheless, I have heard too many white lesbians and gays, perhaps clinging to a myth of innocence, maintain that they "don't have a racist bone in [their] body." Many have no close friends who are black, and others socialize only in white environments. Because white is the societal norm, most of these people never question if the few blacks whom they do see represent the vast majority of blacks, straight or gay. They seldom question if there should be more blacks in their church or favorite restaurant or nightclub or circle of friends. To be white and homosexual and not to challenge or question the absence of black lesbians and gays in the culture is itself an element of racism.

The late Marlon Riggs, in his powerful poem "Tongues Untied," may best describe the evolution in attitude of many black homosexuals, and particularly men, in relating to the white lesbian and gay community. He wrote:

In California,
I learned the touch and taste of snow.
Cruising whiteboys, I played out
adolescent dreams deferred.
Patterns of black upon white upon black upon white
mesmerized me. I focused hard, concentrated deep . . .

Tried not to notice
the few images of black
that were most popular:
joke
fetish
cartoon caricature
or disco diva adored
from a distance . . .

Searching, I found something I didn't expect,
something decades of determined assimilation
could not blind me to:

In this great gay mecca,
I was an invisible man, still . . .

CHAPTER SEVEN

Déjà Vu: The Common Language of Racism and Homophobia

"When a man has emerged from slavery," wrote Supreme Court Justice Joseph Bradley, "there must be some stage in the progress of his elevation when he takes the rank of a mere citizen, and ceases to be the *special favorite* of the laws" (emphasis added). So it was that in 1883 the U.S. Supreme Court struck down a post–Civil War law to guarantee blacks access to public facilities. Resurrecting the same argument some hundred years later, in 1995, then Senate Majority Leader Bob Dole admitted, "Slavery was wrong, but should future generations [of whites] have to pay for that [with affirmative action]? Some would say yes. I think it is a tough question." Using a similar argument, Senator Dole opposed President Clinton's plan to allow gays to serve in the military by writing in a letter to the *Washington Times,* "To protect the rights we treasure, we must avoid creating special rights for special groups."

From the moment the Civil War ended in 1865 until the present, America's conservative elite has resisted the inclusion of oppressed groups into their ranks. Still using the same tired, discredited arguments of the nineteenth century, they hardly bother to change the language of their bigotry as their targets change over the years. From Joseph Bradley to Bob Dole, the first line of defense against the civil rights of any group is to label such civil rights as "special rights."

How does it work? The forces of the status quo make deceptively innocent arguments to deny that an oppressed group needs legal protection. "Homosexual activists are running a scam against the American people," claims the Reverend Lou Sheldon of the Traditional Values Coalition. "They want us to believe they don't have the same rights as everyone else. *Do not be deceived, homosexuals are not unprotected!* All citizens enjoy the same protection and rights under the U.S. Constitution."

True enough, the Fourteenth Amendment guarantees "equal protection of the laws" to all citizens, but this tells only half the story. To persuade the public that gay rights laws are unnecessary, Sheldon oversimplifies the protections afforded by the Constitution. The courts have never interpreted the Fourteenth Amendment as *prohibiting* discrimination. Instead, the equal protection clause of the Constitution guides the courts in determining what level of scrutiny to apply when evaluating certain government actions. Because of our nation's history with slavery and segregation, whenever the government classifies or distinguishes people based on race, these classifications are considered "inherently suspect" and the government must articulate a "compelling" interest to defend them. In the most famous example, when state governments segregated schoolchildren by race, the courts held that such government classifications were unconstitutional. This level of judicial review is commonly referred to as "strict scrutiny." This does not mean that all racial classifications violate the law, but does mean that the government must go out of its way to defend them when challenged. Government classifications based on gender (such as an all-male school) require only an "important" government interest to justify them, and this level of judicial review is often referred to as "intermediate scrutiny." Classifications based on sexual orientation, on the other hand, are hardly scrutinized at all. As long as the government has any "rational basis" for a classification, the courts will permit discrimination. Therefore, while it is technically true that the Constitution guarantees to all citizens the equal protection of the laws, the protection afforded for gender and race is much greater than that for sexual orientation.

The equal protection clause did not, on its own, confer specific rights to blacks. The Fourteenth Amendment did not guarantee them the right to vote, to stay in public accommodations, or not to lose a job because of their race. Other laws had to be passed to accomplish these things. Where there are no existing laws, as with sexual orientation, the equal protection clause can be meaningless. Currently, no federal law prohibits discrimination against lesbians and gays in employment, housing, public accommodations, or access to benefits and privileges conferred upon others. Only nine states and the District of Columbia have passed laws barring some form of discrimination against lesbians and gays. In forty-one states—the majority of America—it is still perfectly legal to fire lesbians and gays, deny them a place to stay, or refuse to offer them certain benefits merely because of their sexual orientation. Twenty-four states outlaw sodomy between consenting adults and apply these laws almost exclusively against homosexuals. In nearly half the country, homosexuals are the only people who can be arrested in their bedrooms, carted away from their homes, and taken to jail merely for private, adult consensual behavior.

Even if the Constitution did protect lesbians and gays from government discrimination, it would not prevent private individuals or organizations from discriminating. The Thirteenth Amendment outlawing slavery is the only one of the twenty-six amendments to the Constitution that prohibits both government and private conduct. In contrast, the "equal protection of the laws" guaranteed under the Fourteenth Amendment protects blacks from *government* discrimination, but it leaves employers, landlords, and other nongovernment entities free to discriminate.

When Congress tried to remedy the problem of private discrimination by passing the Civil Rights Act of 1875, the Supreme Court invalidated the law, writing that blacks should be protected "in the ordinary modes by which other men's rights are protected." But there was nothing out of the ordinary about the law the Court invalidated. It merely ensured that blacks could stay in the same inns and public accommodations as whites. In the eyes of Justice Bradley, this meant special rights, but is it possible to imagine African Americans as the "special favorite" of American law in 1883? Had black people fully "emerged from slavery" and its badges of inferiority only eighteen years after the Civil War? Surely, the right of blacks to enjoy public facilities was no more a special privilege than is the right of lesbians and gays to enjoy protection in housing or employment.

Failing to prove that the oppressed group is already protected, opponents of civil rights argue that the existing laws should treat everyone equally. There should be no black or white, straight or gay, they claim. Since we are all just Americans, passing laws designed to benefit one group or another would constitute "special rights" for that group. This argument appeals to our most cherished notion—equality—but to say that everyone will be treated equally is to ignore the fact that some people are more in need of protection than others. Although most Americans do not need to worry that they will lose their jobs because of their sexual orientation, lesbians and gays do fear this because they are usually unprotected in the workplace. It is not enough to say that the laws are the same for everyone when there are no laws to protect anyone who suffers. As the U.S. Supreme Court noted in its 1971 decision *Jenness v. Fortson,* "Sometimes the greatest discrimination can lie in treating things that are different as though they were exactly alike." Although we might all hope for a more equitable society, we know it does not now exist. Without first correcting existing imbalances, equal-treatment requirements freeze and reinforce the inequities of the status quo.

The defenders of the status quo misread history by suggesting that measures to remedy inequality are morally indistinguishable from the inequality itself, and they neglect to consider the structural advantages in place after generations of inequity. Instead, each time a new civil rights law is proposed, they defend as adequate and honorable the earlier law which they previously opposed.

Since most current civil rights laws do not protect lesbians and gays, new laws that include sexual orientation should not be considered as promoting special rights. Some civil rights laws that benefit African Americans, such as minority set-aside programs, can be interpreted as giving "preferences" to blacks. Few people deny that such policies do prefer blacks over others, so instead, what the defenders of minority set-asides do is admit the preference but make a case for its necessity. With civil rights for lesbians and gays, however, no one—not even the most radical gay rights activists—argues for quotas or set-asides or preferences. Most of the major legislative battles over gay rights have merely involved the right of homosexuals not to be discriminated against for who they are. Under no stretch of the imagination could we consider this basic right to be the equivalent of the policies of minority set-asides.

To bolster their argument that everyone should be treated

equally, conservatives contend that because of "special rights" laws and preferences, minorities are actually better off than nonminorities today. Conservatives use the phrase "reverse discrimination" to explain their opposition to new civil rights measures. They see a "zero-sum conflict" in society where each group has a certain number of points and where adding points to any one group will automatically deduct points from other groups. However the points are reapportioned, the sum of the difference must equal zero. If two points are given to blacks, then two points must be taken away from whites. If one point is given to homosexuals, then one point must be taken from heterosexuals.

Using this logic, conservative writer Ben Wattenberg complained in a May 1993 newspaper column, "Many deserving white males have been kept out of government." Never mind the fact that the President, Vice President, Speaker of the House, and Senate Majority Leader have always been white men. Never mind also that white men comprise only a third of the population yet make up 80 percent of Congress, 80 percent of tenured university faculty, 90 percent of the Senate, and 92 percent of the Forbes 400.

To reclaim their innocence, white men have begun to cast themselves in the role of victim in America's ongoing morality play about justice. Not long after civil rights laws began to be enforced against race discrimination, white men began to challenge employer hiring decisions, judicially imposed consent decrees, and affirmative action school admissions policies. The most famous case was the U.S. Supreme Court's 1978 *Bakke* decision, in which a white man successfully challenged his denial of admission to the medical school at the University of California at Davis. The Wattenberg/Bakke line of reasoning assumes that every white person who is qualified for a position should be entitled to one and that nonwhites who earn positions are often unqualified. When the privileges of race are stripped from them, the ruling class begins to see itself as oppressed.

Conservatives apply the same zero-sum logic to the question of gay rights. Bob Dole's warning against "special rights" for lesbians and gays was based on the need to "protect the rights we treasure." From Senator Dole's perspective, equal rights for homosexuals threaten the rights of heterosexuals. Many conservatives argue that gays, like blacks, are actually better off than others in society. Some, such as *Washington Times* columnist Don Feder, have complained that because of liberal censorship "a conscientious Christian or Jew is far more likely to feel uncomfortable in the politically correct workplace of the '90s than the average homosexual." Like Wattenberg, Feder seems to argue that the real oppressed groups are those adversely affected by societal changes designed to accommodate minorities. Feder's claim about gays, like Wattenberg's remarks about blacks, seems unsupported by the evidence. After all, how often does someone lose her job because of her religion? Are large numbers of Christians really being harassed in the workplace or fired from their jobs, as lesbians and gays are? Those who are discriminated against because of their religion at least enjoy the protection of the laws, unlike lesbians and gays. If what makes these religious workers uncomfortable is being challenged by others for their homophobic remarks, then perhaps they should be made to feel uncomfortable. But so, too, should lesbians and gays who make antireligious slurs. The workplace, after all, should not be a firing range for the slings and arrows of prejudice.

Gay rights opponents want to prove not only that homosexuals are better off socially than Christians but that they are better off economically than most heterosexuals. Don Feder claims there is not "a shred of evidence of economic deprivation to support discrimination claims." To fine-tune his point, he twists the words of homosexuals themselves to show that discrimination is not a problem, as, for example, when he quotes gay business columnist Ed Mickens as saying, "Today, it's rare that anyone gets fired just for being gay." Feder and other opponents of gay rights also cite the gay community's own advertising surveys to suggest that homosexuals need no protection because they are typically wealthier than the general population. Black Republican Joe Rogers cites a 1991 *Wall Street Journal* article to bolster his position that "average income per gay household well exceeds $55,000 per year" and that "on average, homosexuals of all races rank as some of the best educated and most affluent people in the country." To be fair, his assertions are not drawn from thin air. A look at the lesbian and gay media would seem to support Rogers. For example, the National Gay Newspaper Guild openly claims that it can help advertisers target "some of the most affluent, well-educated and brand loyal consumers in the country." The Guild's promotional ads even quote *The Wall Street Journal*'s description of the homosexual population as "the most potentially profitable, untapped market in the U.S. today."

These numbers tell us more about advertising hype than they do about homosexuality. Carlos Stelmach, editor of the gay magazine *10 Percent,* admitted to San Francisco's *Bay Area Reporter* that "on the advertising side we like to be able to say that we [homosexuals] have a lot of money to spend." Two reputable studies contradict the assertion that lesbians and gays earn more than heterosexuals. A 1994 Yankelovich study published in the *Bay Area Reporter* found gay men had median household incomes $2,000 a year less than their heterosexual male counterparts and that the median income for lesbian households was $400 a year less than the amount for straight women. Another 1994 study, published by University of Maryland professor Lee Badgett, found that gay men earn 11 to 27 percent less than their nongay counterparts, according to *The Wall Street Journal.* But none of the estimates of gay wealth by either side is entirely reliable given the difficulty in identifying the gay population and the likelihood that survey results underrepresent lesbians and gays of color, who tend to be less affluent than their white counterparts.

For different reasons, gay publications and antigay conservatives both inflate the wealth of gay consumers. Yet the conservatives who are so quick to quote the gay media about the affluence of its patrons fail to cite the same media's claims about the *size* of the gay population. At least the gay media is consistent in its intent to enlarge the significance of the gay community, while the conservatives decide selectively which evidence to employ. Relying on the same data, the antigay forces and the National Gay Newspaper Guild ultimately reach different conclusions. The antigay troops conclude that homosexuals are not victims of prejudice. The Guild, on the other hand, only wants to sell advertising, even if the methods used to reach that goal conflict with the broader message of the lesbian and gay movement.

Blacks who buy into this antigay economic logic should know that the same brand of skewed statistics used to drum up gay advertising could be used to show that African Americans are not oppressed. Just as gay publishers want to sell advertising, so too do black publishers. Those seeking advertising dollars claim that African Americans are "the leading purchasers of newspapers . . . [who] spend billions of dollars in the major consumer categories." A July 1994 press release from the Journal Newspapers in Pasadena, California, cited statistics that "African Americans spend $5.2 billion on new cars and trucks, $3.9 billion on personal care products and services, $3.3 billion on travel and lodging, $2.5 billion on consumer electronics, $2.5 billion on tobacco products, $1.7 billion on alcoholic beverages, and $1.2 billion on entertainment." With such an impressive display of black economic power, would conservatives claim that blacks no longer need civil rights? Yes. In fact, many conservatives now challenge blacks in their assertions about racism with statistics about economics and class. Pointing to multimillionaires such as Bill Cosby, the late Reginald Lewis, and Oprah Winfrey, these conservatives claim that many blacks actually have more economic power than many poorer whites. Critiquing the U.S. Small Business Administration's programs to aid minority businesses, *The Wall Street Journal* asked in 1994, "Can a minority entrepreneur worth

$64 million be truly disadvantaged?" Ironically, the same conservatives who believe that blacks are already privileged expect black people to join forces with them to oppose gay rights because gays are privileged.

Because economic success does not insulate them from prejudice, minorities in all socioeconomic categories benefit from antidiscrimination laws. American civil rights principles do not hinge on economic status. If economics were the touchstone, then civil rights laws would have been tailored toward the poorer blacks and excluded the black middle class. But instead, all African Americans enjoy the law's protection, regardless of their income.

The bipartisan Glass Ceiling Commission recently reported that "large numbers of minorities and women of all races and ethnicities are nowhere near the front door of corporate America" and found that all minority groups are still "disproportionately represented" among the working poor. However, by focusing attention on a few high-profile examples of "reverse discrimination," conservatives have succeeded in persuading Americans to ignore the widespread socioeconomic disparities that disempower nonwhites, women, and minorities. Thus, in our increasingly fragile world economy, any progress for blacks or gays becomes an easy scapegoat to explain the problems of everyone else.

The opponents of gay rights know that Americans like to think of themselves as fair-minded people. As the *New York Times* reported in December 1994, polls show that most Americans oppose discrimination against homosexuals. But the same polls also show that most people believe gay Americans are already protected. African Americans are equally uninformed. According to a recent poll conducted by Democratic pollster Celinda Lake, 62 percent of blacks did not know that lesbians and gays are unprotected by civil rights laws. Relying on this misimpression, an African-American heterosexual woman in Colorado admitted to me that she had voted in favor of a statewide antigay ballot initiative because she thought that gays were already protected by the law. For the antigay forces to succeed, Americans cannot be allowed to learn that discrimination against lesbians and gays is still perfectly legal and widely practiced. The radical right must distract Americans from such knowledge and convince them that lesbians and gays have sinister objectives.

When all else fails, the forces of the status quo attempt to divide oppressed groups against each other, and blacks and gays have become perfect pawns in this plot. The first step is to contrast the oppression of blacks with that of lesbians and gays. For example, conservative Don Feder writes, "As a group, homosexuals have never been subjected to official segregation, prevented from voting or denied access to public accommodations." Similarly, Joe Rogers makes the point that "no group in America, save Native Americans, can claim comparison to the unfortunate, aching and miserable experience of slavery and segregation suffered by African Americans." While these claims may be true, they miss the point entirely. What difference does it matter that homosexuals have not suffered exactly the type of discrimination that blacks have suffered? Neither women, Latinos, and Jews nor people with disabilities have experienced slavery in this country, but today they are all protected by American law. The basis of legal protection is not that a group must suffer exactly the same oppression as any other group, but merely that no group should be treated unfairly.

Once the oppressions are contrasted, the next step is to convince blacks that their own civil rights are threatened or cheapened by civil rights for lesbians and gays. In a July 1994 press release from the Traditional Values Coalition, the Reverend Lou Sheldon was careful to push as many sensitive buttons as possible to alarm African Americans about gay rights. If the Employment Non-Discrimination Act (ENDA) were passed, Sheldon warned, "homosexuals, bisexuals, etc., would be given the same 'minority status' as people of minority races." To reinforce his point, Sheldon added, "In the eyes of the law, one's sexual orientation would be equal to someone else's skin color."

By such statements, Sheldon fans the flames of societal prejudice by suggesting that blacks should be offended by the comparison to homosexuals. But what would be the danger if lesbians and gays were protected by the law just as African Americans are? Sheldon also misstates the effect of the bill on existing law. The law does not create a "minority status," as Sheldon suggests. Although he cautions that race and sexual orientation would become equal, this comparison is legally meaningless and false. The passage of ENDA would not change the level of judicial scrutiny applied to race or sexual orientation. Even with ENDA, governments could make all sorts of constitutionally permissible distinctions based on sexual orientation that would deprive lesbians and gays of certain benefits. It is hard to imagine, but Sheldon somehow does, that this set of affairs would equate blackness with homosexuality.

Sheldon appeals to the black community's ignorance and fear, arguing that ENDA was designed to "force Americans into accepting homosexuality as an acceptable lifestyle or face punishment." Not surprisingly, the act does nothing of the sort; in fact, compared to other laws such as the sweeping Civil Rights Act of 1964, ENDA is quite modest. It prohibits antigay discrimination in employment, but would allow such discrimination to continue in housing, public accommodations, government benefits, and numerous other areas. The bill exempts small businesses, does not apply to domestic partner benefits, prohibits quotas and preferential treatment, does not apply to the military, and would not apply retroactively. Like Title VII of the 1964 law, ENDA would not apply to religious organizations; but unlike Title VII, it also would not allow litigants to prove discrimination unless they proved actual disparate *treatment* rather than permitting statistical evidence that employment practices had a disparate *impact*. Sheldon's claim that the bill is designed to force Americans to accept homosexuality distorts the extremely limited scope of this legislation.

The similarity of Sheldon's argument to the anti–civil rights arguments gives us some indication of the real agenda behind the antigay rights movement. In 1964, Representative Thomas Abernethy of Mississippi objected to the Civil Rights Act, arguing, "If [the black man] demands the right to be hired he has to recognize somebody else's right not to hire him." Similarly, Senator John Tower of Texas complained that the 1964 law "would attempt to deny to millions of employers and employees any freedom to speak or to act on the basis of their religious convictions or their deep-rooted preferences for associating or not associating with certain classifications of people." The complaints ring as loudly today against homosexuals as they did yesterday against African Americans.

Another argument used to support discrimination emphasizes the importance of traditional values. In the 1986 case *Bowers v. Hardwick,* appealing to the "millennia of moral teaching," Chief Justice Warren Burger invoked traditional values to support his opinion, concurring with the majority, which upheld the state of Georgia's antisodomy law. The Supreme Court reasoned that since sodomy had been a criminal offense in all the original thirteen states when the Bill of Rights was ratified and had been forbidden by all but five of the states when the Fourteenth Amendment was passed, it would be "facetious" to claim that sodomy rights were "deeply rooted in this nation's history and tradition." What makes this argument so problematic is that it answers prescriptive questions with descriptive analyses. In other words, it answers *what should be* by describing *what is,* thus never probing deep enough to get to the question of whether *what is* actually *should be.*

The Court's emphasis on yesterday to determine our rights today raises troubling reminders of the notorious 1857 Dred Scott decision. In the Dred Scott case, the Court ruled that Scott, a former slave, could not be considered a citizen of the state of Missouri. As in *Bowers,* the *Scott* Court refused even to address the question of what the law should be. "It is not the province of the court to decide upon the justice or injustice, the policy or impolicy, of these laws," the decision read. Instead, the Court relied heavily on the past, explaining that when the country was founded, blacks "had for more than a century before been regarded as beings of an inferior order, and altogether unfit to associate with the white race . . . and so far inferior, that they had no rights which the white man was bound to respect." Citing the Declaration of Independence, the *Scott* Court said "it is too clear for dispute, that the enslaved African race were not intended to be included."

The framers of the Constitution clearly did not include blacks or gays in their vision of freedom, but this does not mean that all future generations of Americans must be guided by those same principles. In fact, American courts have learned to look beyond the intent of the nation's founders in determining racial justice. When the Bill of Rights was ratified in 1791, many states segregated blacks from whites in public places, and many prohibited blacks and whites from marrying each other. These restrictions endured nearly a hundred years after the "equal protection" clause of the Fourteenth Amendment took effect in 1868. Using the logic of the *Bowers* Court, it would have been "facetious" for blacks to argue that the right to marry outside their race or walk through desegregated facilities had been deeply rooted in history and tradition. Nevertheless, the Supreme Court's 1954 *Brown v. Board of Education* decision struck down laws that segregated public schools, while in 1967, the Court's decision in *Loving v. Virginia* held unconstitutional laws prohibiting blacks and whites from marrying each other. In *Brown,* Chief Justice Warren, writing for a unanimous Court, limited the significance of history in deciding modern cases. He wrote, "We cannot turn the clock back to 1868 when the [Fourteenth] Amendment was adopted, or even to 1896 when *Plessy* was written. We must consider public education in the light of its full development and its present place in American life throughout the Nation." Similarly, in

Loving, the Court said that although historical sources "cast some light" on the intent of those who wrote the Fourteenth Amendment, the framers' intent is "not sufficient to resolve the problem." The Court recognized that the ignorance and prejudices of the past should not dictate the law of the present. In stark contrast, the *Bowers* Court was content to rely upon the will of the nation's founders, even though the men who drafted the Constitution in the eighteenth century could know very little about sexual orientation, since the concept did not even exist until a century later.

Relying on definitions from the past to resolve the problems of the present often requires circular reasoning. For example, in the *Loving* case, the state of Virginia argued that it could outlaw marriages between blacks and whites because marriages between blacks and whites were not marriages. And why were they not marriages? Because Virginia law said they were not. Similarly, in *Singer v. Hara,* a Washington state court found that marriages between two people of the same sex were not marriages *because* marriage was defined as "the legal union of one man and one woman." The court made no attempt to justify the definition in light of the gay couple's legal challenge. Instead, the court repeated, "the relationship proposed by the appellants does not authorize the issuance of a marriage license because what they propose is not a marriage." The reference to the traditional definition of marriage missed the point because the very issue in *Singer* was not whether marriage *had* been defined by the state to preclude two men or two women from marrying, when clearly it had. The real issue, however, was whether such an exclusive definition was constitutional or legally justifiable.

The court seemed to suggest that the traditional definition of marriage was so universal and long-established that it need not be fully demonstrated or proven by the court. But the court's attempt to imply that marriage had always consisted of a bond between a man and a woman is still subject to some question. As John Boswell writes in his landmark book *Christianity, Social Tolerance, and Homosexuality* (1981), "Half-truths are more misleading than whole lies, and the historian's greatest difficulties are presented by slight twists of meaning in translations which appear to be complete and frank." In a subsequent book, *Same-Sex Unions in Premodern Europe* (1994), Boswell challenges the historians' traditional understanding that heterosexual marriage had always been licensed and homosexual marriage prohibited. Explaining that attitudes toward homosexuality shifted from toleration to rejection during the Middle Ages, Boswell cites an ancient Hittite law that apparently regulated the conditions of homosexual marriage, the recorded existence of hundreds of gay marriages in ancient Rome, and other evidence indicating that gay marriages were far more widespread in both ancient and early Christian societies than is now widely believed.

To rely on history without critically examining it is no way to run a courtroom, but this type of logic is used commonly when we discuss issues of sexual orientation. Chief Justice Burger, writing in the *Bowers* decision, could hardly contain his contempt for homosexuals as he described the historic perception of sodomy as "an offense of 'deeper malignity' than rape, an heinous act' the very mention of which is a disgrace to human nature . . ." Burger's argument might be reduced to the following question: No one has ever liked homosexuals, so why should we? But to continue an injustice toward lesbians and gays merely because of a history of opprobrium makes as much sense as outlawing interracial marriage because of the tragedy of Othello and Desdemona. The *Loving* Court realized this, but the *Singer* court did not. The telling difference is that *Loving* was a case about race, while *Singer* was a case about sexual orientation.

The contrast between the results in the two cases is most clear when we compare the actual language the two states used to defend their systems of marriage. In *Singer,* the state of

Washington claimed that its marriage restrictions did not constitute gender discrimination because the restriction applied both to men and women. The court explained:

> [T]he state points out that all same-sex marriages are deemed illegal by the state, and therefore argues that there is no violation of the ERA so long as marriage licenses are denied equally to both male and female pairs.

This argument echoes the argument the state of Virginia made to defend its antimiscegenation statute years before. In *Loving,* the Supreme Court wrote:

> [T]he State contends that, because its miscegenation statutes punish equally both the white and the Negro participants in an interracial marriage, these statutes, despite their reliance on racial classifications, do not constitute an invidious discrimination based upon race.

Washington and Virginia each argued that their marriage restrictions were fair because they did not single out a protected group (women in Washington and blacks in Virginia) for discrimination. Instead, they argued, the laws applied equally to all people. Women as well as men were restricted from same-sex marriages in Washington, and blacks as well as whites were restricted from interracial marriages in Virginia.

Both states missed the point that marriage is a legal fiction which can be modified at will by the state. To the extent that the state closes off the options for two adults who want to join themselves in marriage, it *chooses* the types of relationships it wants to sanction. The Supreme Court understood this when it rejected Virginia's argument by finding that the miscegenation law was "repugnant" to the Constitution "even assuming an even-handed state purpose to protect the 'integrity' of *all* races." On the other hand, the *Singer* court concluded that "the societal values which are involved in this area must be left to the examination of the legislature." The *Loving* Court adopted a broad and activist view of the role of the judiciary that challenges and pushes societal values toward justice, but even with this precedent to stand on, the *Singer* court took a narrower view of judicial power and refused even to question societal values.

The shallow reasoning used by the *Singer* court and its unwillingness to probe deeper questions of right and wrong demonstrate that lesbian and gay concerns are as easily dismissed by the courts today as African Americans' concerns were dismissed by the Supreme Court in the Dred Scott case. Using the flimsiest of arguments to rationalize their hatred of gays or blacks, the ruling class teaches both groups that their concerns are not even worthy of serious response.

Our society also devalues the concerns of the oppressed by expecting a minority to sacrifice basic human rights to the will of the majority. The right to earn a living, participate in the political process, and serve in the military have all been circumscribed by the prejudices and convenience of the majority. For instance, although most Americans believe homosexuals should be hired as salespersons, only 44 percent think they should be hired as clergy, only 42 percent accept them as elementary school teachers, and only 47 percent accept them as high school teachers, according to a 1989 Gallup Poll. Lesbians and gay men are thought to pose a special risk to society when they take on certain responsibilities. As schoolteachers, lesbians and gays threaten to disrupt the orderly workings of the school, molest schoolkids, recruit them to homosexuality, and teach them that homosexuality is normal. In Tacoma, Washington, a federal court found the complaints of one student and three teachers were sufficient grounds for school administrators to determine that a gay teacher's continued presence would "create problems." As soldiers or intelligence officers, lesbians and gays are perceived as a threat in that they may engage in sexual activity or disrupt the esprit de corps of the troops, as a federal court said in *Ben-Shalom v. Marsh,* or be blackmailed because of their homosexuality, an argument made in the 1990 case *High Tech Gays v. Defense Ind. Sec. Clearance Office.*

In 1987, the New Hampshire Supreme Court upheld the constitutionality of a legislative bill that barred lesbians and gays from adoption of children and from foster care "to eliminate the 'social and psychological complexities' which living in a homosexual environment could produce in such children." Similarly, a 1986 Arizona appeals court upheld a lower court decision that found a bisexual man "nonacceptable" to adopt children because the environment created for the children would be "inimical to the natural family." In 1994, Virginia courts stripped Sharon Bottoms of her natural-born son because of her homosexuality and openly lesbian relationship. The same arguments about disrupting a child's normal life are used by anti-integrationists opposed to interracial parents. But in the case of *Palmore v. Sidotti,* the Supreme Court rejected the claim that a white child could be stripped from its white, divorced mother because she remarried a black man. The Court admitted the "risk that a child living with a stepparent of a different race may be subject to a variety of pressures and stresses not present if the child were living with parents of the same racial or ethnic origin." But in spite of the pressures, the Court concluded that removal of the child for these reasons would be unconstitutional. "The Constitution cannot control such prejudices but neither can it tolerate them," the Court said. "Private biases may be outside the reach of the law, but the law cannot, directly or indirectly, give them effect." What the Court seemed to suggest was that racial prejudice, and not their parents interracial marriage, was the source of the problem for the child. Using the same logic, we can conclude that antigay prejudice, and not her mother's lesbian relationship, is the real danger facing the child of Sharon Bottoms.

The preferences of the majority usually do not justify the trampling of the rights of a minority. In 1982, for example, the courts rejected an argument from Continental Airlines that its passengers preferred thin female flight attendants as a justification for its hiring decisions. In the political process, Congress in 1965 prohibited states from imposing ballot-access restrictions that diluted black votes. Thirty years later, however, leaders of the religious right placed measures on the ballot in a dozen states that would eliminate the few existing laws that prohibit sexual orientation discrimination. As for the military, President Harry Truman ended segregation of the armed forces with a 1941 executive order that said "the democratic way of life within the Nation can be defended successfully only with the help and support of all groups within its borders." Two years later, the military decided that lesbians and gays need not apply.

The arguments against gays in the military provide one of the clearest examples of the common language of racism and homophobia, and the logic in each argument is flawed. As far back as the Civil War, generals "feared that the presence of black soldiers in the army would create a disharmony and drive away white volunteers," according to Kenneth Karst. In a 1991 *UCLA Law Review* article on "The Pursuit of Manhood and the Desegregation of the Armed Forces," Karst explains that black manhood "suggested a new and disquieting form of rivalry, and so the Union cause had to be 'a white man's war.'"

An "internal memorandum" from the Army surgeon general, leaked to the *Washington Times* in May 1993, found that "open integration of homosexuals into the military will increase the likelihood of bringing in members of the group with the very highest risk of acquiring HIV: male homosexuals." Similarly, in 1948, Senator Richard Russell opposed integrating blacks in the military because "the incidence of syphilis, gonorrhea, chancre and all other veneral diseases is appallingly higher among the members of the Negro race than among members of the white race." Both arguments would unfairly exclude a whole group of people merely because some of them had diseases. In addition, since homosexuals already serve in the military, the argument about HIV fails to explain why allowing gay men to serve openly will suddenly increase the likelihood that they will be infected. A better policy would be to test all soldiers and treat those with diseases rather than excluding and stigmatizing whole groups.

In the 1990s, Senator Dan Coats argues that lesbians and gays will create problems of sexual attraction in the military. He and other supporters of the gay ban seem to fear that homosexuals will force themselves on other soldiers. A similar concern prompted Senator Theodore Bilbo in the 1940s to complain that "the only thing in which [black soldiers] are interested is the social relations. They want white wives, they want to sit down at the white man's table, they want to sleep in his bed." Each argument assumes that the members of the despised group are unable to control their sexual drives. Perhaps more offensively, the arguments assume that heterosexuals and whites are the envy of all others. Lawrence Korb, former assistant secretary of defense in the Reagan administration, contradicted this argument when he testified to Congress in March 1993. "There's a body of evidence that shows that not every gay man is attracted to every other man, or the same for women," he said.

Opponents of the gay ban argue that lesbians and gays will introduce immorality into the forces. In the 1990s, Brigadier General Jim Hutchens warns, "Requiring those whose religious and moral teaching unequivocally opposes homosexuality to serve with practicing homosexuals is to be cynically insensitive." Likewise, in the 1940s, Representative Carter Manasco of Alabama quoted an article in the *Alabama Baptist* to show that blacks did not belong with whites in the military because "purity of race is a gift of God." Both comments miss the point made by Dr. David Marlowe, a military psychiatrist, at a 1993 congressional hearing. The whole principle of the military, he said, is "to demonstrate to young people who come in from the highly individualistic, self-serving society we live in [that] their survival, success and achievement is profoundly bound up in their relationships with and their interdependence with the other members of the group."

General Colin Powell warns against using the military for social experimentation by allowing gays to serve openly. A similar point was made by General Omar Bradley in 1948 when he said that "the Army is not out to make any social reforms." Appealing to public opinion, General Bradley said the Army would change its policy only "when the nation as a whole changes it." The military may not be the perfect place for social reform, but in our system of government, the military's biases must bend to the needs of the public, and not the other way around.

As all the various arguments have been discredited over time, the supporters of the gay ban, like the supporters of racial segregation, resorted to arguing for the will of the majority to defend the continued discrimination against homosexuals in the military. In the 1940s, two Army studies showed that more than 80 percent of white soldiers opposed racial integration, while in the 1990s, 74 percent of enlisted personnel oppose lifting the ban on homosexuals in the military. Hiding behind the amorphous, catch-all phrase of "unit cohesion," supporters of the gay ban argue that lesbians and gays serving openly would make other soldiers feel uncomfortable. Senator Sam Nunn, a supporter of the gay ban, even conducted field hearings of the Armed Services Committee (which he chaired) on board a navy submarine to illustrate the crowded living conditions of the troops. "They are living in close quarters and don't have any place to get away from each other," Senator Nunn observed. Noting that "there is no more intimate relationship known to men than that of enlisted men serving together at the squad level," Senator Russell used this observation in 1948 to defend the segregation of blacks.

The most clever "majority will" argument appears to be based on the interest of the minority, "for their own good." For example, a Marine Corps major has warned that lifting the ban on gays in the military would "cause unnecessary deaths [of gay soldiers] in combat." In another instance, Marine Colonel Fred Peck, shortly after learning that his twenty-four-year-old son was gay, testified to Congress, "I've spent twenty-seven years of my life in the military, and I know what it would be like for him if he went in. And it would be hell. I would be very fearful that his life would be in jeopardy from his own troops." What these comments indicate is not a failure of the homosexual soldiers, but a failure of the military's own system of discipline and behavior. Just as white soldiers threatened not to take orders from black soldiers, heterosexual soldiers today threaten not to take orders from homosexual officers. "The young officers who attempt to explain how homosexuality is an 'alternate' lifestyle instead of a deviate lifestyle will quickly lose the respect of the Marines and a bit of their own honor in the process," wrote Major Arthur Corbett in the January 1993 issue of the *Marine Corps Gazette*. Former Arizona senator Barry Goldwater, a conservative Republican, doubts this will happen. In a 1993 op-ed piece in the *Washington Post,* Goldwater wrote, "The military didn't want blacks in integrated units, or women, and now it doesn't want gays. Well, a soldier may not like every order, or every member of his or her unit, but a good soldier will always follow orders—and, in time, respect those who get the job done."

Over time, some views about lesbians and gay men might change if they are allowed to serve openly in the military. The same arguments used to deny blacks full entry into the armed forces did not finally prevent the military from achieving a more impressive record at diversity than has most of society. "In the last two decades the military has achieved notable improvements in racial harmony by devoting time, energy and money to the vexing problem of race relations," the *New York Times* reported in April 1995. With a similar investment of energy, surely the military's code of discipline could overcome any threat to unit cohesion.

When they are asked about the comparison between gays in the military and the integration of blacks in the military, the facile, dismissive response of the gay ban supporters provides another example of how the concerns of lesbians and gays are often not taken seriously. "Racial injustice and discrimination are indefensible. Exclusion of gays is different," wrote Bernard Trainor and Eric Chase in a March 1993 op-ed piece for the *New York Times.* They do not tell us why the two are different, even though the very words of the arguments sound exactly the same. Instead, we are simply expected to trust them. Likewise, Senator Strom Thurmond gave a two-word response when asked by the Associated Press (AP) in 1993 about the similarities between the gay ban and the segregation of black soldiers: "No comparison." Thurmond, however, provides a living reminder that the same people who oppose civil rights for lesbians and gays today opposed civil rights for African Americans years ago. As the governor of South Carolina forty-five years ago, Thurmond was an outspoken opponent of ending racial segregation in the armed forces, the AP reported. So why should we believe that Thurmond now appreciates the principle of equal opportunity in the military? According to Thurmond, because General Powell, the first black chairman of the Joint Chiefs of Staff, agrees with him.

Although most of the arguments used against blacks in the military have been discredited, the same words have not been discredited when used to oppress lesbians and gays. As Moritz Goldstein wrote in *Deutsch-jüdischer Parnass,* "We can easily reduce our detractors to absurdity and show them their hostility is groundless. But what does this prove? That their hatred is *real.* When every slander has been rebutted, every misconception cleared up, every false opinion about us overcome, intolerance itself will remain finally irrefutable." Just as the Jews learned about the Nazis, homosexuals and blacks should learn that the prejudice of their oppressors is often irrational. We should not assume that reason will always persuade our enemies to understand us, and by acknowledging this fact, we might learn to overcome the fear and frustration of our failure. Appeals to reason or to the nature of the universe have been used throughout history to enshrine existing hierarchies as proper and inevitable," writes Harvard professor Stephen Jay Gould. "The hierarchies rarely endure for more than a few generations, but the arguments, refurbished for the next round of social institutions, cycle endlessly." Remarkably, the forces of the status quo are able to perpetuate existing hierarchies by using the same failed arguments against different groups. If the arguments against integrating blacks into the military made no sense, they make even less sense for gays, who, unlike blacks in the 1940s, are already integrated and serving in the military. In 1989, the Pentagon itself estimated that nearly 200,000 lesbians and gay men were in the armed forces.

The emphasis on "majority will" arguments in the 1940s and again in the 1990s indicates the failure of arguments questioning the *ability* of black soldiers or gay soldiers. No one suggests that lesbians and gays are incapable, or undisciplined, or insubordinate. Instead, the whole argument for the ban now rests on the preference of the heterosexual soldiers not to serve with homosexuals. It is heterosexuals and not homosexuals, we are told, who will become incapable, undisciplined, or insubordinate merely because of the knowledge that homosexuals will be permitted to serve openly. General Colin Powell stressed the "majority will" argument when he said, "I've got to consider what you say to a youngster who might come and say, . . . 'General, in the most private of my accommodations, I prefer to have heterosexuals around me than homosexuals.'" Senator Carol Moseley Braun, the first black woman in the U.S. Senate, replied, "This is what you say to that youngster, General Powell. Tell him that the greatest danger he faces is not his private accommodations. It is from the forces of hate and fear in this country that forty years ago would have denied to you [General Powell] the opportunity to lead . . . Wish him a long and distinguished career in the service, and tell him that by the end of his forty years in uniform you hope he will have seen as many changes for the better in our military and the imperfect society it defends as you have in yours."

CHAPTER EIGHT

One More River to Cross

Traveling in a direct path from Cairo, Egypt, at the northern end of Africa, a thousand miles south to Khartoum, the capital of Sudan, it is possible to cross the Nile River four times. The river then snakes along various paths into Ethiopia and Uganda, stretching out for another three thousand miles from Khartoum. To some, these may seem to be many different rivers. Instead, they are all part of the same waterway, the world's longest river—the Nile.

   Traveling through human history from the earliest tribal and ethnic warfare to the present, it is possible to cross a river many times. From the ethnocentrism of nationalism to the anti-Semitism of the Inquisition to the racism of American slavery, the river breaks off into the tributaries of sexism, xenophobia, and homophobia. Some imagine these currents to be separate bodies of water, but they are all the same. They are all a part of the river called prejudice. Like the Nile, it is deceptive, taking on many different shapes, and it naturally appears different at various places along its vast expanse. At some points it is deep and wide and forbidding, while at other points it is not as intimidating. But all of us, black and white, straight and gay, must cross this river to survive.

If current trends continue, homophobia will not be the last acceptable prejudice but, rather, the most currently acceptable one, and even this dubious distinction is being challenged by the resurgence of open racism and xenophobia. The words of the Negro spiritual called "One More River" do not necessarily say that the river to be crossed will be the last river to cross. Instead, they suggest that the river may be merely the next in a series of rivers to cross. Whether homophobia becomes the last river and not just one more river depends on all of us.

Many Americans would have us believe that homophobia and heterosexism do not threaten America's commitment to justice in the way that racism did and still does. Either they do not concern themselves with homophobia or they unapologetically practice it themselves. Many African Americans are part of this group. By critically examining racism and distinguishing it from homophobia, they conclude that the latter is a river that need not be crossed. And while they are correct to note differences between the waters, they miss the point that both racism and homophobia flow from the same polluted source—they are not the same, but they are part of the same river. "If bigotry is in the society against gays, can you really believe that society is going to be treating blacks well or women well?" Congresswoman Eleanor Holmes Norton asks. Using her own metaphor, she adds, "This is a fabric. You can't cut off a piece of it and say, 'Okay, y'all are free, no more bigotry as to you.' It doesn't work that way."

When it comes to sexual orientation, many of us have allowed our brains to be hijacked by others—by our peers, our family members, and especially our clergy. We often challenge discrimination against blacks, but we do not question the same form of discrimination practiced against homosexuals. We are quick to censure our peers if they make racist remarks, yet we barely flinch at the scorn heaped upon lesbians and gays. We distance ourselves from religious zealots who twist the Scriptures to mask their racism, but we dare not even examine the bias and misinterpretation that support religious homophobia. By refusing even to consider the alternatives to what we have been taught, we preclude the possibility of our own emancipation from the shackles of other oppressions.

Ignorance is oppression's greatest ally and freedom's greatest enemy. When Frederick Douglass was still a young slave in Maryland, he learned what he called the pathway from slavery to freedom: "If you teach that nigger . . . how to read, there would be no keeping him. It would forever unfit him to be a slave." He realized that "education and slavery were incompatible with each other." Exposed to the light of reason, the myths and stereotypes about blacks and gays do not easily survive either. We learn that blackness is not all about color, that homosexuality is not all about sex, that blacks are no more homophobic than whites, and that homosexuality does not inoculate whites against racism any more than blackness inoculates blacks against homophobia.

We all must know that our minds are trapped in the prejudices of our society, for only through this knowledge can we attempt to resist these influences. Homophobia afflicts not only heterosexuals but also homosexuals, who internalize, expect, accept, and often believe the negative rhetoric directed at them. Racism also works its tricks on blacks and whites both, leaving blacks with a slave mentality of obsequiousness, obedience, and inferiority. Before we can respond to the prejudices of racism and homophobia in others, we must first confront the internalized hatred inside ourselves. We must challenge the self-hatred that teaches us that our lives are less valuable than others merely because we are different and therefore despised.

"To make a contented slave," Frederick Douglass wrote, "it is necessary to make a thoughtless one. It is necessary to darken his moral and mental vision, and, as far as possible, to annihilate the power of reason. He must be able to detect no inconsistencies in slavery; he must be made to feel that slavery is right; and he can be brought to that only when he ceases to be a man." The tools of oppression have not changed much in 150 years. The same mental castration techniques needed to oppress black slaves are now employed to oppress modern-day homosexuals. They, too, must be convinced not to think for themselves. Social norms must dictate to homosexuals that they not challenge the inconsistencies of homophobia, and heterosexism must remain altogether beyond question. Homosexuals must be brought to believe that they are somehow subhuman or that their behavior is unnatural. All these conditions are necessary for oppression to continue.

One night during the period I was writing this book, I dreamed that I was walking around a huge outdoor theater that looked like a sprawling motel complex. Near the parking lot in the middle of the complex stood a man telling jokes for the entertainment of the surrounding audience. One of his jokes was about homosexuals. I froze when I heard the word "gay" and listened tentatively as he continued to speak. The audience laughed and clapped at his first joke, and suddenly I found myself clapping too. But as he started the second joke, a voice inside me said, "No, this is wrong." I could no longer endure the abuse, and I felt I needed to do something. I walked toward the comedian and cupped my hands over my mouth. With the loudest noise I ever remembered making, I simply started to yell, "Boooooo! Booo! Booooooooooo!" To my surprise, the entire audience joined in, but I could not tell if they were booing me or the comedian. It was only as the comedian stepped back and ran behind a glass door that I realized the audience was supporting me and standing up against the comedian's homophobia.

This dream woke me up on Saturday morning, January 28, 1995, the night after I watched a homophobic performance by a comedian on *Russell Simmons' Def Comedy Jam*. The comedian said he supported gays in the military because without them who would be there to help you when you're stuck in the jungle and a snake bites your dick. "Who's gonna suck that shit outta there," he asked, " 'cause I damn sure ain't gonna do it." I was disturbed when I heard the comment, but I actually felt strangely relieved that it wasn't as homophobic as it could have been. I put the joke out of mind and had no idea that it was still there until I woke up from my dream a few hours later.

I do not usually remember my dreams, but this was the second one in a week I had remembered. In the other dream, I stood up in a church and told the minister, "I am a Christian and I am a homosexual. And I am not ashamed of my Christianity. And I am not ashamed of my homosexuality." I was nearly beaten up that evening for violating church taboo. But in this new dream I was being supported by the people around me. Both dreams center around the same theme: standing up in front of an audience of unknowns and challenging the prejudice of the speaker to whom we are listening. Perhaps the dreams expose the frustration of being faced with these personal moral dilemmas so often. But perhaps also they raise a question that all people, black or white, straight or gay, should ask themselves: "What will happen if we stand up?"

What will happen if heterosexuals come out of their closets of fear and challenge the homophobia around them? What will happen if homosexuals come out and let their friends and family members know who they are? Will they be beaten up, or will they be supported? And is it better to suffer the outrageous fortune or to oppose it? As Thomas Jefferson wrote in the Declaration of Independence, "All experience hath shown

that mankind are more disposed to suffer while evils are suffer-
able than to right themselves by abolishing the forms to which
they are accustomed."

To fight homophobia and racism, we must continually challenge and push ourselves. "I force myself to do things," says
Dr. Elias Farajaje-Jones, who is black and very openly gay.
When he marched through New York in the Stonewall 25 procession in the summer of 1994, he wore a T-shirt he describes
as explicitly gay. "To wear down in the Village and everything
is very cute and charming," he says, "but I was staying with a
friend of mine that lived in Harlem." He thought about "duck-
ing into" his friend's apartment to change his shirt, but then
decided "if Stonewall means anything, it means that you
should walk in this neighborhood with this on."

Dr. Ron Simmons turns the tables on homophobia by re-
casting homosexuality from some blacks' perception of it as a
weakness into an indictment of white oppression. He charges
that homophobia is an attitude that black males have adopted
largely from the white culture and white religion. "Why should
Africa's descendants base their lives and their future on the
Koran, or the Bible?" he asks. According to Simmons, "The
Koran is not an artifact of African culture, it is Arabian. And
the Bible in its present form was given to us by white slavemasters." Cheryl Clarke, on the other hand, while agreeing that the
dominant culture imposes homophobia on the black community, cautions in an essay in the book *Home Girls,* "We cannot
rationalize the disease of homophobia among black people as
the white man's fault, for to do so is to absolve ourselves of the
responsibility to transform ourselves."

In challenging the bigotry around them, black lesbians and
gays must also be willing to define themselves, and not be
defined either by other people's stereotypes or by their own
fear of those stereotypes. But some stereotypes resonate because they speak an essential truth, even though they may be
manipulated by others. Some homosexuals are promiscuous.

Some black gay men are flaming queens. Some gay women dress as men, and some gay men dress as women. For black homosexuals to pretend not to see the diversity in the black gay community would set a dangerous precedent. If stereotypically masculine black gay men refuse to acknowledge effeminate black gay men as part of that community, why should straight African Americans be any more willing to acknowledge black lesbians and gays as part of the larger black community? Often we fear that acknowledging the fringe elements in our community will threaten the broader objectives of our struggle. We communicate this fear by claiming to be just as rigidly traditional as our oppressors. But this approach makes us less revolutionary and more evolutionary. We do not rebel, but instead evolve into that which we claim to challenge.

Frederick Douglass recalled in his autobiography a critical incident with one of his slavemasters, Edward Covey, a professor of religion with a reputation as a "nigger breaker." On an early Monday morning in the summer of 1833, in retaliation for an act of insubordination, Covey entered his horse stable and caught hold of Douglass's legs and attempted to tie them. But at that moment, Douglass recalled later, "from whence came the spirit I don't know—I resolved to fight . . . I seized Covey hard by the throat; and as I did so, I rose." Covey "trembled like a leaf" as Douglass unexpectedly resisted. They fought for nearly two hours, until both men were fatigued. Nevertheless, for the duration of Douglass's service, Covey never laid a finger on him in anger. In a turning point in his life as a slave, Douglass had learned the lesson of resistance.

Douglass's words express the challenge that faces all oppressed people at some point in their lives—to suffer oppression or to resist. I chose Douglass not because his experiences parallel those of modern-day homosexuals, for clearly they do not. The enslavement of blacks, with its total degradation of self and humanity, is not comparable to the situation of homosexuals, black or white, today. But precisely because the slave's

experience was so thoroughly dehumanizing and so catastroph-
ically oppressive, all others who have suffered since may find
comfort in the lessons of those who survived.

Fighting homophobia need not involve physical struggle—
often the greatest battles are psychological. For lesbians and
gays, black or white, the most difficult battle is whether or
when to come out and to whom. I know because I struggled
with this dilemma for many years, and in some instances, I still
find myself struggling. The first person I told was my mother,
but then it took a year before I could work up the courage to
tell my father; and when I did so, I wrote a letter rather than
talking to him. I wrote:

> We in this family don't communicate as well as we
> should, but I think we have our ways of expressing our
> feelings and fears without ever saying them. For exam-
> ple, I know that you and the rest of the family are very
> proud of me, even though you don't often say so, be-
> cause I just *know*. I can feel your pride even when
> you're silent . . . But pride is like a double-edged
> sword: it cuts both ways. On the one hand, the family
> has been so confident for me that pride cut away all my
> fears of failure. On the other hand, the family seems to
> expect me to do so many great things, I never felt I
> could live up to my expectations. Sometimes, I can't
> even live up to my reputation.
>
> I always thought this was a secret. I thought no one
> wanted to know if I was scared or unsure of myself.
> Everybody just expected me to be a perfect kid. But
> the more I think about it, the more convinced I be-
> come that you can't hide anything from your family.
> No matter what you try to conceal, your family always
> knows about it. They may not talk to you about it, but
> they know. This is our family's way of communicating
> without talking.
>
> Every now and then, we manage to fool ourselves

even when we're not fooling anybody else. We tell ourselves everything is okay and we even believe this sometimes. Meanwhile, everybody else around notices our private agony and struggle. We live in glass closets, all the while thinking nobody can see inside. Until one day you step outside your closet and realize people are looking inside. I think I've had that one day . . . I stepped outside my closet and realized people know more about me than I was willing to admit about myself. I think you are one of those people who knows about me. But just in case you don't know or aren't sure, I'm telling you that I'm gay . . .

I had no idea how my father would react to that letter, and I had worked up so much anxiety about it that a strongly negative reaction would not have surprised me. Whatever his reaction, I was prepared to accept the consequences. I was still the same son he had raised. I had always been gay, even when I was afraid to realize it. The only difference about me in coming out was that I had decided to share more of myself with my father. The risk of rejection was less a concern than the prospect of living the rest of my life as a lie. As Frederick Douglass said, "I prefer to be true to myself, even at the hazard of incurring the ridicule of others, rather than to be false, and incur my own abhorrence." When I did come out, my father responded by sending me a note. It was the first and only note he ever sent me, and he told me he loved me and supported me.

The simple act of lesbians and gay men coming out of the closet is the most powerful weapon in the war against homophobia. Poll after poll indicates that people are more likely to support the civil rights of lesbians and gays if they know someone who is gay. Seventy-one percent of those surveyed who knew someone gay said that homosexuals should be allowed to serve in the armed forces, while only 61 percent of all Americans felt this way, according to a February 1994

Newsweek poll. Sixty-one percent of those who knew someone gay said homosexuals should be hired as elementary school teachers, while only 47 percent of all Americans agree with that statement. "By coming out, gays and lesbians are able to show Americans just how mainstream we are," says Wes Combs, the program director of National Coming Out Day, held each year on October 11. Combs identifies three separate stages of coming out. First, in the *personal* stage, the individual realizes he or she is gay. Second, in the *private* stage, the individual begins to share this information with a select group of others, usually on a one-on-one basis. Third, in the *public* stage, the individual comes out to even more people outside of a protected circle of confidants.

For black lesbians and gays, coming out is often more difficult than for whites. Blacks must contend with issues of racism that compound their struggles with homophobia, and most blacks are already so obviously identified by their race that they are reluctant or unwilling to identify themselves further by their sexual orientation. These complicating factors help explain why fewer blacks than whites identify as lesbian or gay, but they do not lessen the need for black lesbians and gays to come out as well. As long as the white gay community continues to exclude and ostracize black homosexuals, as long as the black community denies their existence, and as long as opponents of civil rights attempt to drive a wedge between the two communities, those who are both black and gay can play a significant role against bigotry merely by saying who they are. For African Americans, concerned that the allegiances of black lesbians and gays lie outside the black community, only when black homosexuals come out will they see this is not the case. "Loving each other as men does not make black gays any less dangerous to the racist status quo," Dr. Ron Simmons says. Indeed, Black Panther Party leader Huey Newton recognized twenty-five years ago that lesbians and gays can be "the most revolutionary" in challenging the political power structure.

With all the efforts being made to divide minorities, it is

important to remember that the real enemy is injustice, not each other. Homophobia, not homosexuality, leads some lesbians and gays to engage in risky and self-destructive behavior. Homophobia, not homosexuality, leads many of them away from their families, their communities, and their places of worship. And when closeted black lesbians and gays continue to deceive themselves with unsuccessful marriages and families, it is homophobia, not homosexuality, that threatens the survival of the African-American family.

The enemy within us is often more threatening than the enemies surrounding us. But that internal enemy is not homosexuality but, rather, the hurtful way we treat one another. Physically, spiritually, and intellectually, blacks are warring against each other instead of supporting each other. In Vidor, Texas, after the force of the federal government had been brought in to integrate a previously all-white housing complex, one of the first black residents was killed not by an angry white resident but by another black person. "The most lethal danger facing African-Americans in their daily lives is not white, racist officials of the state, but private violent criminals, typically black, who attack those most vulnerable to them without regard to racial identity," Harvard law professor Randall Kennedy wrote in an April 1994 op-ed piece in *The Wall Street Journal*. In fact, the Justice Department reports that even though black males aged twelve to twenty-four represent only 1.3 percent of the population, they account for 17.2 percent of all single-victim homicides. The black community faces many different threats—from poverty to substandard housing to joblessness to substance abuse to disease to homicide to family breakdowns—where blacks are disproportionately represented against the general population. Homosexuality is not one of those threats. But when African Americans participate in or even tolerate sexual orientation bias, they exclude many of their brothers and sisters in the black family from fuller participation. With barely one foot in the white straight man's door, some African Americans kick down other minority groups and members of their own group who are still struggling to grasp the doorknob.

But despite the homophobia among blacks, Dr. Ron Simmons urges black lesbians and gays to avoid angry confrontational approaches in challenging this prejudice. Rather, he says, "we must show them through compassion and understanding that one can be gay and be socially, culturally and politically useful. We can be gay and committed to 'Blackness,' committed to the liberation of black people."

Blacks and gays have much to learn about each other and about those who are both black and gay. Although I was lucky to find my way home, many other black lesbians and gays are still searching for their homes. Only when African Americans, the lesbian and gay community, and families accept black homosexuals and love them for who they are will these now separate families regain many of their members. In so doing, they will help some to find their way back home and discover that many others are already there.

ABOUT THE AUTHOR

A 1992 graduate of Harvard Law School, Keith Boykin served for two years as special assistant and director of specialty press for President Clinton, acting as the principal liaison and spokesperson between the White House and the minority media, including the African-American and gay media. Currently, he serves as executive director of the National Black Gay & Lesbian Leadership Forum. He lives in Washington, D.C.